Voting for Russia's Governors

Voting for Russia's Governors

Regional Elections and Accountability

under Yeltsin and Putin

Andrew Konitzer

Woodrow Wilson Center Press
Washington, D.C.

The Johns Hopkins University Press
Baltimore

EDITORIAL OFFICES

Woodrow Wilson Center Press
Woodrow Wilson International Center for Scholars
One Woodrow Wilson Plaza
1300 Pennsylvania Avenue, N.W.
Washington, D.C. 20004-3027
Telephone: 202-691-4010
www.wilsoncenter.org

ORDER FROM

The Johns Hopkins University Press
Hampden Station
P.O. Box 50370
Baltimore, Maryland 21211
Telephone: 1-800-537-5487
www.press.jhu.edu/books/

2 4 6 8 9 7 5 3 1

Library of Congress Cataloging-in-Publication Data

Konitzer, Andrew.
  Voting for Russia's governors : regional elections and accountability under Yeltsin
and Putin / Andrew Konitzer.
    p.   cm.
  Includes bibliographical references and index.
  ISBN 0-8018-8299-0 (alk. paper)
  1. Voting—Russia (Federation)   2. Elections—Russia (Federation)   3. Political
participation—Russia (Federation)   I. Title.
  JN6699.A5K66   2005
  324.947′086—dc22   2005026855

Woodrow Wilson International Center for Scholars

The Woodrow Wilson International Center for Scholars, established by Congress in 1968 and headquartered in Washington, D.C., is a living national memorial to President Wilson. The Center's mission is to commemorate the ideals and concerns of Woodrow Wilson by providing a link between the worlds of ideas and policy, while fostering research, study, discussion, and collaboration among a broad spectrum of individuals concerned with policy and scholarship in national and international affairs.

Supported by public and private funds, the Center is a nonpartisan institution that establishes and maintains a neutral forum for free, open, and informed dialogue. Conclusions or opinions expressed in Center publications and programs are those of the authors and speakers and do not necessarily reflect the views of the Center staff, fellows, trustees, advisory groups, or any individuals or organizations that provide financial support to the Center.

The Center is the publisher of *The Wilson Quarterly* and home of Woodrow Wilson Center Press, *dialogue* radio and television, and the monthly newsletter "Centerpoint." For more information about the Center's activities and publications, please visit us on the Web at www. wilsoncenter.org.

Contents

Tables and Figures   ix

Preface   xi

1   *Russia's Regional Electorate: Jurors in a Corrupted Court*   1
    Regional Elections: A Failed Institution?   7
    Accountability, Elections, and Economic Voting   10
    A Second Look at Elections and Regional
       Executive Accountability   13
    The Context   15
    Data Sources   18
    Structure   20
    Notes   23

2   *Assigning Responsibility*   28
    A Few Words Regarding the "Portability of Concepts"   29
    Accountability   31
    Accountability for What?   36
    Economic Voting   39
    Economic Voting in Russia and Eastern Europe   46
    Economic Accountability in an Evolving Context   54
    Methodological Decisions   61
    Looking Ahead   64
    Notes   65

3   Sploshnie Vybory: *A Guide to Russian Regional
    Executive Elections*   71
    The Rules of the Game   72
    Incumbent Electoral Success in the Yeltsin and Early-Putin Eras   82

Not Entrenched . . . but "Fortified"? 88
Incumbent Success and Regional Status 94
The Elections through the Lens of the Accountability Criteria 96
The Next Step 98
Notes 99

4 *The Russian Jurisdictional Voter: Evidence from
Ul'ianovskaia Oblast* 103
The Socioeconomic and Political History of Ul'ianovskaia Oblast 104
A First Look at Jurisdictional Support in Russia's Regions 125
The Ideal Subnational Jurisdictional Voter 128
A Preview and Summary of Results 131
Casting Stones within a Federal Context 142
Conclusions 147
From Behavior to Outcomes 149
Notes 149

5 *Aggregate Economic Performance and Election Outcomes* 158
Data Sources 159
Preview and Summary of Results 160
Test Variables and Controls 162
Model and Final Results 167
Elected versus Appointed Executives 171
Notes 172

6 *Russia's Regional Executive Elections in
Comparative Perspective* 174
Theoretical Expectations . . . and Disappointments 175
Ukraine 180
Preview and Summary of Results 183
A Closer Look at Ukraine's Appointee System 184
Conclusions 189
Notes 190

7 *Making the Worst of a Bad Situation?* 194
Five Post-Yeltsin Challenges . . . and Putin's Solutions 197
Toward a System of Appointed Regional Executives 231
Conclusion 233
Notes 234

Appendix: Methods and Measures 241
Aggregate-Level Indicators 244

Index 247

Tables and Figures

Tables

3.1	Russia's Regional Elections at a Glance, 1995–2001	84
3.2	Appointed versus Elected Incumbents	86
3.3	Evolution of Regional Election Laws across First and Second Elections	90
3.4	Percentage of Elections Contested by a Given Number of Candidates by Election Year	93
3.5	Wins and Losses by Federal Subject, 1995–2001	95
3.6	Number of Candidates in "Final" Election Round, 1995–2001	96
4.1	Early Economic Indicators for Ul'ianovskaia Oblast	107
4.2	Responses to Economic Evaluation Questions, Ul'ianovskaia Oblast, September 2000	119
4.3	Logistic Regression Model for Incumbent Support	139
4.4	Responses to the Question "Please rate who, in your view, most affects conditions within our oblast"	144
4.5	Support by Economic Assessment	145
4.6	Party Support	146
5.1	Russian Incumbent Regional Executive Probability of Winning, Total Effects	168
6.1	Ukrainian Regional Executive Turnover, Odds Ratios	188
7.1	Regional Executive Election Results for 2003 by Party Support	224
7.2	Saint Petersburg's 2000 and 2003 Elections	230

Figures

1.1   The Russian Federation's Administrative Boundaries   16
2.1   The Accountability Game   34
2.2   Responses to the Question "Which of the following problems
      concern you most?"   38
4.1   Electoral Geography of Ul'ianovskaia Oblast's 1996 Regional
      Executive Elections   115
4.2   Electoral Geography of Ul'ianovskaia Oblast's 2000 Regional
      Executive Elections   126
4.3   Support Calculi, Ul'ianovsk Oblast, 2000   132
4.4   Support for Incumbent by GTRK Volga Viewership   143
5.1   Incumbent Electoral Success   161
5.2   Scattergram Showing Cook's Distances, Incumbent
      Win/Loss Model   170
6.1   Quarterly Ukrainian Regional Executive Turnover,
      June 1995–December 2000   182
6.2   Ukrainian Regional Executive Turnover,
      June 1995–December 2000   184

Preface

From their inception in the early 1990s, the popular elections for regional executives that Vladimir Putin's administration legislated out of existence on December 12, 2004, had alternately evoked hopes for a new decentralized democratic order where regional managers would be held accountable to their electorate; fears of political and economic disintegration; ridicule as a facade for backroom dealings among regional and central elites; and finally exhaustion as voters grew weary of endless dirty campaigning for elections over which they felt they had little control. Periodic calls for the elimination of the elections could be heard almost from the very moment that the regional contests became the norm around 1995 and 1996. However, these calls reached a crescendo during the Putin administration's first term in office, and the end came amid a wave of terrorist attacks and another major effort to transform the Russian Federation's still shaky political institutions. As the justifications for this apparently undemocratic act spilled forth, it became apparent to many observers and citizens that what Russia had given up was not a bulwark against centralized oppression and poor governance but an albatross whose legitimation of regional elites' theft, corruption, and rent-seeking behavior had nearly led the country to political and economic ruin.

Nonetheless, the condemning tone of those surrounding the Putin administration smacked of political expediency, and criticism both from abroad and from a small but vocal group of Russian commentators and political actors (some with their own sense of political expedience) suggested that Russia's experience with regional executive elections was not as dreadful as portrayed by the institution's detractors. Furthermore, for many observers, the new institution of quasi-appointments carried no guarantee of better governance or less corruption. How would the regional electorate profit from trading self-interested regional political elites for self-interested political elites in faraway Moscow? Would the waste and graft that allegedly consumed the election process be lessened by moving the selection process into regional legislatures and backroom negotiations? What was actually being lost or gained through this radical change in Russia's federal institutions?

This study constitutes my initial attempt to answer some of these questions by analyzing the record of Russia's past decade of regional executive elections from the standpoint of accountability for regional living standards. The choice of indicators reflects both my sense, developed over years of field research, of the regional voters' primary interest and evidence drawn from numerous surveys indicating that bread-and-butter issues remain the primary concern of the Russian electorate. However—particularly in the context of a complex and poorly defined federal structure—merely identifying what the voter cares about provides little indication as to whether he or she can or will hold appropriate policymakers responsible for these outcomes. Poor information and a misunderstanding of the country's admittedly confused system of governance could result in the inability to place blame for pertinent outcomes. Furthermore, even if the voter can "vote appropriately," there is also an entire array of tools and methods whereby incumbents, federal authorities, and challengers could channel election outcomes and effectively shield themselves from an electorate whose interests do not match their own.

Having painted a portrait of the laws and history surrounding Russia's regional executive elections, I present a set of analyses that seek to answer how Russia's regional voter decided to support or oppose an incumbent; to what extent micro-level economic voting decisions translated into election outcomes; and, through a comparison to the system of appointed regional elections concurrently operating in Ukraine, whether elections were a better promoter of accountability than presidential appointments. The results are surprising. Despite the rhetoric surrounding the Putin administration's decision to eliminate popular elections, the contests held from 1996 through 2001 yielded an element of accountability and seemed to outperform the system of appointees in neighboring Ukraine.

The book ends with an examination of Putin's initial attempts to fix the problems evident during the Yeltsin era and speculates on the future of a Russia without popularly elected regional executives. I argue that what began as an apparently rational effort to close loopholes in election laws and provide better oversight of regional contests rapidly degenerated into an effort to remove political opponents through the arbitrary application of tougher legal constraints. This "interim period" from 2001 to 2004 replaced a system of sometimes corrupt regional election processes with frequent and equally self-serving interventions by political actors in Moscow. Though some of Russia's more notorious regional lords lost their positions in the process, many equally culpable but more politically reliable leaders found renewed strength, and the regional electorate appeared to lose interest in a process increasingly controlled by the Kremlin. Looking ahead to the future under a system of quasi-appointments, I draw on Ukraine's experience to speculate about the interests and incentives guiding the new selection process and find little basis for optimism.

Work on this book began as my dissertation at the University of Pittsburgh's Department of Political Science. In the process, I indebted myself to an ever-growing circle of friends, colleagues, and organizations. A full listing might constitute a small work in itself, but I wish to specifically acknowledge as many as possible of those who gave of their time, resources, and expertise. I apologize to any whose names I have inadvertently omitted.

Starting with those on this side of the world, I wish to thank my dissertation adviser Jonathan Harris and committee members David Barker, Dan Berkowitz, and Ron Linden, whose insights, patience, and guidance carried me through all stages of the process. The University of Pittsburgh's Department of Political Science and Center for Russian and Eastern European Studies provided invaluable support, and I am particularly grateful to Bob Donnorummo and Bob Hayden for offering me unique opportunities to work in parts of Russia that at the time were less accessible for someone at my stage of professional development. Had it not been for my appointment as field director for the Samara-Pittsburgh public servant training partnership in Samara, I might have never left the confines of Moscow and Saint Petersburg and found my new interest in Russia's provinces.

I also owe a debt to numerous American research, funding, and government organizations. Funding for my field research was provided by the ACTR/ACCELS Regional Scholar Exchange Program, the Institute of International Education, and the U.S. Department of Education's Foreign Language and Area Studies program. The Kennan Institute provided me with a year of research support and fruitful exchange as well as an excellent working environment, and I am particularly grateful for the assistance and collegiality shown by Blair Ruble and Margaret Paxson. Joe Dresen and Erin Hofmann made arrangements for a number of presentations in Washington, and Lindsay Collins shared her administrative skills and friendship.

Other colleagues and acquaintances offered their support by reviewing drafts of the book; by offering comments and suggestions at various workshops, seminars, and conferences; or by providing useful contacts for my field research. Robert Orttung and an anonymous reviewer made a careful reading of the book and offered excellent advice and insightful critiques. Susie Baker arranged two very productive presentations at the U.S. Department of State; Lucan Way offered invaluable contacts in Kyiv; and numerous conference participants, discussants, and anonymous reviewers presented their views on various aspects of the project.

Moving on to Russia and Ukraine, the number of colleagues, friends, and acquaintances who offered support defies a comprehensive listing, but I wish to acknowledge those who took particular pains to provide access to critical data and offered their knowledge and insights into Russian society. In Samara, Vladimir Zvonovskii shared his data, contacts, and extensive knowledge of the regional political scene. As a colleague and friend, Vladimir was always open to my inquiries and gave generously of his time. Lydia Goverdovskaia and Sergei Perov provided their friendship, administrative support, and contacts in Samara and Ul'ianovsk. Viktor Kuznetsov shared data and information from the Samara Oblast' administration and always found time in his busy schedule to answer often mundane questions. Evgenii Molevich and Sergei Agapov also offered invaluable insights and documentation. The staff at the Samarskaia Oblast Library put aside their surprise over my endless photocopying requests and patiently helped me gather information. Finally, I wish to express particularly heartfelt thanks to Larisa, Tanya, and Gennadii Smirnov for their immeasurable love, friendship, and patience.

In Ul'ianovsk, Aleksandr, Ol'ga, and Vladimir Kazantsev offered wonderful hospitality and research support, introducing me to a region where I knew very few people. Valentin Bazhanov provided his time, contacts, and friendship at various stages of the project, as well as frequent updates while I was back in the United States. Igor Egorov shared his knowledge of regional developments and introduced me to individuals working in the oblast administration and local academic institutions. Gennadii Antontsev, Sergei Gogin, and Vadim Shishkin also made invaluable contributions of their time, resources, and information. Finally, Valentina Shuvalova provided data support and the raw material for the Ul'ianovsk survey analyses.

Aside from the assistance and kindness shown to me in the Samarskaia and Ul'ainovskaia Oblasts, I am also grateful for the help of others during briefer trips and collaborations. Iurii Marchenko, Viktor Stepanenko, and

Olena Yatsunska offered their insights and critical data about Ukraine. Sergei Kaliagin generously gave of his time, home, and contacts during a brief but very enjoyable visit to Perm. Finally, Boris Firsov, Grigorii Golosov, and Valentin Mikhailov provided sage advice, invaluable data, and good company either in Moscow or in Washington.

Of course, this work would never have been realized in its current form without the assistance and patience of the Woodrow Wilson International Center for Scholars and the Woodrow Wilson Center Press. I owe a particular debt of gratitude to Joseph Brinley and Yamile Kahn for their excellent editorial support and their patient, detailed responses to my questions. These and all the above-listed individuals made critical contributions to the current work, and all errors or omissions in the final product are solely my own.

Finally, I wish to express my immense love and gratitude for my wife, Maja, my father and mother, Rich and Judy Konitzer, and my sister, Dolores Abreu. Maja's patience and encouragement carried me through the last months of this project, and she is a source of inspiration for all my personal and professional endeavors. My mother and father gave selfishly of themselves to help me develop and grow in all aspects of my life and my sister has always been there with her love and friendship.

Voting for Russia's Governors

Chapter 1

Russia's Regional Electorate: Jurors in a Corrupted Court

Ninety-nine percent of the campaigns in Russia pass quietly and peacefully. Every four years, there are eighty-eight regional leaders elected. Let's count on our fingers the instances of actual scandals: Kursk, Primore, Rostov, Krasnoiarsk. . . . That's all. But there's an entirely different problem. After a scandal, the region becomes like scorched earth, the people's distrust of all elections gains monumental strength. So after a show like in Krasnoiarsk or Nizhnii, you need some time for the territory to cool, to calm down.

—Boris Nadezhdin

No matter what Veshniakov, the federal prosecutor, and anyone else have tried, election results are still resolved by telephone calls, money, and bandits. In order to eradicate corruption, governors must be appointed.

—Vladimir Zhirinovskii

On a crisp October day in 2000, a veteran of the Great Patriotic War entered his polling place in the city of Kursk, expecting to once again cast his vote for the region's popular and outspoken incumbent, Aleksandr Rutskoi. Upon entering the polling place, he glimpsed at the poster of candidates hanging on the polling station wall and was surprised to find an "X" over the governor's picture—merely a day before the election, Rutskoi had been struck from the ballot. For the veteran, the choice now came down to a list of unknown individuals—he had never even considered voting for anyone except Rutskoi.

A month later, as the November snows continued to accumulate, an elderly resident of Ul'ianovsk sat down to watch the evening news. The burners on the stove were lit, not only to warm some water for tea but to also compensate for the cold radiator standing beneath the icy window. On

1

the kitchen table, her son's copy of *Ul'ianovsk Segodnia* carried a headline berating the oblast (region) administration for the region's energy crisis. On the television, GTRK Volga broadcast an interview with an irritated Governor Iurii Goriachev, who casually suggested that the mayor's office had stolen budget money targeted for municipal heating subsidies. The pensioner pulled her blanket a bit closer, contemplated the upcoming mayoral and gubernatorial elections, and swore to vote against both incumbents.

Another winter day in December 2000 found voters in Brianskaia Oblast puzzling over a list of candidates on their region's gubernatorial election ballot. Those who intended to cast their vote for Governor Iurii Lodkin found two "Iurii Lodkins" on the ballot. Was it Iurii Dmitrievich or Iurii Evgen'evich? Others, expecting to vote for the governor's main competitor, faced a frustratingly similar problem. During the campaign, many had not bothered to note whether they supported Nikolai Denin or Aleksandr Denin. The biographies on the polling place poster offered little assistance —Nikolai Denin was the director of the company "Snezhka," while Aleksandr Denin directed the company "Snezhko."

A few weeks later, a twenty-year-old disc jockey stood on his balcony in the city of Tula contemplating the lit end of a cigarette. The son of a small entrepreneur, he loathed the stone-faced apparatchiks who, almost a decade after the collapse of the Soviet Union, continued to rule his region. Aside from the occasional pronouncement attacking the DJ's favorite local nightclub as a "den of drugs and loose morals," the oblast authorities had done absolutely nothing for the region's youth, catering instead to the more politically active pensioners and veterans. Yes, it was probably time for a change, but he feared the polling stations. Some of his friends warned him that representatives from the military draft board would be there.

On another October day in 2003, a couple in Saint Petersburg watched, for the fourth time that day, as President Vladimir Putin held a meeting with the temporarily furloughed Northwestern District presidential envoy, Valentina Matvienko. Mayor Vladimir Yakovlev had "voluntarily" resigned for a position in Moscow, and elections were scheduled to take place in a matter of weeks. A voice-over indicated that Putin and Matvienko discussed Saint Petersburg's 2004 budget. The couple wondered why the president was working through next year's city budget with a mayoral candidate. And didn't someone mention that the challenger (What was her name?) was a strong contender?

Across more than 200 regional elections that occurred in post-Soviet Russia from 1992 through November 2003, millions of Russian voters were challenged to play a key role in achieving the goals of democratic decentralization under conditions that fell far short of the ideals posited by analysts and theorists in the social sciences. They faced opaque budgets, tangled policy jurisdictions, crooked incumbents, vote fraud, a dearth of reliable mediated information, and constant *uncertainty*—uncertainty that their candidate would survive until election day, uncertainty that their incumbent would remain in office until voted out, and uncertainty that the party-less candidate, recently plucked from obscurity, would be any more trustworthy than the incumbent that he sought to replace.

This book provides an account of the Russian voter's struggle and an analysis of the potential for subnational electoral accountability in post-Soviet states. It begins with a discussion of the theoretical promises of decentralization and the potential to use the ballot box as a means to punish or reward incumbents for their success as stewards of their policy jurisdictions, and it goes on to demonstrate through survey and aggregate analyses of a sample of elections from 1996 to 2001 how Russian voters managed to eke out a modicum of electoral accountability under often abhorrent electoral conditions.

The nature of post-Soviet Russia's political, social, and economic development had created a hostile environment for the type of accountability envisioned by many Western proponents of political devolution. Throughout the Boris Yeltsin era and into the first year of Vladimir Putin's rule, Russian federalism exhibited elements of uncontrolled decentralization, or what Kathryn Stoner-Weiss refers to as "creeping regional autonomy."[1]

Such a condition was characterized by chaotic budget relations; a fragmented legal, political, and economic space; and the creation of regional political subsystems that varied from progressively democratic to strongly authoritarian. The federal government's weak position vis-à-vis the regions resulted in a larger number of de facto and de jure concessions, which only exacerbated the disintegrative process resulting from regional executives "taking all the independence they could handle."[2] After 1996, regional executive elections constituted one of the few relatively consistent political phenomena across all regions. Yet, within this institution, the variation in election rules, political environments, and a multitude of other factors once again emphasized the true extent of Russia's political fragmentation.

Furthermore, this very fragmentation, and the federal government's inability—or unwillingness—to impose uniform political, economic, and social standards on regional elites resulted in a growing sense that elections, in a country of "regional autocracies," could only act as a mass-based rubber stamp for the ruling elite. A popular image arose among academics, journalists, and the public at large of regional executives sitting at the center of local power networks, ruling for the good of their clique, paying only symbolic attention to the living standards of their constituents, and yet still demonstrating an ability to weather even the most challenging election campaign.

However, the results of this study challenge the last of these perceptions and cast a new light on the role of elections in promoting regional-level accountability during the Yeltsin and early Putin eras. Despite the use of nearly every conceivable underhanded election tactic, incumbents' abuse of administrative offices, a barren regional civil society, and budgetary confusion that challenged even skilled economists to make assessments of performance, regional voters more often than not sanctioned poorly performing incumbents and rewarded good stewards with another term in office. In fact, the very disintegrative process, which at various times seemed to threaten the Russian Federation with the fate of its Soviet predecessor, perhaps even heightened the public's perception regarding the salience of regional executive elections and spurred it on to participate in an active and well-considered manner. With Yeltsin's very public incapacitation, and the rather apparent cross-regional diversity in living standards, voters in regional elections understood that their governor or republican president was the first, and perhaps only, line of defense from increasing deprivation. Having recognized the salience of the elections, the biggest challenge was then to overcome the accountability barriers erected by executives intent on maintaining their often lucrative offices. According to the results of this study, the voters apparently enjoyed greater success than the conventional wisdom on the subject had suggested.

But, unfortunately, the story does not end there. The popular perception regarding the "failure" of regional democratic institutions, particularistic agendas, and the desire to rein in regional elites drove Russia's second presidential administration, under President Putin, to implement a series of reforms aimed ostensibly at fixing the ailments of Yeltsin-era federalism. In a series of efforts beginning with the May 13, 2000, decree establishing seven federal districts under the tutelage of a new institution of district-level presidential representatives, the new president, Central Election Commission, and Duma set out to force regions to bring existing regional laws into compliance with federal legislation, give the president the power to both remove regional executives and disband legislatures, limit regional executives to two consecutive terms in office, place restrictions on media behavior during regional elections, strip governors of their power to appoint directors of regional broadcast stations, and strengthen the role of political parties in elections and regional-level policymaking processes.[3] And this list of changes includes only those pieces of legislation and presidential decrees that were actually implemented.

Other reforms—including the elimination of executive elections and a return to a system of appointed governors—were debated, but they stalled at various stages in the policymaking process.[4] Still, as indicated by statements from Aleksandr Kazakov, the representative from the Committee of the Federal Council on Matters of the Federation and Regional Politics (Komiteta Soveta Federatsii po delam Federatsii and regional'noi politiki), the idea of establishing a system of appointed regional executives was still very much alive throughout Putin's first term. In a September 2003 roundtable presentation, Kazakov provided the following set of considerations, which led him to conclude that Russia would see the establishment of regional appointees during Putin's second term:

> First, in this case there will be no need for federal districts and presidential envoys. Secondly, there would be a big economic savings on elections. Thirdly, and this is perhaps the most important, appointments to positions by Presidential order are the only possibility for the majority of governors to keep their posts . . . and as far as the overwhelming majority of governors have already proven their loyalty to the Kremlin, soon after the presidential election we should expect from them a petition requesting that they be appointed to their posts. And there will be no kind of "black PR" during elections. Everything will eventually come to this. This proposition . . . will be supported by the central government . . . these are simply pragmatic things.[5]

Following Putin's reelection in March 2004, many observers expected a further consolidation and concentration of power under the president. Events quickly bore out these concerns. In the wake of a series of terrorist attacks—including the simultaneous downing of two airliners, a bombing at the Rizhskaia metro station in Moscow, and the tragic seizure and subsequent storming of a school in Beslan—Putin announced to a session of the Cabinet of Ministers his plan to reform Russia's political structures. Aside from eliminating single-mandate districts during Duma elections (thus moving exclusively to proportional representation), and establishing a "public chamber" for the presentation of citizens' initiatives, the president's list of reforms included the elimination of popular elections for regional executives, and their replacement with a system of appointment similar to the one used for selecting the prime minister. According to this method, the president would recommend a candidate for regional executive to the region's legislature, which would then vote to approve or reject the candidate. If the legislature rejected the candidate, the post would be temporarily occupied (probably by the president's initial candidate) until the president put forth the candidate for a second or, if necessary, third legislative vote. In the event that the candidate was rejected three times, the president would have the right to disband the regional legislature, forcing new elections (from this point on, this system of selecting executives will be referred to as "quasi-appointment," in place of the more awkward, official "election by recommendation of the president").

After nearly five years of speculation and conjecture regarding Putin's plans for regional executive elections, 2004 marked the end of Russia's decade-long experiment with elected governors and republican presidents. On December 12, Russia's Constitution Day, President Putin signed into law a set of proposals to replace the system of elected regional officials with the system of quasi-appointments outlined above. Before his signing, the bill sailed through three readings in the State Duma, propelled in large part by the substantial United Russia bloc that had controlled the legislative body since the 2003 Duma elections.

Opposition to the reforms proved desultory and ineffective. Earlier, on September 28, a group of twenty-two deputies and political activists led by Vladimir Ryzhkov sent an open letter to the Constitutional Court asking it to evaluate the constitutionality of the proposed reforms and present the results of its deliberations to the Duma before the legislative body's vote. The Court quickly responded—not directly, but through its press service—indicating that it could only act on "official complaints or inquiries from citizens regarding existing laws."[6] Outside Moscow, legislative assemblies and executives in a handful of regions came out against the stipulation that, in the event that an assembly failed to approve the president's candidate, the organ would be disbanded and new elections called. Despite these protests, this particular stipulation remained intact and was included in the final law.[7]

There were also some acts of popular protest in the provinces, with demonstrations in Saint Petersburg, Izhevsk, Volgograd, Stavropol, Ekaterinburg, Irkutsk, Tomsk, and elsewhere. However, these demonstrations generally attracted fewer than 500 individuals, and many provinces featured pro-reform rallies in place of, or in direct opposition to, the protests.[8] Considering public opinion polls at the time, the low turnout at antireform demonstrations might have been expected. According to the Public Opinion Foundation (Fond Obshchestvennoe Mnenie, or FOM) surveys of residents from Russia's oblasti, *kraia* (territories), and republics, when respondents were asked in mid-September for their reaction to the president's proposals, 29 percent responded "positive," 37 percent responded "negative," and 35 percent "hard to say." By the beginning of December, the positions had reversed; 36 percent now supported the proposals, 35 percent were undecided, and 29 percent responded negatively.[9]

Russia's federal government quickly and resoundingly rejected regional elections, trading what appeared to be a corrupted and ineffective institution for the promise of stability, order, and efficiency. This left analysts, critics, and pundits to answer the question of what has been lost and gained by Russia's decision to reverse the decentralization of the past decade and bound further down the road to a unitary state. Was the elimination of popular elections a setback for Russian democracy, or had the institution become so corrupted that the system of appointments would yield analogous or even better outcomes? In attempting to answer this question, this book will not only offer a eulogy of sorts for Russia's regional elections but will also suggest clues to the future of a Russia with appointed regional bosses.

Regional Elections: A Failed Institution?

Much of the justification for the effort to recentralize Russia lay with the general argument that the current system of federal relations had been at least partially responsible for the stalled economic and political reforms that plagued the country during the latter half of the 1990s. According to these arguments, the evolution of control to the regions had resulted in the construction of what academics had come to see as regional "fiefdoms" and "regionalized autocracies."[10] Critics also pointed out that the addition of popular elections only served to legitimize the role of leaders who—through a combination of dirty tricks and proincumbent election laws passed through submissive regional legislatures—largely controlled election outcomes.

During a decade of well-publicized scandals and the abuse of so-called administrative resources, a wide consensus arose that regional executives were effectively accountable to no one. Reacting to President Putin's September 2004 initiatives, the leader of the Rodina faction, Dmitry Rogozin, made more specific mention of the "fiefdoms" charge, indicating that the change to a system of appointments would avoid "the blackmail of Russian

State organs from the side of destructive barons and oligarchs."[11] As vice chairman of the Federation Councils Commission for Coordination with the Accounting Chamber, Sergei Ivanov stated, "Right now, . . . the governor does not serve his region, but instead, the region serves its governor. An expression has even appeared: During the first term, the governor works, and during the second, he rules."[12] Western analysts also have questioned the worth of regional election institutions. Eugene Rumer, a senior fellow at the National Defense University's Institute for National Strategic Studies, argues that

> Putin's move to appoint, rather than elect, regional governors is hardly a major blow to Russian democracy. Elected governors, once hailed as guarantors of Russian federalism and a hedge against an all-powerful central state, have acquired a reputation as feudal barons. . . . Gubernatorial elections from Moscow to Vladivostok have come to symbolize the unholy alliance between money, politics and, in some instances, crime, as well as the "administrative resource."[13]

Nonetheless, aside from ample anecdotal evidence from the past decade of provincial political contests that demonstrated the fundamental crookedness of Russia's regional executive elections, there were few attempts to systematically examine whether the high-profile scandals, and executives' structural control over regional election processes, had indeed eliminated all elements of accountability. Had these elections become so corrupted that they had ceased to perform the function of holding executives responsible for their policies? If so, were the Putin administration's proposals to eliminate these elections actually justified?

This study attempts to tap into these questions by examining the relationship between a fundamental human interest—one's material well-being—and support for Russian regional executives. The choice of this particular focus allows me to draw inferences not only about the degree to which elections function as accountability mechanisms but also to explore fundamental questions about regional-level voting behavior in transition states, the role of economics in determining electoral outcomes ("economic voting"), and the empirical basis for some of the more strident claims of the democratic decentralization literature.

Through a multimethod approach combining quantitative and qualitative analyses, I present an exploration of Russian regional executive election voting behavior and outcomes. The cornerstones of this analysis are three chapters that include individual-level analyses of regional citizens' popularity functions and aggregate-level analyses of the relationship between regional-level economic indicators and election outcomes from 1996 to 2001 in Russia and the requisites of regional executive turnover in unitary Ukraine. The analyses result in two intriguing conclusions. First, comparative sociotropic assessments of regional performance are prominent in citizens' decisions to support or not support their given incumbent. Second, through aggregate-level analyses using a new indicator of *relative* regional economic performance, it appears that these individual-level decisions translated (albeit imperfectly) into aggregate regional-level outcomes, indicating a pattern of support partially dependent upon regional growth.

These results suggest three important points. First, contrary to some of the literature that applies economic voting theses to Russia and other formerly socialist countries, there is evidence of retrospective economic voting at the *subnational* level. Second, the particular manner in which economic factors affect election outcomes indicates that it is exactly *policies* that matter. Executives in historically or geographically well-endowed regions were not automatically guaranteed reelection. Third, though incumbents in poorly performing regions possessed a range of instruments to essentially shield themselves from a disgruntled electorate, poor performance was still "punished" at the polls—regional elections in the Russian context were not fundamentally flawed, but the institutions left much room for manipulation.

Together, these outcomes bear important implications for the changes being implemented in Russia's federal, regional, and local structures of governance. The public debate surrounding the series of reforms currently under way in Russia has included frequent references to the "obvious failure" of existing regional institutions to yield accountability for subnational policymakers. More specific culprits have included poorly defined policy jurisdictions, political elites' control over the election process, a biased and unprofessional media, underdeveloped regional party structures, and poor federal oversight in the areas of election campaigns and budget implementation.

For the most part, the Putin administration has correctly identified the elements of post-Soviet political, social, and economic life that are major obstacles to the realization of electoral accountability. However, in many cases, the central authorities' initial efforts to provide a "cure" proved worse than the illness. Beginning from assumptions about the abject failure of regional elections, the regime's reforms amounted to a heavy-handed backlash, combined with frequently arbitrary efforts to realize specific political goals, that threatened to destroy the benefits of decentralization eked out during the initial decade of the post-Soviet era. During President Putin's first term, there was growing evidence that increasing central government intervention was actually *weakening* elections' ability to function as accountability mechanisms—arbitrary intervention in regional electoral campaigns and the apparent invincibility of United Russia–backed candidates threatened to sever the tenuous link between regional performance and incumbent success. Ultimately, the administration moved to an even more decisive measure: altogether eliminating the elections.

Accountability, Elections, and Economic Voting

Naturally, any study focused on electoral accountability and economic voting must begin by establishing some working definitions of the relevant concepts. Turning first to the issue of accountability, Bernard Manin, Adam Przeworski, and Susan Stokes's work on accountability and elections provides a useful and simple definition that I utilize as one of the foundations of this study:[14]

> Governments are "accountable" if voters can discern whether governments are acting in their interest and sanction them appropriately, so that those incumbents who act in the best interest of citizens win reelection and those who do not lose them [*sic*]. Accountability representation occurs when (1) voters vote to retain the incumbent only when the incumbent acts in their best interest, and (2) the incumbent chooses policies necessary to get reelected.[15]

However, though Manin, Przeworski, and Stokes's working definition gives a broad sense of accountability as an act of holding policymakers responsible for the outcomes of their policies, it also begs a number of critical questions. First and foremost, the task of defining what is in the "best interest" of citizens and determining how incumbents should act to satisfy these interests presents a challenge to any social scientist attempting to operationalize this concept. "Best interests" may be tied to personal power; morals and ethics; a sense of security; desires for various forms of pleasure; religion, ethnicity, and national identity; or any number of other factors. Such an infinite multitude of potential interests forces any researcher investigating the accountability question to choose specific types of interests that he or she feels to be relatively more "universal" than others. Thus, for the purposes of this study, I follow in the footsteps of many other students of accountability by choosing to explore the degree of accountability for citizens' *material welfare.*[16]

A number of considerations warrant this choice. First, economic concerns are consistently salient among a majority of Russia's citizens. One survey conducted in January 2001 by VTsIOM (the All-Russian Center for Public Opinion Research) asked respondents "which of the problems existing in today's Russian society makes you most anxious?" Issues related to the economy dominated, with 79 percent answering "price increases"; 43 percent, "unemployment"; and 40 percent, "crisis in the economy" (respondents could choose more than one category). With such responses occurring even against the backdrop of the Russian economy's post-1999 economic upturn, it is clear that economic issues continue to occupy the minds of most Russians.

Second, as will be further discussed below in the section on governors, regional economic performance constitutes one of the perceived primary areas of responsibility for regional governments. In this respect, the popular Russian idea of the governor as *khoziain* (literally, a manager or lord)[17] offers a suitable indication of the popular conception of the governor's role as the administrator of the regional economy.[18] Though one frequently meets this term in media reports, interviews, and casual conversations about regional politics, survey evidence provides additional backing for the sense that regional voters most often see their executives as economic managers. A VTsIOM study (cited by Vera Tolz and Irina Busygina) after the elections of 1995–96 asked individuals who they thought were the winners of the most recent cluster of gubernatorial elections. Though 32 percent answered "politicians," a full 46 percent answered "effective economic managers."[19]

Third, an investigation of accountability for economic outcomes is a worthy pursuit in and of itself, opening the way for contributions into a much wider set of literature in economics, federal studies, and policymaking. As will be discussed further in chapter 2, whether or not regional executives are accountable for economic outcomes has important implications for the shape of reforms in Russia as a whole. The Russian economy is no greater than the sum of the economies of its individual units, and if territories are controlled by rulers facing little incentive to pursue development-oriented policies, then the entire country suffers.

Finally, economic performance constitutes one of the more easily *measurable* indicators.[20] Voters naturally have other important issues to consider—like the incumbent's personal reputation; policies toward minority populations; and the building of hospitals, churches, and schools—but economic indicators are both universal and more or less standardized across units. Hence, economic performance can offer a useful first step into more detailed and sophisticated examinations of elections and accountability.

The focus on the link between elections and economic conditions necessarily connects this study to the social sciences' so-called economic voting literature.[21] To generalize in the broadest terms, the core argument of this literature is that economic conditions *of some type* have an impact on elections *in some fashion*. Nonetheless, as will be discussed in more extensive detail in chapter 2, this rich literature presents a number of challenges to the simplest "It's the economy, stupid!" thesis.[22] Following upon the seminal works of Kramer and of Kinder and Kiewiet, the social sciences witnessed a steady accumulation of evidence in favor of the idea that voters *somehow* take considerations of economic performance into account when deciding whether to support or oppose their political leaders. However, a consensus on the microfoundations of these decisions proved elusive, and the entire economic voting school was periodically jolted by studies indicating that there was little or no relationship between the economy and election success. Hence, even at the more salient and thoroughly examined national level, there remains a lingering uncertainty about the existence and potential effects of various economic voting calculi in any society.

Moving to the *subnational* level, the logic of economic voting becomes even more complicated. The fact that local economies find themselves embedded within a larger national economy (which itself is embedded in the global economic system) raises even greater challenges for voters—who must determine not only whether they are better off than in a given period in the past but also whether these positive or negative outcomes can be attributed to national, regional, or local government actions. As will be discussed in chapter 2, studies of subnational economic voting have returned very mixed results, with a relatively stable balance between findings indicating the presence of economic voting calculi and those indicating that other factors, like party affiliation, trump considerations of local economic conditions. Indeed, despite their continued recognition as the very bedrock of democracy, political parties play a rather contradictory role in the subnational economic voting and accountability question.

Although political parties provide all the benefits of a useful "information shortcut" for voters, this shortcut may discourage these same voters from making the effort to assess local conditions.[23] As a result, loyalty to national political parties is simply transferred to the local level, resulting in elections that are more akin to "local referenda" for national parties than to contests based on local performance. This tendency to vote with one's party rather than one's pocketbook presents problems not only for the economic voting literature but also for proponents of decentralization—who argue that by bringing policymakers "closer to home," decentralization allows citizens to exert more control over local decisionmaking. If voters lean too heavily on the party affiliation shortcut, they may forfeit their role as local watchdogs.[24]

Given that researchers conducted many of the above-mentioned studies in advanced Western democracies where established institutions and norms of behavior result in the most "rationalized" political systems currently in existence, it should perhaps come as no surprise that economic voting and accountability have a very mixed record in "transition" countries such as Russia.[25] Boris Yeltsin's 1996 election victory came about despite the fact that he reigned over a wrenching four-year collapse of his country's economy. The 1990s witnessed a constant flow of media stories and editorial comments detailing how yet another governor or republican president had sailed through a reelection bid while continuing to run his or her region into the ground. Casual observations were backed by tepid results from studies attempting to measure the degree to which Russians were economic voters, and whether actual election results were indeed promoting accountability for economic conditions. The culprits varied from the naïveté of Russia's new voters to weak party systems to poorly established norms of competition to fraud and other more insidious means of controlling election outcomes.

Regardless of the specific cause, there arose a growing consensus, evident in countless journalistic and academic accounts, that the endlessly unfolding election contests in Russia's regions did little or nothing to promote accountability and that the voters were mindless puppets in an electoral performance created to legitimize the predetermined outcomes of inter-elite struggles behind the scene. By the end of the 1990s, this conventional wisdom held regional executive contests in such low regard that many policymakers and commentators saw little to lose in transferring to a system of quasi-appointed governors.

A Second Look at Elections and Regional Executive Accountability

This study reopens the debate regarding the role of elections in holding governors accountable for regional economic performance by applying both updated and entirely new types of data to the question. Looking back at the evolution of economic voting studies in advanced industrial democracies, it seeks to overcome the methodological divide between aggregate level and individual level in that literature (see the discussion in chapter 2) by offering analyses on both levels. In the process, I present the first analysis of regional-level survey data focusing on the relationship between respondents' evaluations of regional and personal economic evaluations and their assessments of acting incumbents.

This new approach to the regional-level economic voting question allows me to not only determine whether economic factors play *any* role in incumbent support but also to examine which types of factors are most important (i.e., sociotropic vs. "pocketbook" issues, relative vs. absolute sociotropic evaluations), and how these factors weigh against other more "noneconomic" issues. The results of such an analysis have especially important implications for the regional-level accountability issue. To hold incumbents responsible for the outcomes within their various policy jurisdictions, not only must voters take economic issues into account, but they must also consider and give salience to the *correct types* of economic issues.

However, an analysis of individual voting behavior in one region fails to capture the broader patterns of executive fortunes that ultimately interest the majority of regional election observers. And examining only one case naturally increases the risk of drawing spurious conclusions influenced in part by the specificities of single observations. Hence, taking a lead from earlier analyses by Steven Solnick, Grigorii Golosov, and others, I also provide aggregate-level examinations of the full range of elections that occurred from 1996 to 2001.[26] For this purpose, I developed a database that includes more than 100 socioeconomic and political variables that cover various aspects of regional socioeconomic development, regional political behavior, and candidate characteristics.[27] This data source provides the raw materials for a series of multivariate analyses examining the relationship between socioeconomic conditions and incumbent electoral fortunes and the relative explanatory leverage of these indicators versus other noneconomic factors. The results of the analyses present a number of challenges to existing understandings about regional executive elections and accountability, indicating that not only did Russian voters go to the polls to "punish or reward" their regional executives but also that this behavior managed to manifest itself in actual election outcomes—governors in well-performing regions were more likely to hold onto their posts.

However, recent research by specialists working within the theoretical framework of "market-preserving federalism" suggests that Russia and other formerly socialist states would nonetheless benefit from a system of centrally appointed regional governments. Therefore, to study more closely how Russia's performance measures up to a similar state with appointed regional executives, I conclude the quantitative analyses with a comparative exploration of executive turnover in Ukraine, where I examine the requisites of central-government-controlled executive turnover and compare the outcome with the results from the Russian case. The results provide further support for the contention that, for all of its failings, Russia's system of regional elections served an accountability function better than the possible alternative of appointed regional bosses.

The Context

Given its focus upon electoral accountability in Russian regional executive elections, a full discussion of Russian federalism lies beyond the purview of this study. However, a brief overview of Russia's federal structures here provides the necessary context for the reader and gives some sense of the Russian Federation's existing complexities.

This study focuses on the politics, economics, and electoral processes of Russia's eighty-nine regions, which at points throughout the study will also be referred to as "provinces," "subnational units," and "federal subjects" (see figure 1.1 for administrative boundaries). At the time of writing, the Russian Federation consisted of five different types of federal subjects that, within Russia's asymmetrical federal structure, enjoyed different rights and privileges. These included twenty-one republics, six territories (*kraia*), forty-nine provinces (oblasti), two "cities of federal significance" (Moscow and Saint Petersburg), one autonomous oblast, and ten autonomous districts (autonomous *okruga*).

As will be discussed in further detail in chapter 2, the oblasti and *kraia* enjoyed roughly similar status as subnational administrative units whose boundaries were not determined by the existence of any particular ethnic or national group. "Ethnic" republics and autonomous *okruga* ostensibly existed to represent the interests of the titular minority within their borders, but beyond that the similarities largely ended. Autonomous *okruga*, which are often contained within the territories of other oblasti and *kraia*, are regulated by the vague and potentially contradictory article 65 of the Russian Constitution, which makes them subject to both the federal government and

Figure 1.1. The Russian Federation's Administrative Boundaries

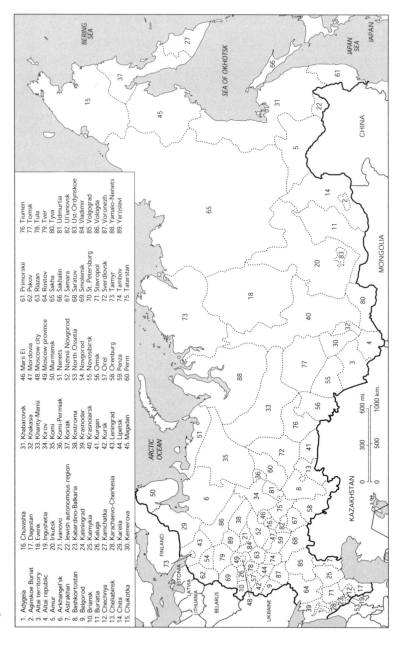

1. Adygeia
2. Aginskoe Buriat
3. Atai territory
4. Atai republic
5. Amur
6. Arkhangel'sk
7. Astrakhan
8. Bashkortostan
9. Belgorod
10. Briansk
11. Buriatia
12. Chechnya
13. Cheliabinsk
14. Chita
15. Chukotka
16. Chuvashia
17. Dagestan
18. Evenk
19. Ingushetia
20. Irkutsk
21. Ivanovo
22. Jewish autonomous region
23. Kabardino-Balkaria
24. Kaliningrad
25. Kalmykia
26. Kaluga
27. Kamchatka
28. Karachaevo-Cherkesia
29. Karelia
30. Kemerova
31. Khabarovsk
32. Khakasia
33. Khanty-Mansi
34. Kirov
35. Komi
36. Komi-Permiak
37. Koriak
38. Kostroma
39. Krasnodar
40. Krasnoiarsk
41. Kurgan
42. Kursk
43. Leningrad
44. Lipetsk
45. Magadan
46. Marii El
47. Mordovia
48. Moscow city
49. Moscow province
50. Murmansk
51. Nenets
52. Nizhnii Novgorod
53. North Ossetia
54. Novgorod
55. Novosibirsk
56. Omsk
57. Orel
58. Orenburg
59. Penza
60. Perm
61. Primorskii
62. Pskov
63. Riazan
64. Rostov
65. Sakha
66. Sakhalin
67. Samara
68. Saratov
69. Smolensk
70. St. Petersburg
71. Stavropol
72. Sverdlovsk
73. Taimyr
74. Tambov
75. Tatarstan
76. Tiumen
77. Tomsk
78. Tula
79. Tver
80. Tyva
81. Udmurtia
82. Ul'ianovsk
83. Ust-Ordynskoe
84. Vladimir
85. Volgograd
86. Vologda
87. Voronezh
88. Yamalo-Nenets
89. Yaroslavl

Source: Adapted from map appearing in Grigorii V. Golosov, *Political Parties in the Regions of Russia: Democracy Unclaimed* (Boulder: Lynn Reiner, 2004).

the ruling authorities of the federal subject within which their territory lies. Furthermore, article 5 of the Constitution indicates that the autonomous *okruga* are equal in status to all other regions.[28]

Throughout the 1990s, the republics enjoyed a special status within the Russian Federation, both through privileges granted by the Russian Constitution and through the signing of bilateral treaties between individual regions and Moscow. Aside from their being among the first federal subjects with elected regional executives (in most cases, "presidents"), these regions also boasted their own constitutions, which often provided them with greater prerogatives vis-à-vis other federal subjects over various policymaking jurisdictions or exempted them from responsibilities facing regional administrations in the oblasti and *kraia*.

Treaty negotiations added to these differences, giving the republics greater power over natural resources within their territories, securing subsidies from the federal government, and offering more control over taxes collected within their boundaries. As Kahn indicates, republican authorities essentially used their (often dubious) status as representatives of potentially problematic ethnic minorities as leverage in negotiations with Moscow. In addition to, and partly as a result of, the economic and fiscal privileges outlined above, this status also gained republican administrators a certain immunity from central government intervention, allowing them to even set up quasi-authoritarian regimes within their territories.[29]

The elections to be examined in this study span a period from 1991 to 2003, with the quantitative section in chapter 5 dealing primarily with the period from June 1996 to April 2001. This choice of election period for the quantitative analysis was largely driven by the fact that a number of the economic variables, particularly gross regional product, were only available for this time span at the time of writing. Because the economic data are presented on an annual basis beginning at the end of 1995, and the measures employed in the aggregate-level analyses are measures of change over the year before the election (thereby requiring that a measure be drawn from the year before), I examined only those cases that held an election within six months of the end of 1996 (thereby drawing on change in the economic indicators from December 1995 to December 1996) and the first four months of 2001 (the latter drawing on change from December 1999 to December 2000 and also reflecting the fact that the April elections marked the end of the 1999–2001 regional executive election cycle).[30] Other data availability issues arose from the fact that separate economic indicators are often not provided for autonomous *okruga* that are contained within other federal subjects.

Hence, the aggregate-level data analyses in chapter 5 represent a subset of elections across this period for which complete data were available.

Finally, a few words are in order regarding my use of the term "cycles" in this analysis. Though Golosov's election cycles represent the actual ordering of elections in a region (first, second, and third cycles represent first, second, and third elections), my use of the term coincides more closely with that of Steven Solnick and others who focus on the fact that Russia's regional executive election history has resulted in election schedules that place more than half the regions' elections in an intensive year-long election cluster.[31] This factor allows analysts to compartmentalize Russia's decade-long regional executive election history into periods of intense electoral activity (1996–97, 1999–2001, 2004–5) during which a large number of regions underwent elections under roughly similar national conditions.

Hence, though the quantitative analyses examine the entire period from 1996-2001 using year dummies to control out factors specific to a given year, the more descriptive sections of this work often feature references to first (1996–97) and second (1999–2001) election cycles with an eye toward explaining how the general context of regional executive elections changed over time. For the purposes of this study, this approach is perhaps more useful for delimiting changes across time than one that simply looks at regions' first and second elections. Depending on the timing of the first election, a region's second election could very well fall before or after a major change in the national political and economic environment, and so one region's second election might occur under external conditions remarkably different from another's (e.g., turning points might include the 1998 financial crisis, Putin taking office, or the elimination of appointees). Speaking of general trends in terms of the 1996–97 and 1999–2001 election clusters largely eliminates this problem and allows me to focus on the impact of changes on key factors by examining regions subject to the same external and internal factors during a relatively brief period of time.

Data Sources

Moving on to the empirical raw material for these analyses, all electoral, political, and candidate characteristic data for the quantitative analyses are drawn from a number of sources, including the official Web site of the Russian Central Election Commission,[32] as well as official Russian Central Election Commission Publications, such as *Vybory glav ispolnitel'noi vlasti sub'ektov Rossiiskoi Federation: Elektoral'naia statistika*, the two-tome *Vybory gosudarstvennoi vlasti sub'ektov Rossiiskoi Federatsii 1997–2000: Elektoralnaia statistika*, and a CD-ROM collection of election results called *10 let izbiratel'noi sisteme Rossiiskoi Federatsii, Vybory v Rossiiskoi Federatsii 1993–2003: Elektoralnaia statistika*.[33] Additional information was drawn from Grigoryi Belonuchkin's "Politika" Web site,[34] and from the Web site for *Regiony Rossii: Politika i Kadry*.[35] Further data on individual regions' elections were drawn from numerous online central and regional-level news pieces and analyses.

Economic data, performance assessments, and economic policy information were drawn from the state statistical agency (Goskomstat and its regional affiliates), Ministry of Finance materials, and official documents of various regional administrations. Of particular use were regional economic yearbooks, Goskomstat's annual *Regiony Rossii* economic data collection, and budgetary data provided by Aleksei Lavrov of Russia's Ministry of Finance. Ukrainian regional-level performance indicators were drawn from Derzhkomstat's *Statistichnii Shchorichnik Ukraini: 2002* and other official documents. Russian regional budgetary data employed in the regional survey/case analyses were drawn from both official regional sources and federal figures (often providing wildly different assessments). Official documents and economic policy assessments from Russian and Western scholars, regional administrations, federal state servants, and media-based policy commentators helped define dynamics in regional economic performance and federal fiscal relations, identify which organs were responsible for which outcomes, and determine how various policies influenced these dynamics. Works by TACIS,[36] regional and federal-level newspapers, broadcast media, the Laboratory for Regional Analysis and Political Geography at Moscow State University, the Ekspert Institute,[37] a number of publications from regional administrations (both print and Internet based), and the Middle Volga Science Center–Ul'ianovsk are just some of the more frequently consulted sources.

Along with accessing data sources for the quantitative analyses, this project also involved a great amount of fieldwork to become familiar with elections and with economic and financial issues at the regional level. Extensive interviewing with regional political figures, bureaucrats, businesspeople, and academics from Samara, Ul'ianovsk, Nizhnii Novgorod, Perm, Kazan, Saratov, Moscow, Saint Petersburg, Kyiv, and other areas of Russia and Ukraine provided critical insights into the working of election systems, interbudgetary finance, and economic trends. Many hours were spent poring over legislation and decrees to determine how the electoral and fiscal institutions had evolved in the course of the 1990s.

Thanks to the ever-growing amount of information on the Internet, I was also able to monitor elections in regions of all parts of Russia by accessing electronic versions of national and regional newspapers. Election analyses, electronic and otherwise, provided general background information for the past decade of elections. Together with the national and regional media sources, these helped color the statistical data, pointed out potential sources of anomalies in the results, and indicated causes for unexplained variance in the models. As with any theory-driven quantitative analysis, the models presented in the chapters below contain substantial error terms, and the included predictors only account for a portion of the variation in the dependent variable. Having become well acquainted with the situation "on the ground" and glimpsing the many essentially unquantifiable idiosyncrasies of some of my cases, I at least gained a respectable grasp of what the models do *not* (and perhaps *could* not) explain.[38]

Structure

Including this introduction, this book consists of seven chapters. Chapter 2 expands upon the literature briefly discussed above, examining both the issue of accountability and previous work on economic voting in the advanced industrial democracies, former Eastern Bloc countries, and Russia's regions. In the process of this review, I note that though the literature has a rich history, it is still marked by heretofore-unresolved divisions, inconsistent results, and a paltry treatment of former socialist cases—especially at the regional level. Greater attention is given to the handful of regional-level studies with an eye toward identifying their main weaknesses. The chapter concludes with an application of key elements from the previously discussed literature to the issue of economic voting in Russia's regions at the end of the first post-Soviet decade, essentially presenting the arguments to be tested in the later quantitative chapters.

Chapter 3 acts as an introduction to the more quantitatively oriented chapters that follow. I start by offering a brief history of the development of the institution of elected governors in Russia. After this, I provide a detailed comparison between the 1996–97 and 1999–2001 elections. Special attention is given to differences in the legal, federal-level political, and economic backgrounds of each given election phase. Further information is provided regarding variations in incumbent success across different types of federal subjects, variations in the levels of competitiveness across different elections, and the extent to which officeholders resorted to incumbent-friendly election laws between election cycles. The material from this chapter thereby provides a background against which to assess the results of the following three quantitative chapters.

Chapter 4 presents the first of the two quantitative studies with analyses of preelection survey data drawn from Ul'ianovskaia Oblast. It begins with a survey of political and economic processes and events in the region during the past decade of its postsocialist development. Then I offer a series of regional-level survey data analyses (the first such study), using binomial logistic regression models to predict support for incumbents on a simple "support/nonsupport" dichotomous dependent variable. The results of these analyses indicate that for this case, respondents going into the election were very conscious of economic factors when assessing their incumbents. Moreover, respondents appeared to make use of sophisticated evaluation methods, with comparative sociotropic considerations strongly related to incumbent assessments. These results, drawing on heretofore unexploited data and methods (for the Russian case), present remarkable new evidence regarding economic voting in Russia and indicate that, contrary to previous studies at the federal level, Russian citizens do in fact employ relatively complex economic popularity functions.

Chapter 5 builds upon the results of the survey analyses to determine whether these outcomes translate into aggregate-level patterns for all elections that occurred from 1996 to 2001. Using data drawn from the election database mentioned above, and employing a new measure of *relative* regional economic performance, I run a series of logistic regressions to determine whether and how economic factors influenced the outcomes of these elections. Again, the results challenge the conclusions of previous studies, especially Solnick's analysis of the 1996–97 election cycle. The relative change in the adjusted wage measure provides a statistically significant predictor for the change in the probability of an incumbent's electoral win, whereas such factors as regional ideological preferences played little role in predicting said outcomes. The results of this chapter provide the first solid evidence of a link between regional economic performance and incumbent electoral success during the set of elections from 1996 to 2001.

In chapter 6, I situate the results of the previous analyses within a more explicitly comparative framework. To address an important recent debate arising from the market-preserving federalism literature, I compare the relative effectiveness of Russia's regional executive elections in holding regional policymakers accountable for economic outcomes to that of the unitary state of Ukraine. Scholars working within the theoretical framework of market-preserving federalism have recently suggested that elections in states pursuing economic reforms are a hindrance to progrowth policies. However, studies by a number of China specialists, and the results of my own analyses in Ukraine, indicate that the act of placing powers of appointment in the hands of central governments does not guarantee that these governments will make appointments and dismissals on the basis of economic criteria. I therefore conclude that there is little evidence to support the contention that appointments provide a better tool for spurring subnational economic growth.

Chapter 7 recapitulates the findings of the previous analysis, identifies five challenges confronting regional-level electoral accountability at the beginning of the Putin administration's first term, describes the efforts undertaken by the administration to deal with these challenges, and presents the implications of these efforts for regional accountability. The period from 2001 to 2004 marked an interim between Yeltsin-era elections and the final elimination of elections in December 2004. During this period, the administration took steps to eliminate certain election tactics, rein in the unrestricted abuse of administrative resources, clarify policymaking jurisdictions, control regional media outlets, establish national party structures in all Russian regions, and intervene to eliminate "problem governors."

Unfortunately, as argued in chapter 7, these efforts often undercut rather than enhanced electoral accountability. The abuse of administrative resources became the sole domain of United Russia party allies. Policy jurisdictions were clarified, but perhaps at the expense of local self-government. Media outlets—particularly those that opposed Kremlin-backed candidates—were temporarily muzzled and continued to face pressure from federal authorities. Regional-level United Russia party organizations provided poor information shortcuts for voters and acted as powerful electoral machines for any incumbent or challenger who affiliated with them. And finally, more and more frequent federal intervention undercut interest in elections by enforcing the perception of federal government dominance. The system of regional executive elections that existed in 2004 was a far cry from the elections of the Yeltsin and early-Putin eras, and federal authorities were increasingly in a position to determine the outcomes of regional elections.

The study ends with a speculative discussion regarding the potential shape of a Russia without regional executive elections. On the basis of the evidence drawn from the quantitative analyses and the lessons from the Ukrainian case, I argue that Putin's initiatives will have an adverse effect on regional-level electoral accountability—creating a situation in which regional leaders are sanctioned and rewarded for their region's electoral performance during national elections ("getting out the vote") and for their personal loyalty to the Kremlin rather than for their success as regional managers. In spite of the ample shortcomings of the Yeltsin and early-Putin eras' regional executive elections, my analyses indicate that the system as it existed from 1996 to 2001 still delivered an element of regional account-ability, forcing executives to focus on the particular needs of their juris-dictions. Putin's proposed system of officials "elected by recommendation of the president" will shift the focus of policymaking away from the regions and roll back some of the modest gains of Russia's post-Soviet political transformation.

Notes

1. Kathryn Stoner-Weiss, "The Russian Central State in Crisis," in *Russian Politics: Challenges of Democratization,* ed. Zoltan Barany and Robert Moser (Cambridge: Cambridge University Press, 2001).

2. Studies focused on Yeltsin- and Putin-era federalism include Stoner-Weiss, "Russian Central State in Crisis"; Alfred Stepan, "Russian Federalism in Comparative Perspective," *Post-Soviet Affairs* 16 (2000): 133–76; Jeffrey Kahn, *Federalism, Democratization, and the Rule of Law in Russia* (Oxford: Oxford University Press, 2002); Steven Solnick, "Federal Bargaining in Russia," *East European Constitutional Review* 4, no. 4 (1995): 52–58; Daniel Treisman, *After the Deluge: Regional Crises and Political Consolidation in Russia* (Ann Arbor: University of Michigan Press, 1999); V. B. Khristenko, *Mezhbiudzhetnye otnosheniia i upravlenie regional'nymi finansami* (Moscow: Izdatelstvo Delo, 2002); Peter Reddaway and Robert Orttung, eds., *Dynamics of Russian Politics: Putin's Reform of Federal–Regional Relations* (Lanham, Md.: Rowman & Littlefield, 2004); Elizabeth Pascal, *Defining Russian Federalism* (Westport, Conn.: Praeger, 2003); Mikhail Stoliarov, *Federalism and the Dictatorship of Power in Russia* (London: Routledge, 2003); Graeme Herd and Anne Adlis, eds., *Russian Regions and Regionalism: Strength through Weakness* (London: Routledge Curzon, 2003); Vladimir Gelman et al., *Avtonomiia ili kontrol'? Reforma mestnoi vlasti v gorodakh Rossii, 1991–2001* (Saint Petersburg: European University in Saint Petersburg, 2002); and Daniel Kempton and Terry Clark, eds., *Unity or Separation: Center–Periphery Relations in the Former Soviet Union* (Westport, Conn.: Praeger, 2002).

3. See (in order) Ukaz Prezidenta Rossiiskoi Federatsii "O polnomochnom predstavitele Prezidenta Rossiiskoi Federatsii v federal'nom okruge" (May 13, 2000, N 849); Federal'nyi zakon, "O vnesenii izmenenii i dopolnenii v Federal'noi zakon: Ob obshikh printsipakh organizatsii zakonodatel'nikh (predstavitel'nikh) i ispolnitel'nikh organov gosudarstvennoi vlasti subektov Rossiiskoi Federatsii" (signed by the State Duma on July 19, 2000), *Rossiiskaia Gazeta,* August 1, 2000, 6; and Federal'nyi zakon, "O vnesenii

dopolneniia v federal'nyi zakon: Ob obshikh printsipakh organizatsii zakonodatel'nikh (predstavitel'nikh) i ispolnitel'nikh organov gosudarstvennoi vlasti subektov Rossiiskoi Federatsii" (February 8, 2001, N 3-F3). For commentary on the federal government's attempts to implement legislation easing the process of removing governors, see Irina Skliarova, "Podpisei ne ponadobitsia: Pravitel'stvo namereno uprostit' protseduru otstavki gubernatorov," *Vremia Novostei,* November 3, 2003, 4. The term limit issue has been the topic of frequent waffling by the president and federal authorities. Elections for key regional executives like Shaimiev in Tartarstan apparently resulted in changes to the law allowing for third and even fourth terms in some cases. See Ivan Rodin, "Regional'naia politika Kremlia opiat' meniaetesia?" *Nezavisimaia Gazeta,* February 6, 2001, http://www.ng.ru/politics/2001-06-02/1_change.html. For a very intensive analytical treatment of Putin-era federative reforms, see Gordon Hahn, "The Impact of Putin's Federative Reforms on Democratization in Russia," *Post-Soviet Affairs* 2 (2003): 114–53.

4. The issue of returning to regional executive appointments has appeared in a number of media and academic discussions. For an example from Duma debates, see the discussion surrounding Vitalii Vladimirovich Lednik's presentation of an amendment eliminating elected governors in *Gosudarstvennaia Duma: Stenogramma zasedanii,* February 15, 2001.

5. Pavel Dul'man, "Garmonii ne khvataet," *Rossiiskaia Gazeta,* September 25, 2003.

6. Irian Romancheva, "Zor'kin otvetil Ryzhkovu cherez press-sluzhbu: Konstitutsionyi sud otkazyvaetsia reagirovat' na reformu konstitutsiunnykh osnov strany," *Nezavisimaia Gazeta,* October 1, 2004. Viktor Khamraev, "Vertikal: Prezident postavil deputatov v privychnoe polozhenie po voprosu o vybornosti gubernatorov," *Kommersant Daily,* September 30, 2004.

7. Pavel Dul'man, "Novosti: Dlia kogo zakon zapisan," *Rossiiskaia Gazeta,* December 15, 2004.

8. Andrei Riskin, "Regiony vstupilis' za konstitutsiiu," *Nezavisimaia Gazeta,* October 29, 2004.

9. The survey question asked, "If heads of regions will be elected not by residents, but by regional legislative assemblies upon the recommendation of the President, will this have a more positive or more negative effect?" See "Reforma regional'noi vlasti," *Baza Dannykh FOM,* December 9, 2004.

10. Henry Hale, "The Regionalization of Autocracy in Russia," in *Harvard University Program on New Approaches to Russian Security Policy Memo Series,* ed. Erin Powers, Memo 42 (Cambridge, Mass.: Harvard University, 1998). The practice of referring to Russia's regions as "fiefdoms" of their respective executives has become a commonplace throughout region-focused stories and analysis. I am unaware of who initially applied this characterization.

11. "Politiki o reforme gosvlasti, predlozhennoi V. Putin," *RosBiznesKonsalting,* September 13, 2004, http://top.rbc.ru/news/daythemes/2004/09/13/13142357_pv.shtml.

12. "Politiki o reforme gosvlasti, predlozhennoi V. Putin."

13. Eugene Rummer, "What Democracy Can Putin Destroy?" *Christian Science Monitor,* September 29, 2004.

14. Bernard Manin, Adam Przeworski, and Susan Stokes, "Elections and Representation," in *Democracy, Accountability, and Representation,* ed. Adam Przeworski, Bernard Manin, and Susan Stokes (Cambridge: Cambridge University Press, 1999), 29–54.

15. Manin, Przeworksi, and Stokes, "Elections and Representation," 40.

16. Jose Antonio Cheibub and Adam Przeworski, "Accountability for Economic Outcomes," in *Democracy, Accountability, and Representation*.

17. Though the term *khoziain* translates literally into "manager," it generally conveys a sense of a patriarchal "boss" who will manage the affairs of a given organization. Vera Tolz and Irina Busygina make a similar point in their study of conflicts between regional governors and central authorities. See Vera Tolz and Irina Busygina, "Regional Governors and the Kremlin: The Ongoing Battle for Power," *Communist and Post-Communist Studies* 30, no. 4 (1997): 405.

18. In a poll conducted in December 1996 by FOM, respondents were asked about which qualities a governor must posses. A total of 64 percent of the respondents indicated that he or she must be a good *khoziastvennik*. See Anna Petrova and Anna Vorontsova, "Vserossiiskaia izvestnost': U Iuria Luzhkova i Borisa Nemtsova," *Baza Dannykh FOM*, December 26, 1996, http://bd.fom.ru/report/map/of19965103.

19. Tolz and Busygina, "Regional Governors and the Kremlin," 421.

20. This is by no means to say that regional (or national, for that matter) economic indicators are *easy* to measure. Such indicators ignore the true extent of the shadow economy, are subject to some manipulation by regional statistical agencies, and have been the subject of much revision throughout the first post-Soviet decade. Furthermore, economists continue to debate the exact meaning of official economic indicators and whether they are indeed a precise representation of the actual trends in the post-Soviet economy. My main point here is to indicate that, among the field of other measures of regional conditions, economic indicators are the only standardized and consistently measured indicators available and therefore present the best option for a cross-regional study including each of Russia's eighty-nine regions.

21. Among the myriad studies of economic voting are such works as Gerald Kramer, "Short-Term Fluctuations in U.S. Voting Behavior, 1896–1964," *American Political Science Review* 65 (1971): 131–43; Donald Kinder and D. Roderick Kiewiet, "Sociotropic Politics: The American Case," *British Journal of Political Science* 11 (1981): 129–61; Stanley Feldman, "Economic Self-Interest and Political Behavior," *American Journal of Political Science* 26 (1982): 446–66; Stephen Weatherford, "Economic Conditions and Electoral Outcomes: Class Differences in the Political Response to Recession," *American Journal of Political Science* 22 (1983): 917–38; Morris Fiorina, "Economic Retrospective Voting in American National Elections: A Micro-Analysis," *American Journal of Political Science* 22 (1978): 426–43; Howard Bloom and Douglas Price, "Voter Response to Short-Run Economic Conditions: The Asymmetric Effect of Prosperity and Recession," *American Political Science Review* 69 (1975): 1240–54; Edward Tufte, "Determinants of the Outcomes of Midterm Congressional Elections," *American Political Science Review* 69 (1975): 812–26; Edward Tufte, *Political Control of the Economy* (Princeton, N.J.: Princeton University Press, 1978); Raymond Fair, "The Effects of Economic Events on Votes for the President," *Review of Economics and Statistics* 60 (1978): 159–73; J. R. Hibbing and J. R. Alford, "The Electoral Impact of Economic Conditions: Who Is Held Responsible?" *American Journal of Political Science* 25 (1981): 423–39; and George Stigler, "General Economic Conditions and National Elections," *American Economic Review* 63 (1973): 160–67.

22. This phrase, immortalized in a sign hanging in Bill Clinton's "War Room" during the 1992 Clinton-Gore election campaign, now appears regularly in academic and popular discussions regarding the role of the economy in election campaigns.

23. Samuel Popkin, *The Reasoning Voter* (Chicago: University of Chicago Press, 1991), 51.

24. Studies of subnational economic voting (which are further discussed in chapter 2 below) include Robert Stein, "Economic Voting for Governor and U.S. Senator: The Electoral Consequences of Federalism," *Journal of Politics* 52 (1990): 29–53; Stephen Turret, "The Vulnerability of American Governors, 1900–1969," *Midwest Journal of Political Science,* 15 (1971): 108-132; John Chubb, "Institutions, the Economy, and the Dynamics of State Elections," *American Political Science Review* 82 (1988): 133–54; Malcolm Jewell and David Olson, *Political Parties and Elections in American States* (Chicago: Dorsey, 1988); Michael Lewis-Beck and Tom Rice, *Forecasting Elections* (Washington, D.C.: CQ Press, 1992); L. R. Atkeson and R. W. Partin, "Economic and Referendum Voting: A Comparison of Gubernatorial and Senatorial Elections," *American Political Science Review* 89 (1995): 99–107; Richard Niemi, Harold Stanley, and Ronald Vogel, "State Economies and State Taxes: Do Voters Hold Governors Accountable?" *American Journal of Political Science* 39 (1995): 936–57; and Karen Remmer and François Gélineau, "Subnational Electoral Choice: Economic and Referendum Voting in Argentina, 1983–1999," *Comparative Political Studies* 36 (2003): 801–21.

25. One can divide the economic voting literature focused on transition states into two broad categories: those that look at the effect of economic performance and standard of living on support for *institutions* (i.e., the market, free elections); and those that focus on these factors' impact on support for parties and candidates. Because this study does not examine support for institutions per se, I will only discuss this literature briefly in chapter 2. For examples of this literature, see the discussion in chapter 8 of Richard Rose, William Mishler, and Christian Haerpfer, *Democracy and its Alternatives* (Baltimore: Johns Hopkins University Press, 1998). For another study of economic and political institutional support in Russia, see James Gibson, "Political and Economic Markets," *Journal of Politics* 58 no. 4 (1996): 954–98. For examples of studies examining the linkage between economic conditions and support for individuals or parties, see Timothy Colton, "Economics and Voting in Russia," *Post-Soviet Affairs* 12 (1996): 313–14; Timothy Colton, *Transitional Citizens: Voters and What Influences Them in the New Russia* (Cambridge, Mass.: Harvard University Press, 2000); Timothy Colton and Michael McFaul, *Popular Choice and Managed Democracy* (Washington, D.C.: Brookings Institution Press, 2003).

26. Steven Solnick, "Gubernatorial Elections in Russia, 1996–1997," *Post-Soviet Affairs,* 14 (1998): 48–80; G. V. Golosov, "Povedenie izbiratelei v Rossii: Teoreticheskie perspektivy i rezultaty regionalnikh vyborov," *Polis* 4 (1997): 44–56; Andrew Konitzer-Smirnov, "Incumbent Election Fortunes and Regional Economic Performance during Russia's 2000–2001 Regional Executive Election Cycle," *Post-Soviet Affairs* 19 (2003): 46–79; Christopher Marsh, "Social Capital and Grassroots Democracy in Russia's Regions: Evidence from the 1999–2001 Gubernatorial Elections," *Demokratizatsiya: The Journal of Post-Soviet Democratization* 10 (2002): 19–36; Bryon Moraski and William M. Reisinger, "Explaining Electoral Competition across Russia's Regions," *Slavic Review* 62 (2003): 278–301.

27. See the appendix to this volume for the coding of key indicators in the database.

28. Grigorii Golosov, *Political Parties in the Regions of Russia: Democracy Unclaimed* (Boulder, Colo.: Lynne Rienner, 2004), 57–59.

29. Kahn, *Federalism, Democratization, and the Rule of Law in Russia.*

30. In previous analyses, I also experimented with longer time lags, including changes

in indicators during the incumbent's term. As in the bulk of the economic voting literature, these approaches yielded weak results, once again indicating that voters appear to have roughly year-long memories of economic conditions.

31. Golosov's focus on the role of parties in both regional legislative and executive elections also makes his choice of definitions more appropriate for his subject material. The two types of elections rarely overlap.

32. See the Web site for the Central Election Commission of the Russian Federation, http://www.cikrf.ru/m_menu.htm.

33. Central Election Commission of the Russian Federation, *Vybory glav ispolnitel'noi vlasti sub'ektov Rossiiskoi Federatsii: Elektoral'naia statistika* (Moscow: Ves' Mir, 1997); Central Election Commission of the Russian Federation, *Vybory gosudarstvennoi vlasti sub'ektov Rossiiskoi Federatsii 1997–2000: Elektoralnaia statistika, tom 1–2* (Moscow: Ves' Mir, 2001); Central Election Commission of the Russian Federation, *10 let izbiratel'noi sisteme Rossiiskoi Federatsii, Vybory v Rossiiskoi Federatsii 1993–2003: Elektoralnaia statistika,* CD-ROM (Moscow: Mercator Group).

34. Grigoryi Belonuchkin's "Politika" Web site, http://www.cityline.ru/politica/vybory/re00t.html; and http://www.cityline.ru/politica/vybory/re01t.html.

35. *Regiony Rossii: Politika i Kadry* (Regions of Russia: Politics and Cadre) published weekly bulletins on regional elections and politics; http://www.materik.ru/mfpp/polika.

36. TACIS is the European Union's Technical Assistance for the CIS [Commonwealth of Independent States] Countries program. A particularly useful TACIS publication was A. Granberg, ed., *Regionalnoe razvitie: Opyt rossii i evropeiskogo soiuza* (Moscow: Ekonomika, 2000).

37. Along with the Laboratory for Regional Analysis and Political Geography at Moscow State University, the Ekspert Institute, the Union of Industrialists and Entrepreneurs, and the Moscow National Bank created the investment guide *Predprinimatel'skii klimat regionov Rossii: Geografiia Rossii dlia investorov i predprinimatelei* (Moscow: Nachala Press, 1997). In addition to providing a useful guide for investors, the text offers a comprehensive examination of regional political, economic, and social climates, a range of socioeconomic and political data, and ratings for all regions. In addition to this, the Ekspert Institute publishes yearly regional ratings similar to those in the more inclusive guide.

38. Although more of these idiosyncrasies are discussed in later chapters, here I offer the case of Briansk as one example. The election there was characterized by the candidacy of three "clones"—individuals with names similar to those of other prominent candidates or political figures. Hence, the incumbent, Iurii Evgen'evich Lodkin, was "cloned" by his challenger Iurii Dmitrovich Lodkin. The strongest challenger to the "real" Iurii Lodkin, Nikolai Vasil'evich Denin, was "cloned" by another challenger, Aleksandr Vladimirovich Denin. See Boris Zemtsov, "Piarom po reitingu," *Nezavisimaia Gazeta,* December 14, 2000, http://www.ng.ru/regions/2000-12-14/4_reiting.html.

Chapter 2

Assigning Responsibility

Yes, an elected governor is always a major political figure. . . . But he must first of all tend to administrative problems: the budget, development of industry, villages, and the social protection of his citizens.

—Vladimir Solomonov

A governor must be a manager. If a region is like a giant conglomerate, he must understand how it functions.

—Konstantin Titov

Before casting their ballots, voters in any country face a series of difficult decisions that they must make using less-than-perfect information. Even assuming that economic well-being features prominently among her primary concerns (itself a simplification), the voter must resolve questions as to which elements of "economic well-being" she should focus upon, how to assess these elements, and who ultimately holds responsibility for outcomes related to these issues. She might define economic fortune in terms of wages, employment, prices, the provision of social benefits, or a host of other considerations.

The process of assessing performance within the realm of any one of these elements of economic well-being brings its own uncertainties. Will the individually fortunate voter cast her ballot for an incumbent even as the rest of society sinks into abject poverty? If not, how might the she evaluate the state of society? Finally, assuming that she properly assesses the prevailing conditions, the voter must choose among an expansive list of causes, including the policies of mayors, governors, legislatures, and presidents; wars; global economic downturns; and any number of other external factors.

Given this tumult of complex decisions, one might forgive analysts for concluding that "individual voters today seem unable to satisfy the requirements for a democratic system of government outlined by political theorists."[1]

This chapter describes how social scientists have grappled with these and other issues in their attempts to understand the economic accountability problem. First, I discuss recent formulations of accountability offered by Adam Przeworski, Susan Stokes, and Bernard Manin. Then I link the discussion of accountability to economic voting by presenting a survey of the economic voting literature drawn from the advanced industrial democracies. In the process, I identify currently underexamined areas within this literature, particularly those pertaining to the issue of economic voting in subnational elections. Next, I explore the much smaller collection of works dealing with economic voting in Russia. Of particular importance is the discussion of work by Steven Solnick, Bryon Moraski and William Reisinger, and Grigorii Golosov, some of the few scholars who deal exclusively with the issue of gubernatorial elections in Russia. Finally, I seek to place the present study within the framework of the just-described literature, indicating that this research provides the first multimethod, extensive analysis of a crucial factor in the political and economic development of Russia's regions: economic voting and executive accountability for economic performance.

A Few Words Regarding the "Portability of Concepts"

At the end of the first decade of post-Soviet governance in the former Soviet Union, one sees a divide between what are commonly known as "area specialists" and "comparativists." In the crudest of terms, area specialists are generally portrayed as possessing a detailed yet unstructured knowledge of the post-Soviet milieu and a weaker grasp of the methodologies and theories guiding the various disciplines with which they are associated. A stereotypical comparativist descends upon a region about which he or she knows very little and blithely applies theories and concepts drawn from his or her respective field. An area specialist (again speaking in hyperbole) produces reams of detailed description about cases and events that are of little interest to anyone outside the scholar's immediate circle. A comparativist improperly operationalizes hypotheses (which themselves are often inappropriate to the case at hand) and then misinterprets the results of generally quantitative analyses because of his or her ignorance of the region's specificities.

Although the intellectual conflicts surrounding this issue have essentially reified these polarized types (see the debates surrounding Cohen's *Failed Crusade*[2]), one should bear two points in mind. First, most scholars fall somewhere between these two extremes. Few stereotypical comparativists could even present (let alone publish) analyses bereft of any knowledge of the region's various idiosyncrasies without experiencing the ire and even ridicule of their area-knowledgeable colleagues. Conversely, the strictest area specialist, in an era where Russia qua Russia is no longer of great interest, is simply ignored.[3]

Second, though certain scholars participate in the debate as a means to protect their particular intellectual turf, one should not lose sight of the fact that the real question at hand is the "portability of concepts"—that is, the ability to transport concepts and theories developed and tested in one geographical and cultural space to another. In this respect, scholars are perhaps best to place themselves somewhere near the middle of the area specialist–versus–comparativist continuum, combining knowledge of the region with a grasp of concepts and theories relevant to their respective academic disciplines.

Transporting concepts from one region to another is not an academic heresy. In fact, such activities provide the very raison d'être for all social sciences. Having said this, the process should be conducted as methodically as possible. The dangers exist both that "foreign" concepts will be rejected too readily following a simple appraisal by a regionally knowledgeable observer, or that said concepts will be too readily accepted based on an uncritically examined, yet statistically significant, result.

I take this brief digression as means to essentially preempt any impulsive criticism of the discussion that follows. This study draws upon concepts conceived and developed in the advanced industrial democracies—regions that the author, drawing on his own extensive knowledge of Russia, recognizes as being far removed from the realities of the former socialist countries. Many of these concepts have already been rejected out of hand by scholars whose conclusions were legitimated by their deep understanding of the region rather than a combination of this understanding and methodical hypothesis testing.

Nonetheless, two assertions underlie this study. First, no reasonable, "transported" concept should be accepted or rejected without rigid testing informed by knowledge of the region. This is almost a social scientific axiom, but one that is nonetheless often ignored in practice. Second, Russian gubernatorial elections, like subnational elections throughout the world, are understudied and undertheorized. Hence, if one chooses to approach the topic within the normative conventions of social science, one must necessarily start with tools conceived of and developed in other regions of the world. At the beginning of this study, it appears unlikely that these tools will provide comprehensive and valid "solutions" to questions regarding gubernatorial election outcomes in Russia, but they promise to provide a first step in what I hope to be a longer path of inquiry. To use another "borrower's" words, "as a point of departure—as a guide to pressing *questions* to be posed and to how research into them might be fruitfully designed—the accumulated social science merits attention. The answers to the questions are an empirical matter, not to be prejudged."[4]

Accountability

According to Manin, Przeworski, and Stokes, "The claim connecting democracy and representation is that under democracy governments are representative because they are elected: if participation is widespread, and if citizens enjoy political liberties, then governments will act in the best interest of the people."[5] However, these researchers point out that the representation achieved through elections can take at least two forms, with important implications for both voter behavior and incumbent's incentives.

The first of these is what Manin and his colleagues call "mandate representation." This requires that voters choose candidates and parties based upon policy proposals put forth by the competing individuals or organizations in the course of the election campaign. For mandate representation to function, citizens must choose those policies that they want implemented and must have an understanding of which party or individual will be most likely to implement them; and upon election, the chosen party or individual must go on to implement said policies.

An alternative to the "mandate" approach is what Manin and his colleagues refer to as "accountability representation." According to this view, elections make for representation because they hold incumbents responsible for their performance in the previous term. Elections take on the air of a trial in which the jury/voters pass judgment on the incumbent's past deeds. If the jury is pleased (or at least finds no fault) with the incumbent, then he or she will be rewarded with another term in office.

As Manin and his colleagues point out, both approaches feature their own weaknesses. Mandate representation places very high informational and trust demands on both voters and incumbents. Two basic questions arise when confronted with a pure form of this approach: first, whether incumbents implement the same policies that they promised to implement in the course of the campaign, and second, whether at the time of the elections voters knew what policies were indeed best for them. In light of these questions, Manin and his colleagues present three circumstances under which mandate representation could occur: when politicians and voters have the same interests, when politicians both seek reelection and believe that maintaining their promises will help guarantee this outcome, and when politicians want their promises to be believed in future circumstances.

These three criteria raise serious problems for mandate views of representation. First, with regard to the coincidence of voters and politicians interests, one must confront the fact that, especially in the case of executives, it is very difficult for any politician's interests to truly coincide with that of "the majority." Furthermore, even if such a candidate could be found, there is no guarantee that his or her interests would not change upon entering office. Both interest structures and information change when individuals make the transformation from citizen to political officeholder.

The second criterion poses additional problems. For it to hold, voters must actually know what is good for them; politicians must recognize this and match their promises with the interests of the "decisive voter" (that hypothetical voter whose interests closely coincide with some winning majority); these promises must yield the citizens' expected outcomes; and the citizens must faithfully reciprocate by rewarding the candidate for essentially fulfilling his or her side of the contract.

Finally, the third criterion essentially imposes a straitjacket on incumbents, forcing them to abide by their promises under any circumstances based on the understanding that they will be punished by *any* deviation from their campaign platform.

In sum, Manin, Przeworski, and Stokes indicate that mandate representation is not only impractical but also undesirable. Voters do not have the resources available to gather the information necessary to know what is best for them in the present or future. Furthermore, promises made during a campaign cannot account for future events. If, during a world recession, voters and a candidate conclude a hypothetical "contract" for 1 percent growth in gross national product during the next four years, should voters be satisfied with such a figure during the global economic boom at the end of the candidate's term? During elections, both voters and candidates are operating under information constraints. For voters, some of these restraints will be removed as the term unfolds. However, for candidates, the moment of taking office amounts to a virtual flood of new information and interests. Maintaining the pact between the voter and officeholder would clearly be very difficult, and in fact, the maximizing voter might actually prefer the incumbent to take whatever course of action is necessary to achieve the *best* outcome rather than the one agreed upon during the course of a campaign.

"Accountability representation" essentially eliminates many of the problems posed by the mandate approach. The two necessary conditions for accountability representation are that voters reelect incumbents who act in their best interest and that these incumbents choose those policies that are most likely to result in their reelection. Here, the fact that voters assess incumbent performance at the end of a term eliminates many of the high information and trust requirements of the mandate approach.

Manin, Przeworski, and Stokes pose the accountability issue in game theoretic terms. Office seekers may have a wide variety of reasons for seeking office, but once in power they are faced with a rather simple choice. The officeholder can attempt to maximize the well-being of the voters under the understanding that this will yield a fixed payoff in the form of reelection. Conversely, he or she could "shirk," extracting rents (embezzling funds, enriching one's clique, creating and outfitting a "golden parachute") in the current term with the understanding that he or she will lose the next election.

Further complicating the picture for the officeholder is the fact that he or she will be evaluated on the basis of past events and under conditions that will be known by the voter. Hence, simply conforming to campaign promises made under conditions of mutual ignorance about future conditions will not suffice to win reelection. The reelection-seeking officeholder must purse the best policies for the given conditions, thus maximizing the return for the electorate.

Through a simple game, illustrated in figure 2.1, Manin and his colleagues indicate how accountability representation plays out across different external conditions. Given two types of conditions ("good" and "bad"), the politician chooses between two policies. Policy A provides better results for voters under good conditions, and policy B provides better outcomes under bad ones. Voters will reelect the candidate who pursues the policy that maximizes the well-being of the voters under whichever conditions held for the term in question.

Which policy an incumbent chooses will depend on the payoff as indicated by the first of the two numbers in each of the cells in figure 2.1. The shaded cells indicate incumbents' reelection payoff, which consists of their salaries and the perks of office ($r^* = 1 + e$, where e is some small but

Figure 2.1. The Accountability Game

	Policy A	Policy B
Good conditions	$1 + e, 5$	3, 3
Bad conditions	3, 1	$1 + e, 3$

positive number) plus the incumbent's personal evaluation of holding office ($V = 2$). Incumbents are guaranteed this payoff if they pursue the optimal policies for voters. The numbers in the unshaded cells indicate the incumbents' payoff by implementing the voter's least preferred policies, extracting rents for themselves, and losing the next election.

Accountability is thus enforced under "good conditions" as follows. The incumbent's payoff for choosing the voters' preferred policy A is $r^* = (1+e) +2$. This is greater than the "shirkers payoff" of 3, which the incumbent would have received had he or she chosen the voter's suboptimal policy B, pocketed the rents, and lost the election. In this situation, it is thus in the incumbent's interests to pursue policies that will benefit the voter and ensure the incumbent's reelection.

The equilibrium for this game conforms to a perfect state of accountability through retrospective voting. Voters want to maximize their well-being, incumbents want to hold office, and all parties possess the information necessary to make their respective choices. However, a number of factors may prevent parties from reaching this equilibrium. Despite the fact that they are drawing upon past events, voters may not possess as much information as incumbents. Though Manin, Przeworski, and Stokes refer only to factors like negotiations with foreign governments and demand for exports as things that citizens cannot "observe," I argue that even theoretically observable factors like a small town's economy are the subject of some speculation. Not only may citizens not have the time, resources, or know-how to uncover otherwise observable factors, but they may also have no idea who is responsible for the outcomes that they may observe.

Manin and his colleagues also indicate that some voters are more "myopic" than some formulations of the accountability approach may suggest. To borrow their apt example, "If the economy grows because the government cuts all the trees in the country, the voter will live on champagne during the term, but there will be no trees left to cut."[6] Hence, some voters may interpret the "successes" of the previous term with varying understandings of the legacies of these policies in the future. The information problem again arises, with the voter once more at a disadvantage. In the final analysis, the efficacy of accountability as a means to promote representation is also highly dependent upon the information available to individual voters.

Even so, when juxtaposed against the "mandate" alternative, an accountability approach to representation offers clear normative, methodological, and operational advantages. It better recognizes the information and enforcement costs facing both candidates and voters, and it takes into account fluctuations in policies and conditions over time. Accountability may be an even highly imperfect means for evaluating incumbents, but given the constraints, it is arguably the most viable means by which the majority of voters assess competing candidates.

Nonetheless, certain institutional factors in any democracy may enhance or diminish the viability of elections as accountability mechanisms. In the final stages of their discussion, the authors lay out the institutional and procedural requirements necessary to induce incumbent accountability. These provide a useful set of conditions for evaluating the potential for accountability representation in any setting and constitute the main criteria for accountability in the remainder of this study.

First, voters must possess the ability to assign responsibility for policy and policy outcomes. Manin, Przeworski, and Stokes indicate that responsibility may be obfuscated by such factors as coalition governments, executive and legislative branches controlled by different parties, or cabinet executives. However, once one begins to examine subnational elections, the list of institutions and actors expands to include branches of government and agencies from any number of levels. Undefined jurisdictional responsibilities can become a matter for speculation by both opponents and incumbents seeking to pass the blame or to claim responsibility for policy outcomes.

Second, voters must be able to vote incumbents out of office and replace them with the candidates of their choice. To illustrate this standard, Manin, Przeworski, and Stokes offer such cases as Mexico's Institutional Revolutionary Party, Japan's Liberal Democratic Party, and Bolivia's entire election system. Here, despite the trappings of democracy, the electorate apparently cannot easily vote the incumbent party out of office. However, such circumstances might result from other decidedly "noninstitutional" factors. Incumbents in any given election may put forth a bogus challenger, existing challengers could exit from the race, or the alternative could be so weak that no "real" challenger exists. In any event, a lack of any viable alternative prevents voters from holding incumbents accountable.

Third, politicians need the correct incentives to seek reelection. This requirement speaks to ephemeral party systems in which parties appear to contest the election and then disintegrate by the time the next election rolls around (arguably similar to the Russian case), instances in which incumbents face term limits, or situations where the rewards of office are so low that the only incentive to run is to plunder the office for a term and then exit. Accountability is an iterative game. If the incumbent plays only once, then there are fewer incentives preventing him or her from shirking and extracting rents.

Fourth, an opposition must be present to monitor politicians and inform citizens. This speaks to the all-important issue of information. If an opposing or at least neutral party is not present to "blow the whistle" on the incumbent, then the public lacks sources of information beyond those provided by the incumbent rulers themselves. Having said this, I collapse Manin, Przeworski, and Stokes's fifth category—the media—into this category as well. In terms of accountability, an opposition essentially presents the reverse side of the incumbent's pronouncements. Often, both sides are poor representations of the "true" circumstances. Hence, an independent media (itself a contentious concept) is critical for the provision of more objective, or at least more diverse, interpretations of events.[7]

Certainly any democracy's compliance with these four criteria will vary to some degree or another. However, these conditions provide useful guideposts for the remainder of this study, and their more exact relation to the arguments put forth in this analysis is discussed in further detail below.

Accountability for What?

Having established some criteria for "accountability," the next issue for a primarily quantitative study is to determine how one might tap into the accountability issue in a study with a large sample size (or *N*). Within the political realm, there are countless potential campaign issues, varying across time and geographical space. Gun control may feature prominently in any given American presidential election, but it would hardly rate a mention in Russia. The Russian spring thaw's effect on local streets might provide ample attack-campaign fodder for an April mayoral election, but it would be a harder sell in July. How does one approach the accountability issue without resorting to single case studies?

One approach, utilized here, is to attempt to define some universal interest that would arguably play a role in almost any election campaign. With this criterion, perhaps the first interest that is likely to come to mind is economics. This choice of indicators is guided by a number of considerations, the foremost being the salience of material conditions among voters' other concerns. As Abraham Maslow argued, physiological considerations constitute the most basic interest of nearly all human beings.[8]

Especially under conditions of scarcity, considerations of material well-being generally hold salience over, or at least feature prominently amid, other needs. As indicated in the survey data cited in chapter 1, the Russian electorate is no exception. At the end of 1999, the average wage in Russia was only 77 percent higher than the official poverty level; 29 percent of the population's income placed it below the poverty level, and 42.3 percent of all households' total available resources placed them below the minimal cost of living standard for their given categories.[9]

Looking at trends over the past four years of surveys conducted by VTsIOM, one can clearly see the salience of economic issues in Russian life. Figure 2.2 shows trends in responses to the question, "Which of the following problems of our society most alarm you?"[10] The large percentage of respondents choosing economic factors suggests that these particular issues continue to have a strong hold on the average Russian's psyche. Particularly after the economic crisis in the autumn of 1998, prices increased in salience, being noted by as many as 81.6 percent of respondents in January 2000. In light of such figures, and given the marked gap between concern for these issues and concern for other noneconomic factors, one can confidently state that economic well-being is a strong and consistent concern among Russians.[11]

An additional advantage of focusing on economic issues is that such indicators are some of the more universal and readily available types of data for the cases under consideration. Though Russia's state statistical services have been the subject of some criticism, they still provide the most homogenous and reliable set of socioeconomic measures across regions. Such factors like real wages, arrears, and regional poverty levels are measured in basically the same fashion across regions and thus offer objective indicators of the type of economic conditions facing each region's population.

Figure 2.2. Responses to the Question "Which of the following problems concern you most?"

Percentage
of
respondents

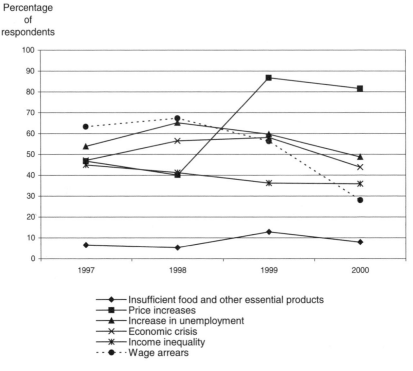

      ♦ Insufficient food and other essential products
      ■ Price increases
      ▲ Increase in unemployment
      ✕ Economic crisis
      ✱ Income inequality
      ● Wage arrears

Source: VTsIOM, *Ekonomicheskie i sotsial'nyi peremeny: Monitoring obschestvennogo mneniia* 46, no. 2 (March–April 2000): 56.

Finally, the choice of economic issues links this study to the abundant economic voting literature, allowing me to draw upon extensive work by other scholars and providing the opportunity to make a contribution to the broader fields of voting and electoral studies. It is thus my intention not only to examine the effectiveness of elections as an accountability mechanism for Russian governors but also to provide insights into the working of economic voting and popularity functions at the subnational level of states undergoing postcommunist economic and political transitions. To my knowledge, this is the first instance of such an application, and it promises to make a significant contribution to our understanding of regional political-economic processes.

Economic Voting

Having made the transition from accountability to economic voting, one should immediately note the history and complexities of the economic voting literatures. Though the argument that economics in various forms affects peoples' support for their leaders spans centuries, it is perhaps best to begin a discussion of the economic voting literature with Kramer's *Short-Term Fluctuations in U.S. Voting Behavior.*[12] Scholars generally consider this article, published in 1971, to be the seminal work in the contemporary economic voting literature. Earlier studies employed vaguely defined indicators, unsophisticated methodology in the form of simple correlations and cross-tabulations, and single-variate tests lacking any means to draw out the individual effects of variables when introduced in conjunction with others. Explicitly drawing hypotheses based on the theories of Downs and Key, Kramer's work provided one of the first methodologically sophisticated and explicitly specified attempts to measure the relative roles of various economic indicators in determining the electoral success of democratic and republican congressional candidates.[13]

In portraying the voters' decision as a choice between two competing "teams" (the incumbent and opposition, or in the American case, Democrats vs. Republicans), Kramer indicated that the next step in any analysis would be to determine the voter's decision rule. Considerations of expendable time and effort, along with evidence from prior studies, suggested that the "typical" voter could not make an informed and rationally self-interested decision based on the gathering of "party platforms and policy pronouncements, legislative voting records, and perhaps expert or authoritative opinions."[14] Instead, Kramer opted for what Fiorina would later call a "retrospective voter."[15] This voter based his or her decision on "readily available information," using the incumbent party's past performance as an indicator of its future prospects. Kramer states:

> If the performance of the incumbent party is "satisfactory" according to some principle standard, the voter votes to retain the incumbent governing party in office to enable it to continue its present policies; while if the incumbent's performance is not "satisfactory," the voter votes against the incumbent, to give the opposition party a chance to rule.[16]

Kramer then presented an equation that depicted party success as a function of incumbency (which embodied certain institutional advantages and disadvantages of incumbency); the "normal" long-term average support for the given party; the difference between a measure of actual incumbent performance and "expected performance" at the beginning of the currently ending term; and finally, an error term that would account for essentially random variance like campaign strategies, foreign events, and the idiosyncrasies of various regional political cultures.

With regard to the "performance" indicator, Kramer was faced with a number of decisions. First, what type of "performance" would be measured? With the focus on economic factors, Kramer chose to examine the relative impact of monetary income, real income, price changes, and unemployment. Each of these would help determine not only if certain types of economic indicators would feature more or less strongly in voters' support for a given party but also how these variables ranked in importance relative to one another. The second decision was how to measure beginning-of-term expectations. Naturally, aggregate-level data precluded the direct measure of such an indicator; so Kramer, assuming that voters would at least expect indicators to remain constant (or in the case of real income, grow at a constant rate) over this period, simply resorted to the percent change in each indicator from the beginning to the end of the concluding term.

Through regression analyses, Kramer demonstrated that "election outcomes are in substantial part responsive to objective changes occurring under the incumbent party; they are not 'irrational,' or random, or solely the product of past loyalties and habits, or of campaign rhetoric and merchandising."[17] Economic factors featured prominently, with incumbent party success rising and falling with economic performance. Real personal income was of most importance, with a 10 percent decrease in per capita real personal income resulting in a 4 to 5 percent drop in the incumbent party's congressional vote (holding other variables constant). Other factors like inflation and unemployment proved largely insignificant. Finally, the "incumbent advantage" only worked in instances where the economy prospered under the current administration. Being an incumbent during an economic downturn essentially canceled out the incumbent advantage.

Kramer's analytical framework set the stage for a whole series of similar aggregate-level analyses from the 1970s through the 1980s. Studies like those of Bloom and Price, Tufte, Fair, and Hibbing and Alford all employed similar aggregate-level analyses (Bloom and Price using state-level data) to consistently demonstrate that economic factors provided a significant amount of explanatory power for midterm and one-year congressional, and even presidential, elections.[18]

Nonetheless, these later pieces also raised a number of problematic issues for the aggregate-level study of economic voting. First, few of the scholars dealt directly with the ecological inference issue. The extrapolation of aggregate results upon individual decisionmaking calculi was potentially problematic.[19] One could measure variation in economic conditions and find correlations with election outcomes, but the actual dynamics occurring between economic factors, the voter, and the elected official remained open to speculation. As Tufte and Kinder and Kiewiet demonstrated, "The aggregate level evidence is necessarily compatible with any number of individual-level models."[20] Had the results of the aggregate analyses proven more consistent, this issue might have been left aside. However, the indeterminacy of the aggregate studies in terms of which types of economic factors most influenced voters,[21] and the magnitude or very existence of economic voting relationships,[22] implored researchers like Kinder and Kiewiet to focus more directly on individual-level analyses.

If Kramer's research stands as the seminal work for aggregate-level studies, then Kinder and Kiewiet's economic voting study provided the foundation for a series of survey analyses.[23] Recognizing that the aggregate-level studies had in fact demonstrated very little in terms of "economic voters'" decisionmaking calculi, scholars turned to survey data to better understand what types of economic fluctuations most influenced individuals and how strongly these factors affected incumbent assessments when compared with other noneconomic factors.[24]

Noting that previous survey-based studies by Logan and Fiorina had indicated that "pocketbook" (based upon an individual's personal economic fortunes) interests played very little role in congressional voting,[25] Kinder and Kiewiet questioned whether economic factors played a role through individuals' assessments of the state of the overall economy, rather than assessments of their own personal economic fortunes.[26] They describe "sociotropic' voters as those who "vote according to the country's pocketbook, not their own" and who "support candidates that appear to have furthered the nation's economic well-being and oppose candidates and parties that seem to threaten it."[27]

Kinder and Kiewiet turned to survey analyses to test their assertions, initially running two separate regression equations: one with survey-based indicators of party affiliation, personal income, and personal experience with unemployment as predictors; and a second with the same set of indicators plus an additional indicator of the respondent's overall assessment of current business conditions as compared with the following year. The results indicated that pocketbook interests played a very minor role in determining the respondent's congressional vote choice falling far behind party affiliation in explanatory leverage. The inclusion of the overall sociotropic assessments indicated that such factors, though still playing a secondary role to party affiliation, made a much stronger impact on congressional vote choice, with poor assessments of overall business conditions significantly and negatively affecting incumbent party support in four of the five elections considered. More detailed investigations of the 1974 and 1976 elections using path analysis offered further evidence against the role of pocketbook issues and in favor of sociotropic interests.

Regardless of Kinder and Kiewiet's findings and the later studies that further support their results, the relative validity of pocketbook-versus-sociotropic voting as well as the use of survey-based analyses as opposed to aggregate-level studies continues to be debated. Other studies preceding and following upon Kinder and Kiewiet's work indicated that pocketbook voting offered a significant predictor for election outcomes in England and France.[28] Sniderman and Brody attributed cross-regional variation to a peculiarly American "ethic of self-reliance."[29] This led Feldman to state that "political evaluations should be affected only when changes in personal well-being are perceived to be a consequence of government policy."[30] Hence, one can expect variation in the relative weight of sociotropic and pocketbook effects, depending upon an individual country's cultural, institutional, and historical milieu. With this in mind, any application of economic voting theory to a new setting necessarily demands that the researcher examine both types of considerations during initial hypotheses testing.

By this point, the reader may have noted that each of the studies utilizing cases from the advanced industrial democracies restricted its focus to national elections. Attempts to apply the economic voting thesis to subnational elections become more popular during the later half of the 1980s, as American scholars recognized the growing authority of state governors within the American federal system. These initial works laid the groundwork for a series of articles that specifically focused on how economics influenced the outcomes of both gubernatorial and state legislative elections.

What specific economic voting issues are raised by the shift to the subfederal level? Generally speaking, analyses of subfederal-level elections allow researchers to examine what I refer to as *jurisdictional issues*—in other words, whether voters recognize the limited jurisdiction of their regional executives and representatives and "punish or reward" incumbents only for those outcomes for which they are (at least conceivably) responsible.[31] As Stein puts it:

The level of government at which an election is held defines the content of the voter evaluations. Historical circumstances as well as constitutional and statutory provisions define the scope of responsibilities for each level of government. Issues associated with responsibilities withheld from a particular level of government, or which are not historically associated with that level of government, are not employed by voters in their evaluations of competing candidates or parties.[32]

Common sense would indicate that jurisdictional issues would naturally play a role in subnational elections. One would not expect a state governor to be "punished" for an unpopular war or the national rate of inflation. Furthermore, as Tidmarch, Hyman, and Sorkin have indicated, press coverage of gubernatorial campaigns tends to focus on issues like taxation, labor, education, crime, and public works that fall within the purview of governors.[33] The case for jurisdictional economic voting would in theory be even stronger if media coverage focused primarily on those functions for which the governor is responsible.

Nevertheless, early work in the United States found little evidence of cross-level jurisdictional considerations.[34] Analyzing the then-popular supposition that American gubernatorial incumbents were becoming "more vulnerable," Turret indicated that, at least for the period from 1900 to 1969, this was not in fact the case. More important, little relationship appeared to exist between variation on a number of economic indicators and four separate measure of gubernatorial incumbent election success. Chubb, examining elections from 1940 to 1982, also indicated that, despite an increase in state governments' responsibility for their states' economic well-being, governors were more susceptible to changes in the national economy than changes in their states' economies.

State economic conditions made a small but significant impact on election outcomes, but such issues as regional party affiliation, the functioning of the national economy under a same-party president, and individual candidate characteristics featured more prominently. Both Turret and Chubb indicated that this last factor, evidenced by a large error term, indicates that candidate characteristics figure more strongly in gubernatorial elections than in elections for other offices. Chubb neatly summarized his findings, saying, "Gubernatorial elections remain contests of party and personality and not of performance—at least not that of the governor and the state."[35]

Studies of so-called second-order elections in Europe demonstrated a similar tendency for voters to essentially transfer their national party preferences to subnational elections.[36] Reif refers to subnational and supranational (referring to the European Parliament) elections as second-order competitions that prove less salient than national contests. Theoretically, these elections might promote accountability for local conditions when voters worry less about the prospects for their favored party to form a national coalition government and more about punishing and rewarding local and regional governments for conditions in their jurisdictions.

However, the empirical record instead indicates that voters transfer their "sincere" national party preference to the local and regional levels, choosing their most preferred party regardless of local conditions simply because these second-order elections are less salient. As a result, second-order elections tend to return weaker results for major national parties but not necessarily because voters feel that the major-party-dominated local and regional party governments are somehow doing a poor job ruling within their jurisdictions. Party affiliation dominates accountability considerations, and once again, the gap widens between the ideal role for local elections and actual voting behavior.

Turning back to the United States, a persistent theme among studies that found little evidence of jurisdictionally oriented economic voting functions was that, despite reforms placing more decisionmaking power into the hands of state governments, governors were still constrained in their abilities to influence the course of state economic development. Even looking at the constraints imposed by the Constitution and statutory precedent, market forces themselves, in the absence of barriers to factor movements, restricted the means by which governors could alter the economic fortunes of their state. Peterson, drawing from models developed earlier by Teibout and Oates, indicated that the freedom of factor flows narrowed the range of taxation policy choices available to each executive.[37] Deviation from the mean would yield a flight of factors to states with more favorable business conditions.[38] Hence, though economic conditions varied from state to state due to any number of geographical, environmental, and historical factors, the fact that governors could do little about both such fixed and other theoretically manipulable factors effectively freed them of responsibility for their state's economic fortunes.

However, more recent studies employing survey analyses indicated that voters and survey respondents were in fact far more "jurisdiction-oriented" than earlier studies of voter behavior suggested.[39] Stein indicates that voters in U.S. states tended to treat gubernatorial elections as a means to register their dissatisfaction with their personal economic fortunes by punishing the president's coparty gubernatorial incumbents (what Atkeson and Partin later termed "national referendum" voting).[40] However, general evaluations of state economic performance were significantly related to respondents' decision to support incumbent governors. This suggested that "voters are aware of the functional responsibilities that differentiate national and state-local governments."[41]

Making an even stronger case for the role of jurisdictional economic voting, studies by Atkeson and Partin, and by Niemi, Stanley, and Vogel, later indicated that even "referendum voting" was less important for gubernatorial candidates than voters' assessments of their state's economic performance. Once again, survey-based data returned results that contrasted with previous aggregate-level studies, and researchers again raised the ecological inference issue as one probable explanation for the contradictory results. Niemi, Stanley, and Vogel even echoed Kinder and Kiewiet's general evaluation of all aggregate-level voting studies, indicating that the results of Stein's analysis might concur with any number of individual-level inductive conclusions.

Given the fact that the studies by Atkeson and Partin, and by Niemi, Stanley, and Vogel, constitute the "latest word" on economic voting in gubernatorial elections, one may conclude the following. First, the presence of jurisdictional economic voting appears to increase as scholars' analyses include a greater proportion of more contemporary cases. This may be an indication of the steadily increasing institutional and jurisdictional strength of U.S. state executives. Second, the case for subnational economic voting appears stronger in studies that employ individual-level analyses. This may indicate that aggregate-level studies are improperly specified, that scholars are drawing spurious conclusions from the results of their quantitative analyses, that survey questions are "guiding" the respondents to the authors' own conclusions, or that election processes and institutions are somehow blocking or filtering the manifestation of individual support calculi in election outcomes (something that U.S. scholars, looking at their own election system, are reluctant to consider).

Finally, as in the surveys of national elections, even those studies that reach the same general conclusions demonstrate that the role of economic voting varies greatly across data sets and studies. Idiosyncratic factors like candidate personalities, regional election "cultures" (aside from simple party affiliation), and campaign strategies—poorly captured in large-N quantitative analyses—appear to play a great role, manifesting themselves in rather large error terms. Despite this list of caveats, recent studies generally agree on one point: Jurisdictionally oriented economic voting plays *some* significant role in the outcomes of gubernatorial elections.

Economic Voting in Russia and Eastern Europe

As indicated in chapter 1, a lack of survey data, disagreement over reliable indicators, the recent nature of Russia's electoral system, and more mundane issues like the dearth of English-language materials regarding elections and economic development have all conspired to limit the number of economic voting surveys undertaken in Russia and other former socialist countries. At the same time, taking just the Russian case as an example, a federation consisting of eighty-nine subjects would seem to provide a very interesting "proving ground" for various permutations of the economic voting thesis. In addition to a wealth of cases featuring a very wide range of conceivable conditions, the fact that these are essentially nascent democratic institutions provides researchers with the opportunity to more closely examine the origins of various voting habits. As Kiewiet and Rivers wrote when discussing the future of economic voting studies, "Further progress is unlikely to come by continued mining of the same types of data in traditional ways. More promising, in our view, will be efforts to identify new sources and types of data that are potentially informative about outstanding theoretical issues."[42]

One can identify a handful of works that took up Kiewiet and River's challenge using data drawn from cases in both Eastern Europe and Russia. Along with more passing treatments of the topic embedded within broader voting studies,[43] these works have focused explicitly on the topic of economic voting in Russia. As with the studies in advanced industrial countries, the works in their entirety employ a variety of methods and draw data from different case elections. As a whole, and again echoing the Western case studies, they indicate that the relationship between economic performance and popular support in Russia is far more complex than conventional wisdom might have us believe.

In his periodic analyses of federal elections in Russian, Timothy Colton provides a number of tests for the role of socioeconomic factors in determining election outcomes.[44] However, as the title suggests, his article "Economics and Voting in Russia" provides one of the first intensive examinations of the economic voting issue in contemporary Russia. Drawing upon the Kinder and Kiewiet's survey-based methodology; Colton runs a series of logistic regressions using survey data gathered from respondents before and just after the 1995 elections. The survey data included questions that tapped into a number of both sociotropic and pocketbook measures of voter interest—issues like attitudes toward various aspects of reform; party affiliation; geographical location; and standard cleavage-based indicators like education, age, ethnicity, and sex.

Six economic variables plus an age indicator were regressed upon voter preferences (support/nonsupport) for each of the five major party categories that contested the election. By themselves, these yielded significant coefficients in eighteen of the thirty economic-indicator-related cells. However, with the introduction of nine other noneconomic variables (1995 party affinity, 1993 Duma party vote, opinion scales regarding various political and socioeconomic reforms), only ten of these eighteen variables maintained their significance. From this, Colton concluded that economic issues constitute a significant but moderate factor in determining respondents' vote choices and were to a large extent "washed out" by the inclusion of other noneconomic variables.

Nonetheless, Colton makes it clear that these tepid results should not be viewed as the "final word" for economic voting in Russia and may partially result from the economic conditions specific to the 1995 election. He suggests that the uniformly low assessments of the Russian economy may have effected the results and indicates how, by essentially introducing greater variance into the economic response measures (increasing the number of individuals giving positive responses on the economic variables), the apparently weak economic variable coefficients can yield significant changes in each party's percentage of the vote. From this observation, he speculates that an improvement in Russia's economic performance could result in a significant reduction in the number of seats occupied by the Communist Party and its allies. His subsequent analyses of Russian voting patterns in the 1995 and 1999 parliamentary and 1996 and 2000 presidential elections revealed much more substantial sociotropic effects at the national level.[45] Taking Colton's studies together, one can argue with some confidence that one sees an element of sociotropic economic voting considerations in

Russian's individual support calculi, but as the 1996 presidential results indicated, these calculi may not be entirely salient nor will they necessarily manifest themselves in election outcomes.

Although their study deals with the economic voting issue only in passing, Clem and Craumer's examination of the regional patterns of electoral behavior in the 1999 parliamentary elections provides some additional evidence in support of the contention that Russians demonstrate a degree of economic voting in national-level contests. In addition to correlation analyses that examine the relationship between party-list voter percentages and factors like urbanization, education, age, percentage of the population employed in agricultural and industrial jobs, and percentage of Russians in each region's population, Clem and Craumer run similar analyses using as independent variables raw and real wages, unemployment, industrial production and change in industrial production, consumption, and percentage of privatized regional housing. On the basis of their Pearson correlation coefficients, these researchers find that regions with higher levels of industrial production, consumption, and raw and real wages tended to vote more for the reform parties and less for the Communists.

Nonetheless, while their results indicate some support for the economic voting theses as a predictor of parties' legislative election success, Clem and Craumer's study is subject to a certain amount of criticism. First, they use only simple correlation analysis, which denies them the means to measure the relative strength of these indicators when other noneconomic factors are present. Second, they provide no readily apparent criteria for determining which relationships support their hypotheses. According to standard statistical procedures, significant relationships (at the .01 level) are evident only between raw and real wages and votes for the Communist Party, Yabloko, and Bloc Zhirinovsky; unemployment and votes for Fatherland–All Russia; industrial production and Yabloko; and housing privatization and votes for the Communist Party, Bloc Zhirinovsky, and the Union of Right Forces or SPS. In their discussion of these results, their choice of relevant relationships appears somewhat random, mentioning some relationships that failed to achieve statistical significance and ignoring others that did.

Furthermore, the researchers offer little by way of explaining both why certain factors were more significant than others and how these factors might conceivably relate to one another. Why might raw wages exhibit a stronger negative relation to Communist Party votes than the seemingly more relevant wage as a percentage of an essential goods basket? What might account for the surprisingly positive relationship between levels of housing privati-zation and support for the Communists? What do the significant figures for the "liberal"/nationalist/opposition Bloc Zhirinovsky tell us in relation to similar results for the more "traditionally liberal" Yabloko? These are just some of the questions which Clem and Craumer's simple presentation of the correlation matrix results leaves unanswered.

Finally, as Clem and Craumer themselves admit, their reliance on aggregate-level data restricts them from making anything more than spec-ulative statements about individual voting behavior. For example, by itself the fact that regions with relatively lower wage levels returned higher votes for Communist candidates says nothing definitive about whether or not it was actually the poorer voters within these regions who were casting votes for the Communist Party. Hypothetically speaking, perhaps combinations of certain sectors of the poor and wealthy managers in old soviet agricul-tural and industrial enterprises (or other conceivable amalgamations) are responsible. Robinson's work on the problem of ecological inference indi-cates that such findings, based exclusively on aggregate-level analyses, are subject to a wide range of both methodological and empirical criticism.[46] Nevertheless, as a first attempt to uncover regional patterns of economic voting for Russian parliamentary deputies, these researchers make a signif-icant contribution to the study of economic voting in Russia using the only data available at the time.

Joshua Tucker's analysis of economic voting within the context of Rus-sia and other ex-communist states represents some of the most recent work on the economic voting issue.[47] Recognizing certain inconsistencies between traditional economic voting theses and the outcomes of recent Russian, Pol-ish, and Hungarian elections, Tucker argued that the traditional literature's focus on incumbent and opposition parties (what he refers to as the "refer-endum model") might be inadequate for studies of postcommunist transi-tions. Instead, he presented an alternative *party-type model* focused upon *reformist* and *old regime* parties. Briefly put, reformist parties tended to benefit from improving economic conditions while old regime parties ben-efited from a worsening economy.

Using regional-level voting and economic data drawn from parliamentary elections in the Czech Republic, Hungary, Poland, Russia, and Slovakia, Tucker tested hypotheses derived from both the referendum and the party-type models. Results of the analyses indicated that, while the incumbent-centered referendum model often failed to accurately predict outcomes, tests of hypotheses derived from the party-type model consistently supported the contention that a link exists between economic conditions and votes for reformist or old regime parties.

Tucker's work stands as an important contribution to the literature on economic voting in postcommunist elections. It provides a fresh look at the traditional economic voting theses and demonstrates a degree of methodological sophistication that distinguishes it from most other studies within the region. However, for the case of 1990s Russia, its utility is limited mostly to Duma elections. As further described below, regional party structures played a minimal role in regional executive elections. Parties seldom nominated candidates for elections, incumbents rarely associated with any given party organization in the course of their term, and campaign endorsements often contradicted official party platforms or lacked consistency across levels of party structure (Hale estimates that, for the period 1995–2000, only 3 percent of regional executives ran with a party endorsement).[48] Simply put, regional executive elections did not present voters with old regime or reformist party alternatives, leaving analysts of regional elections with only the traditional incumbent-based conceptualization of the economic voting thesis.

As with the studies of economic voting in the advanced industrial democracies and developing world, most Russian voting analysts have focused their attention almost exclusively on the national level. With very few exceptions, the study of subnational politics in post-Soviet Russia has focused primarily upon the role of elites or the development of regional political institutions (itself an elite-driven affair).[49] Discussions of electoral processes focus predominantly on the various competing elite groups within a region or city and consist primarily of weighing the various resources available to different actors. In many respects, the closed nature of many regional political systems justifies such an approach. Russia, after all, continues to fall short of any liberal-democratic ideal, and the weak linkages between society and decisionmakers, along with a political culture developed over years of highly centralized rule, make an elite-centered approach a very viable means to understand the workings of contemporary Russian politics.

However, the nearly exclusive focus on elite competition in studies of regional politics and elections completely ignores a crucial aspect of the equation: Voters. Regardless of the apparent disconnect between society and the regional leadership, and the ability of elites to manipulate public opinion and election outcomes, the fact remains that citizens do participate in regional electoral contests, and few studies have been undertaken to determine whether the results of these elections are the exclusive result of the balance of power between different elite groups or whether voters may rely on their own means to assess the regional situation and vote accordingly. As a result, election outcomes are explained in a largely post hoc manner (i.e., this candidate won because he/she was clearly the strongest candidate) that rules out the ability of voters to operate independently of a dominant political elite's interests. Such approaches tend to attribute instances of incumbent victory in the face of "overwhelming discontent" (often not indicating the basis for this assessment) to the incumbent's ability to manipulate the electoral process, and they portray incumbent defeats as the work of some new political elite that somehow managed to mobilize stronger resources to dupe or coerce the voter. In either case, these assumptions are rarely actually tested. Voters were removed from the regional election equation almost immediately after the collapse of the Soviet Union.

Looking at some exceptions to this general trend, Steven Solnick's "Gubernatorial Elections in Russia, 1996–1997" examined three critical questions: (1) whether results could be treated as a proxy of support for then-president Boris Yeltsin, (2) whether there were indications of party identity formation in the regions, and (3) whether economic conditions played a major role in determining outcomes. Focusing only on the third question, Solnick's results indicated that *no* significant relationship existed between regional economic conditions and gubernatorial election outcomes. Correlation analyses for various economic indicators like unemployment, percentage of the population living below the poverty line, and real wage levels indicated that only measures of regional poverty levels and levels of investment had even a weak relationship with the percentage of the vote captured by the incumbent. In fact, of all the variables included in Solnick's regression analysis, only the percentage of voters casting their votes for nationalist and socialist parties in the 1995 Duma elections had any statistically significant relationship to incumbent success. If Solnick's results regarding the economic voting question are truly representative, they suggest that regional executives are politically unaccountable for the economic performance of their regions—a truly discouraging prospect for advocates of democratic federalism.

Grigorii Golosov provided another study of regional executive election success that included an explicit test of an economic voting hypothesis. In his analysis, Golosov examined three different theoretical approaches to explaining incumbent electoral success: "sociological-psychological," "sociological," and "economic voting." Drawing upon the results of correlations between indicators representing each approach and various measures of incumbent success, Golosov concluded that the social-psychological approach —essentially, regional attitudes toward reformers and the Communist opposition, measured as the level of regional support for Yeltsin during the most recent presidential election—provided the most leverage in explaining incumbent success. He found that the economic voting approach provided a weaker but still useful means to predict outcomes on the incumbent success indicators. (The sociological approach, which took into account regional social cleavages and was measured by the urbanization of the regional population, placed a distant third.)

More recently, Bryon Moraski and William Reisinger's examination of regional executive electoral competition also included measures of regional economic performance in the forms of an indicator for the change in the regional consumer price index for 1995 and a static measure of average per capita income for the same year.[50] Though they primarily attempt to gauge the level of democracy rather than incumbent success rates, their proxy measures include a turnover indicator and are hence directly relevant for the study at hand.

Like Solnick, Moraski and Reisinger found little relationship between incumbent turnover and regional economic performance. However, given their choice of measures, this is perhaps unsurprising. Though their chosen economic indicators might offer some means to test whether incumbents are "safer" in particularly well-endowed regions, the indicators fail to capture whether or not voters respond to the direction of economic development (although the change in the consumer price index does provide at least some dynamic indicator) and also ignore the fact that most economic voting studies indicate that voters have difficulty "remembering" economic conditions beyond a year before the election or survey in question (the study examines the set of elections from 1991 to 2000).[51] All told, the economic variables used in Moraski and Reisinger's analysis are poor indicators of the economic conditions surrounding each election, and hence one might expect these researchers to find no significant relationship between the economic indicators and incumbent turnover.

Taking these studies together, a number of general observations can be made regarding the current state of the study of subnational economic voting in Russia. As suggested in chapter 1, both Golosov's and Solnick's insightful analyses are somewhat weakened by a number of unavoidable consequences of both the cases examined and the methods employed. A major factor is the issue of presidential appointments. For instance, every incumbent in each of the thirty-seven cases under examination was appointed by Boris Yeltsin between 1992 and 1996. As Solnick explicitly indicates, with executives so strongly identified with the federal executive and his reforms, the 1996–97 elections were subject to "referendum" voting, whereby incumbents in subfederal positions are assessed not by their own performance or other personal characteristics but upon the basis of the voters' assessment of federal organs and programs. Given President Yeltsin's poor showings at the polls during this period, one might expect incumbents to have faired as poorly as they did, regardless of the conditions in their regions.[52]

To further complicate matters, many of the incumbents had been appointed to their positions just before the election in question (in all fairness, Solnick makes this very explicit in his article). With eleven of thirty-seven instances in which incumbents held office for less than a year, it is difficult to understand how voters could logically hold the executive accountable for the given region's performance. Similar considerations might also account for the results of Golosov's analysis. The measure employed to capture his sociological-psychological approach provides a nearly perfect proxy measure for testing referendum voting. Given the fact that most of the incumbents in his study are Yeltsin appointees, we have every reason to expect there to be some linkage between support for Yeltsin and support for "his" governors. However, this pattern is likely to disappear once incumbents hold office as a result of popular election.

Second, because they only reflect variation within the subset of regions that had an election during a given year, the economic indicators used by Solnick, Golosov, and Moraski and Reisinger fail to fully capture the specific type of *jurisdictional* voting described above. The analysts' models included raw static and, in Solnick's case, dynamic (measuring change over the year before the election) indicators *only* for those regions that had elections during the periods under examination. On the face of things, this choice reflects the logic that support for this incumbent will decline in regions where economic conditions are worse than in other parts of Russia. However, to take the example of Solnick's piece, one should bear in mind that he tests his model against a selection of the thirty-seven cases that underwent election during this first cycle. What is in fact being measured is variation on the independent variable for those thirty-seven cases—not for Russia as a whole.

In more actual terms, and bearing in mind all the ecological fallacy issues involved in aggregate analyses, this suggests that voters in any one of Solnick's case regions weigh their regional performance against the thirty-six other regions that had elections during the 1996–97 election cycle.

Jurisdictional voting, conversely, suggests that voters weigh their region's performance by roughly assessing where their region stands within Russia as a whole. To better capture this concept, one should instead employ an alternate measure representing each region's performance relative to the all-Russia mean for a specified time period before the election. The analyses in chapter 5 employ such a measure.

Finally, as with Clem and Craumer's piece, the exclusive use of aggregate-level data restricts the range of explanations open to exploration.[53] Particularly, though Solnick may demonstrate that no relationship exists between incumbent outcomes and aggregate-level economic performance and though Golosov finds a weak relationship between performance and incumbent success, the use of aggregate-level data prevents both analysts from making convincing statements about the micro-level decisions that implicitly result in their macro-level outcomes. Furthermore, aside from the ecological inference issue, aggregate-level data proscribe the examination of key questions in the economic voting literature that focus on exactly how economic conditions influence support for incumbents. Specifically, one cannot determine from aggregate data either whether citizens are guided by pocketbook versus sociotropic issues, or whether they compare economic conditions across regions instead of simply responding to general fluctuations in regional economic indicators.

Economic Accountability in an Evolving Context

As suggested above, a fundamental problem regarding previous studies of subnational electoral accountability is that they provide only a snapshot of elections during a period of much flux and turmoil. The election cycle of 1996–97 exhibited remarkably different characteristics from elections in 1999–2001, and these differences perhaps disguise more persistent relationships that span the whole range of regional elections. Up until this point, few studies have explicitly examined the course of regional elections throughout this period from the standpoint of electoral accountability. By expanding the entire set of elections under examination, one can not only generate more reliable tests of models but also highlight trends in electoral outcomes across the entire period.

Looking across Russia's first postcommunist decade with an eye toward the evolution of its regional elections, one can identify three stages of development. The first stage begins with the collapse of the Soviet Union in

1992 and stretches through the last elections of Russia's first gubernatorial election cycle in 1997. The political characteristics of this stage include appointments of executives to all of Russia's oblasti and *kraia,* a handful of elections in selected oblasti and *kraia,* and presidential elections in every "ethnic" republic. This period also witnesses the initial economic upheavals of the postcommunist era, along with privatization, the liberalization of prices, and initial ad hoc attempts by regional governments to deal with the rapidly evolving economic situation. The period ends with the first cycle of regional executive elections, which as I argued above were unique in the fact that all incumbents going into the election were presidential appointees. Solnick's analysis of Russia's regional executive elections focuses exclusively on contests held during this period.

The second stage in the evolution of Russia's regional executive elections spans a period from late 1997 through the final elections of Russia's second regional executive election cycle in 2001. A number of changes in the economic and political environment differentiated the first and second stages.

Turning first to the economic sphere, increasing variation among regional performance measures provides one major differentiating factor. Whereas in 1996, economic differences between regions were already significantly higher that those witnessed in many other federations, by the end of 1999 these differences were even greater. Descriptive statistics on per capita gross regional product for the period from 1996 to 1999 offer some indication of the increasing divergence among levels of regional performance. If in 1996 the coefficient of variation (a standardized measure of variation in which the population standard deviation is divided by the population mean) of per capita gross regional product was 0.63, by 1999 this number had grown to 1.17. Hence, variance in per capita regional national product was close to doubling between the first years of each respective election round.

Variation in real wages, though much more subdued, also indicated an upward trend, with coefficients of variation increasing from 0.25 in 1996 to 0.29 in 1999. This would indicate that a number of regions were breaking ahead or falling behind the "pack," and that regional "winners and losers" were becoming further defined as the decade continued. In terms of the economic voting thesis, one might expect that, as variation increased, voters could more readily evaluate their leaders' performance and have a stronger justification to "punish or reward" incumbents based upon these variations. Therefore, we can expect a strengthening of the economic voting component across the two stages.

Second, the absence of "emergency" appointments before the 1999–2001 elections strengthened the case for holding regional executives accountable for the state of their regions. As further elaborated in chapter 3, of the thirty-two races between 1999 and 2001, twenty-three featured incumbents who had held office for four to five years; five featured initial Yeltsin appointments who, after being reelected in the 1996–97 round, were now in their seventh and eighth years; and four featured successors to governors who had either been in office for four (two cases) or eight (two cases) years.

Hence, races were contested either by incumbents or "heirs" to incumbents who had at least served out one full term. This factor eliminates the potentially obfuscating factor in the 1996–97 round of governors who had served for little more than a year in office before their reelection campaign. If voters were unhappy with the regional economic situation in 1999–2001, governors would be hard pressed to argue that they had not served in office long enough to affect the situation. Taking this logic a step further, one would expect economic conditions to especially factor into elections where governors had held their posts for seven or more years.

Finally, while scholars studying the case of U.S. governors debate whether state executives possess enough control over their states' economic fortunes to be held accountable for economic conditions, this appears to be a less contentious issue for the regions of the Russian Federation during the period between 1991 and 2000.[54] Before the reforms implemented by Putin starting in the summer of 2000, many Russian specialists identified a trend toward "local authoritarianism," with the governors' cliques controlling most of the political and economic activities in their regions.[55] According to these specialists and other evidence gathered in the course of my own fieldwork, regional legislatures—the institution that logically would be in the best position to offset executive control—had ceased to perform their balancing function after the events of October 1993.

After Yeltsin's October 1993 showdown with the federal legislature, he ordered all regional legislatures to be disbanded. Elections for new bodies were to be held by March 1994. However, because Russian federal law stipulates that election laws and institutions like the regional election commission are to be implemented and created by both the regional executive and the legislature, the absence of a sitting legislature effectively placed most control into the hands of regional executives. In many instances, executives took advantage of this state of affairs to ensure that election outcomes suited their interests. Furthermore, presidential decrees and federal laws after the October 1993 events maximized the power of executives relative to the new legislatures, effectively "rewarding" regional executives for their loyalty during the parliamentary crisis by giving them substantial powers. As a result of these and other factors, regional legislatures could no longer be considered prominent independent actors in regional policymaking during the period in question.

In financial terms, as of 1998, regional governments were responsible for the following portions of the consolidated budget:[56]

- government administration and municipal self-administration;
- law enforcement and security;
- research and development;
- industry, energy, and construction;
- agriculture and fishing;
- environmental protection and resource preservation;
- transport, roads, communications, and information;
- development of market infrastructure;
- housing and city development;
- early warning systems and disaster relief;
- education;
- cultural affairs;
- mass media;
- health care and physical fitness;
- social policy;
- debt servicing;
- other expenses; and
- targeted budgetary funds.

To finance these budget items, governors accumulated a large proportion of the taxes collected in their regions. According to Aleksei Lavrov, oblasti and *kraia* received 61 percent of the taxes collected on their territory in 1996. Throughout the 1990s, this official figure changed very little, placing Russia well ahead of other federations in terms of the financial resources officially concentrated in the hands of regional authorities.[57]

However, as a number of studies on Russian federalism and interbudgetary transfers have demonstrated, the normative division of responsibilities and finance offers only a partial picture of budgetary federalism during this period. Bilateral treaties between the center and individual regions created a patchwork of budgetary relations. First republics and then oblasti and *kraia* received exemptions from certain taxes, increased regional power over the use of natural resources, and increased federal funding through higher budgetary transfers or extensive federal projects and programs. As aptly demonstrated by Treisman, this created a situation in which center–periphery relations, rather then being characterized by top-down administration, increasingly took on the manner of negotiations between more or less equal parties. With the threat of secession growing in the Caucasus, and the precedent of early bilateral treaties, regions throughout Russia sought to essentially blackmail the center into extending privileges.[58]

Even ignoring the role that the bilateral treaties played in this process, the disorder that followed Yeltsin's pronouncement to "grab as much sovereignty as you need," coupled with Moscow's financial and institutional weakness, essentially shifted much of the decisionmaking on economic policy to the regions. As Darrell Slider states, "While there was no legal or constitutional basis for regions to control the local economies, the lack of central control over regional policymaking and implementation has provided de facto authority in this sphere to regional governments."[59] In addition to the large number of social and economic functions that were officially transferred to the regions, the center's inability to fully finance those responsibilities that it retained placed even more prerogatives in the hands of regional authorities. By 1995, tax offices, military installations, and even the regional-level federal tax authorities found themselves receiving funds either directly from regional budgets or indirectly from the federal budget via the regional budget.[60] A lack of federal funds also had an impact on Moscow's ability to even monitor regional–federal organ relations in the regions and prosecute infractions by regional authorities. Even seemingly banal issues like the provision of office space, purchase of equipment, and utilities could play into the hands of regional authorities in their struggle with the federal organs.[61]

Regional authorities also took it upon themselves to finance their increased responsibilities by levying new taxes or, in cooperation with regional tax authorities, "skimming off" larger proportions of tax revenues than warranted by federal law.[62] Once again, the partial co-optation of federal authorities located in the regions made it extremely difficult for the center to recognize and prosecute infractions. Very often, regions did very little to hide violations, publishing often blatantly controversial legislation in their official periodicals with very little fear of retribution.

The crisis of August 1998, along with increasing sclerosis at the center, only exacerbated this situation. As Stoner-Weiss indicates, the crisis "served to underscore the fact that in practice many regions exercise autonomy beyond what is provided for in the bilateral agreements, the Constitution or existing federal law."[63] In August, interbudgetary relations were largely shattered, with the federal government unable to meet its financial obligations to the regions. The results were even greater autonomy for regional governments, which were forced to essentially "go it alone," covering both their own area of responsibility (albeit with reduced help from the center) plus an even larger portion of those budgetary sectors that where at least normatively the responsibility of the federal governments.[64]

During the postcrisis period, regional governments resorted to a number of "emergency measures," which resulted in them taking on more and more of the trappings of quasi-independent political entities—"border" restrictions,[65] price fixing, and the levying of more taxes and fees that lay beyond their legal prerogative. The effect of the crisis was only exacerbated by the fact that, between April 24, 1998, and August 9, 1999, the Russian federal government was crippled by the "parade of prime ministers"—four newly appointed prime ministers in only eighteen months. With no government lasting more than eight months, federal power was cast into a permanent state of reorganization for nearly two years. During this time, regional governments retained and even expanded the de facto autonomy they had gained immediately following the August crisis.

Finally, as Vera Tolz and Irina Busygina indicate, a respectable portion of a region's economic and fiscal fortunes were attributable to the regional executive's ability to maintain good ties with and extract benefits from key figures in Moscow. Connections with federal political actors might yield larger transfers to the regional budget; federal funding for major projects; tax breaks of various sorts; and the less concrete, but nonetheless very important, means to escape federal scrutiny in instances where regional policies ran against federal laws.[66] For all their implied unseemliness, these backroom dealings were an important factor in regional economic fortunes, and if voters indeed cast their vote according to regional and local conditions, then one must recognize the importance of these dealings in maintaining support for regional executives.

Despite these arguments, it should be recognized that a combination of undocumented financial flows, disagreements over indicators, constant flux, and the very difficulty of defining concepts of "power" have prevented any scholars from presenting a truly convincing and entirely accurate "last word" on the degree of decentralization in 1990s Russia.[67] Nonetheless, Slider echoes the general agreement among scholars studying this issue, stating that "the regions have shown considerable ability to shape the local economic system in ways that deviate from national reform policies" and that "any statistical analysis of almost any indicator of the implementation or impact of economic reforms in Russia will show extreme variation across regions."[68]

In any case, a precise measure of the *degree* of decentralization is not necessary to justify a reapplication of the economic voting thesis to the 1999–2001 elections. Having argued that Solnick's results from the previous election round were partially affected by referendum voting issues, it logically suffices to demonstrate that (1) governors *at least* maintained the same level of control over their regional economies as in 1996–97, and (2) that the basis for referendum voting decreased. The very fact that the decentralization versus centralization debate raged throughout the 1990s and that one of the first priorities of Putin's administration was to "rein in" in the regions provides evidence enough for the first contention—the next paragraph deals with the second.

As a whole, the gubernatorial elections that took place in the 1999–2001 cycle were characterized by weakening bases for referendum voting. In the 1996–97 cycle, every incumbent facing election was a Yeltsin appointee and was thus a potential target for any voters anxious to express their dissatisfaction with the Russian president. The poor showing of these incumbents guaranteed that such a factor would play a negligible role in the 1999–2001 elections. By the time the later elections arrived, original Yeltsin appointees held office in only twelve of the thirty-two cases under examination. Each of these "appointees" now all held office, at least in theory, according to the popular will of the electorate that had turned out for the 1996–97 elections.

Furthermore, the object of the 1996–97 referendum voting, Boris Yeltsin, had resigned from his post almost four months before the first elections. The new president, Vladimir Putin, did not clearly elucidate his relations with any of the incumbents at hand until perhaps the Kursk election of October 2000 (and even this is debatable). Even in this case, and a handful of other instances that followed, the presidential administration made it clear only that they did *not* support certain candidates. Though many candidates understood the potential electoral gains provided by a presidential endorsement and claimed to have the backing of the president, Putin did not provide clear backing for a candidate in any of the elections before 2001.

The third and final stage in the evolution of Russia's regional elections began with the end of Russia's second electoral cycle in 2001 and ended with the signing into law of reforms eliminating regional executive elections on December 12, 2004 (the last election played out in Nenetskii Autonomous

Okrug on February 6 of the following year). One might characterize this stage first by noting the greater level of economic stability and growth experienced by Russia during this period. Regardless of the cosmetic nature of this stability (driven, as many argue, predominantly by oil revenues), few could argue against the contention that this stage exhibited the most steady improvement in regional growth and living standards since the collapse of the Soviet Union. Certainly a number of regions continued to lag behind, but the Russian Federation as a whole experienced a marked increase in productivity and growth.

Alongside these changes in the economic sphere came major changes in the political realm. The most significant developments were related to reforms of regional governing structures, laws, and the federal structure itself as the Putin administration drove home its efforts to increase central control vis-à-vis the regions. Furthermore, in contrast to the second stage, as Putin entered his second and third years of rule, the federal government exhibited an increasing willingness to intervene in regional political affairs and elections. Sitting incumbents like Yevgenii Nazdratenko and Vladimir Yakovlev were lured away from executive office, incumbents running for reelection found themselves targeted by federal authorities or facing candidates with strong central backing, and Moscow violated its own campaign laws stumping for candidates in places like Saint Petersburg.

Before the decision to eliminate regional executive elections at the end of 2004, the impact of many of these efforts was only beginning to be evident, and thus the total impact on the future of regional executive elections will never been known. Nonetheless, as will be demonstrated in chapter 7, initial signs pointed to an increasing sense of central control over regional political affairs that seemed to have an impact on the public's willingness to subject itself to the rigors of Russia's subnational elections. Even as the Kozak Commission's reforms held out the promise of clarifying the jurisdictional confusion facing voters in the previous stages, the nature and content of other federal reform efforts lowered voters' perceived payoff from subjecting themselves to the time and emotional costs imposed by Russia's stark regional civil society.

Methodological Decisions

Given the small number of Russian election analyses, this study necessarily draws upon the experiences of previous American case studies. As indicated in the discussion of the literature above, the economic voting literature at the federal and subfederal levels is split along a methodological divide between individual-level and aggregate-level approaches. Interwoven with this debate is the ecological inference issue, whereby scholars must opt between making often unsupported inferences from more widely available aggregate level data or limiting their selection of cases and undertaking the expense of survey analyses.[69] In the course of my work in Russia's regions, I was fortunate enough to acquire the means to pursue both approaches, gaining the advantages inherent to each and allowing me to offer a more comprehensive picture of the economic voting question in the regions.

Survey-based data offer a means to test hypotheses regarding the information that citizens use in their evaluations of their regional executives. In the same vein as Kinder and Kiewiet's survey analyses, I construct models to determine whether sociotropic or pocketbook issues figure more prominently in voters' decision making calculi. Furthermore, with regard to the jurisdictional issue that I argued was key to the subnational economic voting issue, surveys allow us to determine whether voters differentiate between the economic performance in their particular regions and those of others (what I refer to as *relative* sociotropic voting). Barring a significant indication of such decisionmaking, it would be difficult to argue that incumbent governors are being punished and rewarded for their *own* performance rather than being punished for nationwide economic fortunes and other factors beyond their control. Surveys also allow us to examine the relationship to a number of noneconomic issues both common to all regions and specific to a subset—like the entrance of candidates from security organs in the period 1999–2001.

Nonetheless, though surveys can provide insights into attitudes and opinions, they alone fail to provide an adequate and full picture of regional voting behavior. First, one must bear in mind that these are *not* exit polls. Exit polls have just recently been undertaken in Russia, and usually only in the course of federal-level elections. For the most part, the scarcity of such polls is likely explainable in terms of cost and demand. Russian law prohibits the publication of exit poll results until the day after the election—the same day on which the official result is generally officially announced or "leaked out." Hence, the most conceivable practical role for exit polls is to assess the validity of official results—something that few actors or agencies are willing to pay for and for which, given the questionable track record of exit polls in other countries, the polls themselves are barely adequate. In the instances where exit polls were undertaken in the course of a regional executive election, voters were generally asked for little more than to indicate for whom they voted. Such polls obviously have limited value for a study of this sort. Therefore, aside from taking on the expense and effort (including legal entanglements with local authorities) to conduct exit polls, researchers are left with the option of opinion polls gathered before or sometime after the election. In terms of drawing conclusions about *voter behavior* (as opposed to incumbent popularity), this choice places certain limitations on the validity of the analyses. Not only is the usual risk of misreporting present, but respondents also can always change their minds by the time the election occurs.

Second, these surveys tell us little about the broader patterns of incumbent success throughout the entire Russian Federation. First, representative surveys from each region in which an election occurred during this most recent round are simply unattainable. Quality varies depending upon the local agency conducting the survey (and the restrictions under which local authorities place these organizations), and the expense of obtaining survey results varies from a nominal fee (if the studies were undertaken as part of an order from other individuals or agencies) to several thousand dollars per survey.[70]

As a result, researchers are again left with the choice of either organizing and conducting their own preelection surveys (a very costly, time-consuming, and risky project in the absence of an initial pilot study such as this) or choosing a select number of "representative" surveys. The latter choice brings a number of costs, the most important of which is that though one may be able to make certain generalizations about voting behavior, the fact remains that the data were drawn from a limited set of regions. This raises the possibility that any results are in part determined by the idiosyncrasies of these cases. For instance, in the case examined in this study, both the survey results and the outcome of the subsequent election provided a textbook example of the economic voting thesis in practice. However, looking across the range of other elections in 1999–2001, this relationship was not so readily apparent. If economic factors play such a decisive role, then why did the governor of Tiumenskaia Oblast (where the average worker's wage is 3.3 times as high as the poverty level) lose his reelection bid, whereas the governor of Brianskaia Oblast (where the average worker's wage is only 0.19 times higher than the poverty level) won?

Furthermore, the typical survey questions offer little leverage in determining precisely what types of economic performance play the greatest role in determining outcomes. With a nod toward the average respondent's poor grasp of macroeconomics, surveys ask very general questions about whether the respondent feels that his or her personal or society's economic situation has "improved/gotten worse" over a given period. Available surveys did not include questions concerning the respondents' assessments of other factors like inflation, unemployment, wages, pensions, or wage arrears. At base, these surveys can only assess whether economic factors—broadly speaking—affect respondent's evaluations of the incumbent, whether these factors are mainly pocketbook or sociotropic, and whether the respondent takes jurisdictional factors into account.

The inclusion of aggregate-level analyses similar to that of Solnick's offsets some of the weaknesses in the survey data. First, such analyses allow me to determine whether objective changes in regional economic conditions, as opposed to subjective evaluations by survey respondents (who are at least partially influenced by campaign and precampaign rhetoric), have an impact on incumbent success in elections. Second, by examining variation across a number of economic indicators, one can gain some insights into which particular kinds of economic performance (unemployment levels, percentage of the population living in poverty, real wages, real pensions, etc.) have the most impact on incumbent success. Third and finally, in light of the survey data problems outlined above (particularly the fact that they only suggest who the respondent will vote for in the future elections), aggregate-level analyses provide the only available means to address election *outcomes.* Using this technique, one examines relationships between variations in a number of economic indicators and incumbent success in terms of both the percentage of votes gained and whether the candidate won or lost.

Given the multimethod approach of this study, more specific treatment of the choice of indicators, hypotheses, and cases will be presented in those chapters dealing with the survey and aggregate-level analyses. Subsequent methodological and theoretical discussions will be couched in terms of the literature discussed above, and the reader is encouraged to refer back to this discussion as often as necessary.

Looking Ahead

This chapter's discussion both examined the literature upon which this study was built and indicated how this literature has had an impact on some of the general methodological decisions contained within the study. I addressed the development of key concepts like sociotropic, pocketbook, and relative sociotropic voting, and pointed out additional issues like referendum voting and jurisdictional considerations. Each of these concepts will appear again in later chapters as I develop hypotheses and tests at the individual and aggregate levels.

In the next chapter, I take the reader through an initial examination of both the system of elections and the elections themselves from which the cases under examination were drawn. The chapter outlines the legal structure within which regional executive elections occur and offers a broad spectrum of the conditions and events of the 1999–2001 elections that will assist the reader as he or she navigates the more abstract quantitative analyses of chapters 4 and 5.

Notes

1. Bernard Berelson, Paul Lazarsfeld, and William Mcphee, *Voting: A Study of Opinion Formation in a Presidential Campaign* (Chicago: University of Chicago Press, 1954), 312.

2. Stephen Cohen, *Failed Crusade: America and the Tragedy of Post-Communist Russia* (New York: W. W. Norton, 2000).

3. For more on the so-called area specialist vs. comparativist debate, see the debate in *Slavic Review* between Valerie Bunce and Phillipe Schmitter and Terry Karl: Phillipe Schmitter with Terry Karl, "The Conceptual Travels of Transitologists and Consolidologists: How Far to the East Should They Attempt to Go?" *Slavic Review* 53, no. 1 (Spring 1994): 173–85; and Valerie Bunce, "Should Transitologists be Grounded?" *Slavic Review* 54, no. 1 (Spring 1995): 111–27.

4. Timothy Colton, "Economics and Voting in Russia," *Post-Soviet Affairs* 12 (1996): 313–14.

5. Bernard Manin, Adam Przeworski, and Susan Stokes, "Elections and Representation," in *Democracy, Accountability and Representation,* ed. Adam Przeworski, Bernard Manin, and Susan Stokes (Cambridge: Cambridge University Press, 1999), 29.

6. Manin, Przeworski, and Stokes, "Elections and Representation," 43.

7. Criteria are paraphrased from Manin, Przeworksi, and Stokes, "Elections and Representation," 47–49. The authors also include a sixth category stating that citizens must "have some institutional instruments to reward and punish governments for outcomes they generate in different realms" (p. 49). Because elections remain the single such instrument in all democracies, this largely normative criteria is omitted.

8. Abraham Maslow, *Motivation and Personality* (New York: Harper Brothers, 1954).

9. Goskomstat Rossii, *Rossiiskii statisticheskii ezhegodnik: 2000* (Moscow: Goskomstat, 2000), 157, 163.

10. Respondents were asked to choose from "insufficient food and other essential products, price increases, economic crisis, crime, moral and cultural crisis, environmental degradation, aggravation of inter-ethnic relations, income inequality, fascism and extremism, corruption, weak state power, conflict amongst political leaders, war and civil conflict (particularly in Chechnia), wage arrears, and difficult to say." Data drawn from VTsIOM, *Ekonomicheskie i sotsial'nyi peremeny: Monitoring obshchestvennogo mneniia* 46, no. 2 (March–April 2000): 56.

11. Concern over crime is consistently the most prominent "noneconomic" issue being chosen by 53.8, 49.6, 42.7, and 43.8 percent of the respondents in 1997, 1998, 1999, and 2000, respectively. Other options included "moral and cultural crisis" (26.4, 26.0, 20.3, and 23.0 percent, respectively); "environmental damage" (26.4, 23.5, 12.9, and 20.2 percent); "aggravation of relations between nationalities" (15.3, 12.6, 9.3, and 16.0 percent); "threat of fascism or extremism" (2.6, 3.6, 3.7, and 2.7 percent); "corruption and bribery" (37.8, 31.9, 25.4, and 30.9 percent); "weakness, inadequacy of state power" (40.0, 36.8, 33.6, and 24.3 percent); "conflict among state leadership" (15.4, 11.9, 8.8, and 10.0 percent); and "armed conflict on the borders of Russia, unstable conditions, the situation in Chechnia" (12.3, 7.4, 3.3, and 43.6 percent). See VTsIOM, *Eko-nomicheskie i sotsial'nyi peremeny: Monitoring obschestvennogo mneniia* 46, no. 2 (March–April 2000): 56.

12. For a review of some of the earlier literature, see Gerald Kramer, "Short-Term Fluctuations in U.S. Voting Behavior, 1896–1964," *American Political Science Review* 65 (1971): 131–43.

13. Anthony Downs, *An Economic Theory of Democracy* (New York: Harper Brothers, 1957); V. O. Key, *The Responsible Electorate: Rationality in Presidential Voting, 1936–1960* (Cambridge, Mass.: Belknap Press, 1966).

14. Kramer, "Short-Term Fluctuations," 133.

15. Morris Fiorina, "Economic Retrospective Voting in American National Elections: A Micro-Analysis," *American Journal of Political Science* 22 (1978): 426–43.

16. Fiorina, "Economic Retrospective Voting," 134.

17. Fiorina, "Economic Retrospective Voting," 140.

18. Howard Bloom and Douglas Price, "Voter Response to Short-Run Economic Conditions: The Asymmetric Effect of Prosperity and Recession," *American Political Science Review* 69 (1975): 1240–54; Edward Tufte, "Determinants of the Outcomes of Midterm Congressional Elections," *American Political Science Review* 69 (1975): 812–26; Edward Tufte, *Political Control of the Economy* (Princeton, N.J.: Princeton University Press, 1978); Raymond Fair, "The Effects of Economic Events on Votes for the President," *Review of Economics and Statistics* 60 (1978): 159–73; J. R. Hibbing and J. R. Alford, "The Electoral Impact of Economic Conditions: Who Is Held Responsible?" *American Journal of Political Science* 25 (1981): 423–39.

19. The ecological inference problem was first recognized by Ogburn and Goltra, and later expounded by Robinson. See William Ogburn and Inez Goltra, "How Women Vote: A Study of an Election in Portland Oregon," *Political Science Quarterly,* 34 (1919): 413–33; W. S. Robinson, "Ecological Correlations and the Behavior of Individuals," *American Sociological Review* 15, no. 3 (June 1950): 351–57. For a solution to the problem, see Gary King, *A Solution to the Ecological Inference Problem* (Princeton, N.J.: Princeton University Press, 1997).

20. Tufte, "Determinants"; Donald Kinder and D. Roderick Kiewiet, "Sociotropic Politics: The American Case," *British Journal of Political Science,* 11 (1981): 129–61.

21. Kramer, "Short-Term Fluctuations"; Fair, "Effects"; S. I. Lepper, "Voting Behavior and Aggregate Policy Targets," *Public Choice* 18 (1974): 67–81; R. P. Y. Li, "Public Policy and Short-Term Fluctuations in U.S. Voting Behavior: A Reformulation and Expansion," *Political Methodology* 3 (1976): 49–70.

22. Bloom and Price, "Voter Response"; George Stigler, "General Economic Conditions and National Elections," *American Economic Review* 63 (1973): 160–67.

23. Kinder and Kiewiet, "Sociotropic Politics"; Stanley Feldman, "Economic Self-

Interest and Political Behavior," *American Journal of Political Science* 26 (1982): 446–66; Stephen Weatherford, "Economic Conditions and Electoral Outcomes: Class Differences in the Political Response to Recession," *American Journal of Political Science* 22 (1983): 917–38.

24. The "value added" of survey approaches (like this current one) may be seen in the following quotation from Kinder and Kiewiet: "It is important to keep in mind that all these analyses [author's note: Kinder and Kiewiet were referring to the 1970s American studies] rely upon aggregate-level data—what has been examined is the relationship between *aggregate* economic conditions and *collective* political outcomes. On logical grounds, therefore, the evidence has nothing in particular to say about how economic conditions affect individual voters. The aggregate evidence is necessarily compatible with any number of individual-level models." See Donald Kinder and Roderick Kiewiet, "Economic Discontent and Political Behavior: The Role of Personal Grievances and Collective Economic Judgments in Congressional Voting," *American Journal of Political Science* 23 (1979): 497. For more arguments to this effect, see Tufte, "Determinants."

25. Mikal Ben Gera Logan, "Short-Term Economic Changes and Individual Voting Behavior" (unpublished manuscript, Yale University, 1977); Fiorina, "Economic Retrospective Voting."

26. Kinder and Kiewiet are careful to indicate that the sociotropic vs. pocketbook voting debate is not about "altruism" versus self-interest. Sociotropic voters may very well be acting in their own interest by rationally calculating that a healthy national economy will yield benefits for their pocketbooks. See Kinder and Kiewiet, "Sociotropic Politics," 132.

27. Kinder and Kiewiet, "Sociotropic Politics," 132.

28. Feldman, "Economic Self-Interest"; David Butler and Donald Stokes, *Political Change in Britain* (New York: St. Martin's Press, 1969).

29. Paul Sniderman and Richard Brody, "Coping: The Ethic of Self-Reliance," *American Journal of Political Science* 63 (1977): 501–21.

30. Feldman, "Economic Self-Interest," 240.

31. Though Stein referred to this as the "federalist perspective" on voting, I refer to it merely as "jurisdictional voting," arguing that similar issues are at stake in federal, unitary, and intralevel government comparisons. Other locus-related issues are particularly prevalent in the study of legislatures. In these cases, though jurisdictional issues play some role, another main issue is the fact that legislatures "dilute" responsibility within a larger body containing many different individuals, fractions, and parties. See G. Powell and Guy Whitten, "A Cross-National Analysis of Economic Voting: Taking Account of the Political Context," *American Journal of Political Science* 37 (1993): 391–414; and Anthony Heath and Bruno Paulson, "Issues and the Economy," *Political Quarterly* 63 (1992): 432–47.

32. Robert Stein, "Economic Voting for Governor and U.S. Senator: The Electoral Consequences of Federalism," *Journal of Politics* 52 (1990): 32.

33. Charles Tidmarch, Lisa Hyman, and Jill Sorkin, "Press Issue Agenda in the 1982 Congressional and Gubernatorial Election Campaign," *Journal of Politics* 46 (1984): 1226–45.

34. Stephen Turret, "The Vulnerability of American Governors, 1900–1969," *Midwest Journal of Political Science* 15 (1971): 108–32; John Chubb, "Institutions, the Economy, and the Dynamics of State Elections," *American Political Science Review* 82 (1988): 133–54; Malcolm Jewell and David Olson, *Political Parties and Elections in*

American States (Chicago: Dorsey, 1988); Michael Lewis-Beck and Tom Rice, *Forecasting Elections* (Washington, D.C.: CQ Press, 1992).

35. Chubb, "Institutions," 150.

36. Karlheinz Reif, "Ten Second-Order National Elections," in *Ten European Elections,* ed. Karleinz Reif (Aldershot, U.K.: Gower Publishing, 1985), 1–36; Pippa Norris, "Second Order Elections Revisited," *European Journal of Political Research,* 31 (1997) 109–14; Karleinz Reif, "European Elections as Member State Second-Order Elections Revisited, *European Journal of Political Research* 31 (1997), 115–24; Michael Marsh, "Testing the Second-Order Election Model after Four European Elections," *British Journal of Politics* 29 (1998): 591–607.

37. Wallace Oates, *Fiscal Federalism* (New York: Harcourt Brace Jovanovich, 1972); C. Tiebout, "A Pure Theory of Local Expenditures," *Journal of Political Economy* 65 (1956): 416–24.

38. Paul Peterson, *City Limits* (Chicago: University of Chicago Press, 1981), 47.

39. Stein, "Economic Voting"; L. R. Atkeson and R. W. Partin, "Economic and Referendum Voting: A Comparison of Gubernatorial and Senatorial Elections," *American Political Science Review* 89 (1995): 99–107; Richard Niemi, Harold Stanley, and Ronald Vogel, "State Economies and State Taxes: Do Voters Hold Governors Accountable?" *American Journal of Political Science* 39 (1995): 936–57.

40. In his analyses of elections in a number of former socialist countries, Joshua Tucker uses the term *referendum* voting in a way nearly synonymous with Fiorina's *retrospective* voter, indicating that the election is essentially a *referendum* drawing upon citizens' evaluation of economic performance during the previous term. Because the present study is an analysis of gubernatorial elections, I employ the term *referendum voting* in the more traditional sense found in previous subnational election studies. See Joshua Tucker, "Reconsidering Economic Voting: Party Type vs. Incumbency in Transition Countries," paper presented at the Annual Meeting of the American Political Science Association, Atlanta, September 1999.

41. Stein, "Economic Voting," 52.

42. Roderick Kiewiet and Douglas Rivers, "A Retrospective on Retrospective Voting," *Political Behavior* 6 (1984): 369–91.

43. Stephen White, Richard Rose, and Ian McAllister, *How Russia Votes* (New York: Chatham House, 1996); Timothy Colton and Jerry Hough, eds., *Growing Pains: Russian Democracy and the Election of 1993* (Washington, D.C.: Brookings Institution Press, 1998).

44. Colton, "Economics and Voting in Russia"; Colton and Hough, *Growing Pains.*

45. Timothy Colton, *Transitional Citizens* (Cambridge, Mass.: Harvard University Press, 2000); Timothy Colton and Michael McFaul, *Popular Choice and Managed Democracy* (Washington, D.C.: Brookings Institution Press, 2003).

46. See W. S. Robinson, "Ecological Correlations and the Behavior of Individuals," *American Sociological Review* 15, no. 3 (1950): 351–57.

47. Tucker, "Reconsidering Economic Voting."

48. Henry Hale, "Bazaar Politics: Prospects for Parties in Russia," *Russia Watch* 9 (January 2003): 5–7. See also Mikhail Afanas'ev, "Politicheskie partii v rossiiskikh regionakh," *Pro et Contra* 5, no. 4 (Autumn 2000): 164–83.

49. On some level, this comment applies to nearly every single study of regional-level politics. Some examples include Vladimir Gelman, Sergei Rizhenkov, and Mikhail

Brie, eds., *Making and Breaking Democratic Transitions: Comparative Politics of Russia's Regions* (Lanham, Md.: Rowman & Littlefield, 2003) (this book is an English translation of the original: Vladimir Gelman, Sergei Rizhenkov, and Mikhail Brie, eds., *Rossiia regionov: Transformatsiia politicheskikh rezhimov* [Moscow: Ves' Mir, 2000]); Joel Moses, "Political-Economic Elites and Russian Regional Elections, 1999–2000: Democratic Tendencies in Kaliningrad, Perm, and Volgograd," *Europe-Asia Studies* 54 (2002): 907; Peter Kirkow, *Russia's Provinces: Authoritarian Transformation versus Local Autonomy?* (New York: St. Martin's Press, 1998); Marie Mendras, "How Regional Elites Preserve Their Power," *Post-Soviet Affairs* 4 (October–December 1999): 295–311; Jean-Charles Lallemand, "Politics for the Few: Elites in Bryansk and Smolensk," *Post-Soviet Affairs* 4 (October–December 1999): 312–35; Yaroslav Startsev, "Gubernatorial Politics in Sverdlovsk Oblast'," *Post-Soviet Affairs* 4 (October-December 1999): 336–361; Anne Le Huerou, "Elites in Omsk," *Post-Soviet Affairs* 4 (October–December 1999); 362–86; Leokadiya Drobizheva, "A Comparison of Elite Groups in Tatarstan, Sakha, Magadan, and Orenburg," *Post-Soviet Affairs* 4 (October–December 1999): 387–406; Arbakhan Magomedov, *Misteriia Regionalizma: Regional'nye praviashchie elity i regional'nye ideologii v sovremennoi Rossii—Modeli politicheskogo vossozdaniia "Snizu"* (Moscow: MONF, 2000); Darrel Slider, "Pskov under the LDPR: Elections and Dysfunctional Federalism in One Region," *Europe-Asia Studies,* 51 (1999): 755–67; and Melvin Niel, "The Consolidation of a New Regional Elite: The Case of Omsk 1987–1995," *Europe-Asia Studies* 50, no. 4 (1998): 619–51.

50. Bryon Moraski and William M. Reisinger, "Explaining Electoral Competition across Russia's Regions," *Slavic Review* 62 (2003): 278–301.

51. As stated above, given the fact that Goskomstat often releases complete regional economic data one to two years after the fact, the authors may have chosen this approach to maximize the number of cases under examination. I would argue that the trade-off between the validity of the measure and the number of cases added warrants against such an approach.

52. Despite his election victory, polls conducted throughout 1996 indicated that the president remained unpopular among the population. In a survey by the Public Opinion Foundation (Fond Obshchestvennoe Mnenie, or FOM) conducted in October 1996, only 19 percent of respondents indicated that they "trusted" the president. Anna Petrovna and Anna Vorontsova, "Doverie k Borisu El'tsinu postoianno snizhaetsia," *Baza Dannykh FOM,* October 24, 1996; http://bd.fom.ru/report/map/of19964201.

53. In all fairness, Solnick recognizes the ecological inference problem and notes that "though a definitive conclusion on the regional elections would require individual-level data comparable to Colton's, aggregate regional data also reflect a surprisingly weak sociotropic effect." Steven Solnick, "Gubernatorial Elections in Russia, 1996–1997," *Post-Soviet Affairs,* 14 (1998): 48–80; the citation here is on 69.

54. See Stein, "Economic Voting," 32–34.

55. E.g., see Vladimir Gelman and Olga Senatova, "Sub-National Politics in Russia in the Post-Communist Transition Period: A View from Moscow," *Regional and Federal Studies* 5 (Summer 1995): 211–23.

56. M. V. Romanovskii and O. V. Vryblevskaia, *Biudzhetnaia sistema Rossiiskoi Federatsii* (Moscow: Yurait, 2000), 91.

57. By comparison, regions in Australia received 20 percent of their tax revenues; in the United States, 45 percent; and in Canada, 50 percent. See Aleksei Lavrov, "Budgetary

Federalism," in *Conflict and Consensus in Ethno-Political and Center-Periphery Relations in Russia,* ed. Jeremy Azrael and Emil Payin (Washington, D.C.: Rand Corporation, 1998), 34.

58. Daniel Treisman, "Russia's Tax Crisis: Explaining Falling Revenues in a Transitional Economy," *Economics and Politics* 2 (1999): 145–69.

59. Darrell Slider, "Russia's Market-Distorting Federalism," *Post-Soviet Geography and Economics* 38 (1997): 445–60.

60. Gelman and Senatova, "Sub-National Politics."

61. Iurii Lebedev and Vladimir Kazantsev, series of interviews by the author, October 2000.

62. Treisman, "Russia's Tax Crisis"; Kathryn Stoner-Weiss, "The Russian Central State in Crisis," in *Russian Politics: Challenges of Democratization,* ed. Zoltan Barany and Robert Moser (Cambridge: Cambridge University Press, 2001).

63. Stoner-Weiss, "Russian Central State in Crisis," 118.

64. Stoner-Weiss, "Russian Central State in Crisis," 118–22.

65. According to Evgenia Serova, roughly 30 percent of Russia's regions established some form of border control during the financial crisis. See Evgenia Serova, "Federal Agro-Food Policy in the Conditions of the Financial and Economic Crisis," *Russian Economy: Trends and Perspectives,* November 1998, 22–27.

66. Vera Tolz and Irina Busygina, "Regional Governors and the Kremlin: The Ongoing Battle for Power," *Communist and Post-Communist Studies* 30, no. 4 (1997): 406.

67. Scholars' arguments are also clearly colored by "where they sit" when conducting their research. Interviews with regional authorities or documents published by regional scholars or journalists invariably indicate that the center retains too much power, leaving the regions to cope with too many responsibilities and too few resources. Observers based in Moscow, by contrast, cast blame on regional authorities who possess too much autonomy from the center. Both sides provide convincing statistics to back up their arguments.

68. Slider, "Russia's Market-Distorting Federalism," 449.

69. King offers a solution to the ecological inference problem through the use of precinct-level data. This promises to offer a useful approach for future studies but, due to the unavailability of applicable subregional data, will have to be ignored in favor of more traditional methods for the course of this study. See King, *Solution to the Ecological Inference Problem.*

70. Nonetheless, these costs pale in comparison with the expense of collecting similar data in the United States.

Chapter 3

Sploshnie Vybory: A Guide to Russian Regional Executive Elections

> In meetings with my fellow citizens they cry out ever more loudly that the whole country is busy with elections, only elections and nothing but elections. . . . But we politicians continue to assault them every God-given week.
>
> —Vladimir Lysenko

Sploshnie vybory, meaning "endless elections," gives a sense of the weariness with which some Russians view their nation's entire contemporary election process.[1] Federal structures and staggered campaigns resulted in a seemingly endless series of contests for a bewildering number of positions, and on any given Sunday, someone, somewhere was facing an election. Therefore, before delving into the quantitative analyses of chapters 4 and 5, it is first necessary to present a general road map of Russia's regional executive elections during the period from 1991 to 2001. This chapter gives the basic legal and historical background of these contests, helps situate the subsequent analyses within the context of a more tangible narrative, and provides a baseline for the discussion of Vladimir Putin's efforts to further reform the institution during the period from 2001 to 2004 (chapter 7).

The chapter first describes the federal laws and other legal documents that constitute the normative bases of Russia's gubernatorial elections and then discusses critical changes in the regional and federal institutions that occurred over the course of the past decade. It also addresses some of the inconsistencies between the normative-legal aspects of Russian gubernatorial elections and events "on the ground"—identifying key factors that contributed to this incongruence. This discussion indicates the extent to which regional elections are subject to the machinations of incumbents and challengers and

71

points out the most frequently cited factors contributing to election scandals and other legal infractions during the period under investigation.

The chapter then guides the reader through a brief history of Russia's first decade of regional executive elections. Particular emphasis is placed upon the cross-regional distribution of election laws within the sets of regions undergoing elections, the types of incumbents involved, variations in incumbent success, and the role of certain factors specific to each cycle like the preeminence of Boris Yeltsin's appointees in the 1996–97 round and the effect of Putin's initial efforts to reverse Russia's slide toward decentralization during the 1999–2001 cycle. Elements of this discussion set the stage for later chapters by explaining how changes in incumbent characteristics and the elimination of Yeltsin appointees had an impact on the potential role of economic voting between election rounds and indicating how effective "incumbent-friendly" election laws might have been in securing unpopular incumbents.

The Rules of the Game

During the period under investigation, a complex collection of laws, presidential decrees and sections of the Constitution provided the legal basis for elections in Russia.[2] In addition to laws focused exclusively on election procedures, other aspects of elections were governed by portions of legal documents dealing with issues in other spheres like the mass media (Russian Federal Law, Of Mass Media, June 31, 1997), social organizations (Russian Federal Law, Of Social Organizations, May 19, 1995), and others. The principal guidelines for elections to all organs at all levels of the Russian Federation were laid out in the 1994 and 1997 (modified in 1999) versions of the federal laws, Basic Guarantees of Citizens Electoral Rights and Rights to Participate in Referendums (hereafter, the Basic Guarantees; October 16, 1994, December 19, 1997, and March 30, 1999).[3] These documents codify the principles of free, competitive, and periodic elections through which citizens older than eighteen years and not subject to imprisonment or other criminal proceedings are free to directly participate (or *not* participate) in the selection of their leaders to legislative and executive posts at the federal, regional, and local levels. The laws also described the eligibility requirements for candidates at all levels of government. For regional executive posts, any citizen no younger than thirty years of age, living on the territory of said subject, and not currently imprisoned or undergoing criminal proceedings, is eligible to run for office (other requirements vary by region, with some federal subjects attempting at various times to impose language and residency requirements).[4]

The Basic Guarantees provided the following blueprint for each step of the election process. First, no less than 65 days before the end of the executive's term or no later than 14 days after an unscheduled termination of the executive's rule, the regional legislative body met to set a date for the elections (in the absence of a sitting legislature, the date for the election is defined by the regional election commission). This election announcement had to be made no earlier than 180 days and no later than 70 days before the chosen date. The election date must then be published in the official mass media no later than 5 days after the decision.

Following the election announcement, borders of regional election districts were defined, lists of eligible voters compiled and verified, and electoral commissions created for each district. One of the key players in this process was the regional election commission. As in many federations, Russian election law mandates the creation of electoral commissions at the federal, regional, and district levels, with each level's commission responsible not only for carrying out and monitoring the election process within its jurisdiction but also for monitoring the activities of those commissions at the next lower level.

Regional election commissions were directly subordinate to the Central Election Commission of the Russian Federation and were responsible for providing the basic institutional support for all elections within their given regions. Each regional commission was created on the basis of the principle of parity between the regional executive and legislature, with each political organ appointing half the commission's members. An additional stipulation required that both organs draw no less than one-third of the commission members from the recommendations of each political bloc having a fraction in both the Russian Duma and the regional legislature. Lower (territorial and district) level election commissions were created either by the municipal legislative body under whose jurisdiction the territory or district falls or, in the absence of a legislative body (as in small cities and rural districts), by the regional-level election commission. At the territorial (*raion,* city) and then district levels (below the *raion* and city level), the same guidelines regarding recommendation by political blocs applied. Federal and regional election commissions existed on a permanent basis for a period of no more than five years (at which point, any or all of the members may be reappointed). District-level commissions held much briefer terms, being disbanded no later than five days following the election.

Aside from their responsibilities for creating lower level commissions, regional election commissions also decided the geographical boundaries of election districts. In cooperation with the local (city or *raion*) head of administration, the commissions tallied the number of voters in each geographical area and defined voting district boundaries. By federal law, each district could include no more than 3,000 registered voters. Upon the establishment of these districts, the regional election commission and local executive created district-level election commissions according to the rules described above.

With election commissions now operating at the regional, territorial, and district levels, the essential organizational infrastructure existed to proceed with the next phases of the election process. Candidates had until thirty days before the election date to gather the necessary number of signatures and produce other documents necessary to officially register as candidates.[5] The number of signatures required to register was fixed by regional laws, but it could not exceed 2 percent of the total number of eligible voters within the region. Furthermore, federal law permitted regional legislatures to require that candidates submit financial documents indicating their income and assets. The regional election commission verified both financial statements and lists of signatures. With regard to the latter, candidates were permitted a certain percentage of nonverifiable signatures as determined by the regional legislature. However, this margin of error could not be less than 10 percent or more than 20 percent of the total gathered signatures (candidates could gather up to 15 percent more signatures than required). Furthermore, if the number of verifiable signatures fell short of the total required, the commission rejected the candidate's registration. Finally, financial documents were subject to verification, and discrepancies could also provide a basis for rejecting a candidate's registration (as determined by regional laws).

Upon registration, candidates became eligible to conduct official campaign agitation through the mass media, organized public events, printed materials, and other sanctioned methods. Nonetheless, certain restrictions governed each of these activities. Election law permitted campaign advertisement (aside from placards, signs, and billboards) only up to the last twenty-four hours before the election date. Additional restrictions were placed on the publication of the results of opinion polls, which could only be published up to the last seventy-two hours before the date. Aside from these temporal restrictions, federal election laws attempted to head off the use of so-called administrative resources by restricting candidates from using public office and other positions as bases from which to undertake campaign agitation. For instance, members of the election commissions, charitable and religious organizations, state and municipal officials, the military, and other state and municipal servants were not allowed to carry out campaign agitation *while performing their given duties or using the assets or property of their given organization.*

Federal and regional laws focus particular attention on the use of the mass media for campaigning purposes. The Basic Guarantees divided mass media outlets into two categories. The first included those organs that annually receive no less than 15 percent of their total financing from state and municipal organizations. As recipients of public funds, these organs were obliged to provide free and equal airtime and print space for all registered candidates. The second group of media organs included all those outlets that do not fall into the first category. These organs could provide airtime and printed space for candidates on a negotiated basis, subject only to the requirement that outlets charge equal amounts to all candidates (and that candidates pay for space out of their federally and regionally mandated campaign fund). For both types of media organizations, any candidate's campaign advertisement had to clearly state either that it was paid from the candidate's campaign fund or that it constituted the candidate's use of his or her allotted free advertisement space.

After the 1999 amendments to the Basic Guarantees, federal guidelines also regulated the dissemination of printed materials. Before the 1999 amendments, this process was largely unrestricted, allowing for the anonymous printing and dissemination of slanderous and extortive materials. Following the 1999 amendments, all printed agitation materials had to contain contact information for the publishing organization, the number of copies printed, and the printing date. Furthermore, before disseminating the materials, candidates were required to provide a copy of the material to the regional election commission, along with a description of the area where the materials would be placed. Finally, materials could be displayed on buildings and other public places only with the permission of the owner. No materials could be placed on monuments, historical and cultural buildings, or in or around election commission offices.

As indicated above, candidates could also campaign through meetings with voters, debates, demonstrations, and parades. However, all these public activities were subject to the same restrictions as any other form of mass public meetings. To meet with voters, candidates had to register with local authorities no less than three days before the meeting. Demonstrations and parades are subject to the federal law titled Organizing and Carrying Out Meetings, Street Parades, Demonstrations and Pickets, which required that the organizer register with local authorities no less than ten days before the planned event. For both demonstrations and mass meetings, candidates had free and equal access to public property suitable for the given activity.

Certain types of agitation were prohibited in any form. Candidates could not incite religious, national, racial, or social hatred, or agitate for the overthrow of the government, forced revision of the Constitution, destruction of the state, war, or restrictions on freedom of speech. "Buying votes" was also forbidden and included the provision of free goods and services, money, benefits, or discounts in exchange for votes. Any individual working in connection with a candidate's campaign was also restricted from engaging in any charitable work during the course of the campaign. Candidates or individuals who violated any of these restrictions could be subject not only to disqualification but also to criminal prosecution in accordance with federal and regional law.

On the day of the election, votes were collected and tallied by the district, territorial, and then regional election commissions. In the event that either voter participation failed to exceed the minimum requirement as defined in regional law or, the number of voters casting votes "against all" candidates exceeded those cast for any other candidate,[6] the election was suspended (*nesostoianie*). If legal violations prevented the "establishment of the people's will with certainty," violations invalidated the results in no less than a quarter of the districts, or results were successfully contested in court, the election was declared invalid (*nedeisvitelnyi*).

If neither of these conditions held, then regional law determined the next stage in the election process. In regions with plurality-based elections, the candidate who gained the most votes won. Regions with majority-based elections required that a candidate gain at least 50 percent of the vote to win in the first round. Failing that, the two candidates with the highest number of first round votes moved into the second round, in which the winner was determined by a simple plurality. Upon attaining a "final" result, the regional election commission was then bound to publish the official results of the election within one month of the "final" election date.

Although the above discussion might indicate that Russia's federal voting laws provided a comprehensive framework for elections, in actual fact, regional governing bodies maintained a significant latitude in determining the nature of their own elections. First, as indicated above, many of the remaining normative details regarding regional executive elections were left to the discretion of regional representative bodies. Among other aspects, regional legislatures determined the required turnout level, whether governors were elected for four- or five-year terms, and whether elections were decided by simple pluralities or majorities.

The laws determining the number of allowable consecutive terms in office were also left open to interpretation, and it was not until the October 6, 1999, law—Basic Principles for the Organization of Representative and Executive Organs in Subjects of the Russian Federation—that the federal government established a two-consecutive-term limit (length of up to five years per term) on regional executives.[7] This change naturally raised some concerns among "veteran" executives facing their third-term elections at the end of the 1990s. In response to these concerns and as a concession by the presidential administration to a few strategic regional executives (President Mintimer Shaimiev of Tartarstan being the most frequently mentioned), the law was later (February 2001) reinterpreted to mean that governors could serve two consecutive terms starting from the year in which the law went into effect (that being 1999). Hence, at the time of writing, a number of executives enjoy the opportunity to hold office for as many as *four* consecutive terms.

In addition to the legally sanctioned delegation of election law-making powers, regions gained a further degree of independence from a combination of (often intentionally) ill-defined federal–center relations, neglect, and the simple incapacity of central state organs to monitor election processes (especially during particularly intensive election rounds, as in 1996–97 and 1999–2001). This situation resulted in regional election laws and practices that sometimes blatantly violated the guidelines set out in federal law. Before the creation of the seven federal districts in 1999, the primary federal "watchdog" in the regions was the regional presidential representative. However, these figures, having been chosen from the same regional elite as the acting governor (another concession by Yeltsin to loyal executives in the regions), often actively colluded with regional authorities and could hardly be considered as independent and objective observers for the federal authorities.[8]

Putin's federal reforms in the summer of 1999, which included the creation of new federal districts under the control of presidential envoys, created another institution for monitoring election outcomes. However, throughout the period under examination, this institution remained in its formative stage and the number of instances in which these representatives intervened in elections makes the presidential envoys' impact on the 1999–2001 elections difficult to assess. Summing up the results of a study conducted by a group of specialists roughly four years after the implementation of the *okrug* reforms, Robert Orttung and Peter Reddaway indicate that none of the specialists "has seen the creation of the seven federal *okruga* as a clear success for the Kremlin. At best, they see the results as "mixed" or as having made the existing system work a little better." Furthermore, "the envoys and the *okruga* have not become an indispensable part of the state. . . . Abolishing the *okruga* now would not make a dramatic impact on the political system."[9]

Looking more specifically at the role of presidential envoys in monitoring election outcomes, it is also telling to note that few of the experts in this study even considered any other role for the envoys than as a means to *remove* governors who were at political odds with the president (a role which they have very often failed to successfully perform). Hence, if there is indeed some role for the envoys in guaranteeing free and fair elections, this has taken second stage to the more salient function of settling political scores for the federal government. As will be discussed in chapter 7, such de facto functions contribute very little to the establishment of the rule of law and the promotion of electoral accountability.

Article 63 of the Basic Guarantees provides for the right of individuals and organizations to raise infractions and challenge election outcomes in either an upper-level election commission or in court. Nonetheless, despite the fact that challenges to election outcomes were at least discussed in nearly every election, not a single one of the election decisions was reversed during the period under examination. This fact points to another natural "safeguard" for incumbents—the seemingly endless litigation involved in challenging an election. Candidates, their representatives, or organizations that choose to challenge the validity of an election or to raise an infraction incurred in the course of a campaign, may resort to either the election commission or a court of law.[10] According to the law, cases brought to court in the course of the election must be settled within five days or by the day before the election. Cases brought to court on or following election day must be settled "quickly." In instances in which the plaintiff seeks to contest an election result, a court must render a decision no more than two months following the start of the case.

In practice, this system functioned rather poorly. From the very start of the "official" campaign season, regional courts entered an endless cycle of litigation by incumbents, challengers, and "independent" social organizations. Whether intentionally or otherwise, this process effectively paralyzed regional legal institutions for the course of the campaign. By itself, bringing one's opponent to court became a form of campaign strategy—both discrediting him or her in the eyes of the electorate and raising the uncertainty that the defendant's candidacy would not survive until the election date. Following the election, plaintiffs seeking to invalidate the results of an election faced a nearly insurmountable task. Citizens' lack of interest and fatigue (partially a result of the media's treatment of the endless campaign-period litigation) removed postelection cases from the public eye, leaving courts to handle the case under less scrutiny. Plaintiffs faced nearly impossible demands, being asked not only to demonstrate that an infraction took place but also to "prove" the counterfactual that, had the infraction not occurred, the election result would have ended differently.

The case of gubernatorial candidate Viktor Tarkhov's postelection court case contesting the July 2, 2000, election in Samarskaia Oblast is indicative of just some of the problems facing plaintiffs in postelection court hearings. As discussed in more detail in chapter 7, the region's 2000 elections came about as the result of Titov's surprise resignation in April 6, 2000, following his ill-fated presidential bid. The attempt to challenge the wildly popular Vladimir Putin cost Titov the backing of many of the regional oligarchs upon which he had relied for support for much of the previous decade. With the possibility that the federal government would back a strong candidate by the time that the regularly scheduled elections rolled around in December, Titov opted to resign and force an early campaign in July.

Moving on from the contest's questionable origins (existing election laws did not, however, rule out such tactics), "ex-"governor Titov continued to enjoy many of the "administrative resources" that he commanded during his time in the oblast administration. A review of the oblast administration–supported *Volzhskaia Kommuna* indicated that, even with the governor no longer "officially" at his post, he still enjoyed the full backing of the proadministration media. *Volzhskaia Kommuna* and other media related to the administration continued to report on the ex-governor's activities—especially those with the most "campaign appeal." Furthermore, the campaign was marked by an exceptionally large number of early ballots submitted before election day. Such ballots, collected by district electoral commissions and subject to less scrutiny than the voting undertaken during the actual election, feature prominently in suits challenging the results of electoral contests.

Tarkhov, a notable in the regional petroleum sector, and before the collapse of the Soviet Union, former chairman of the Samarskaia Oblast soviet and executive committee, entered the apparently lopsided fray as Titov's primary challenger. Tarkhov's campaign—backed by the Communist Party and attempting to balance his oligarchic background with populist slogans about saving the vulnerable from Titov's liberal economic policies—was plagued by a poorly defined policy focus, the difficulty of painting one of Russia's most economically successful regions as an economic basket case, and his opponent's overwhelming resources. His bid ended in his winning only 29 percent of the popular vote to Titov's 53 percent.

Following the election, Tarkhov sought to challenge the outcome of the July 2 elections on the grounds that the results were determined by an unusually large proportion of early votes,[11] and the incumbent had both made unfair use of "administrative resources" and meddled in Tarkhov's campaign activities. The case did not make it to court until late September— nearly three months after the election. In the first hearing, the plaintiff's lawyer was asked to indicate exactly when and where the incumbent made use of "administrative resources" and how many individuals these activities could have influenced.

Because there is no law limiting the number of ballots cast before the election, there was little Tarkhov's lawyer could do but to indicate that an "exceptionally large number" of early votes were cast for the incumbent. In his statement, the lawyer stated that it was impossible to find an adequate number of individuals who would take the risk of testifying on Tarkhov's behalf (these would naturally include individuals who were currently working for the administration, which had already sat in office for the three months following the election). As a result, the case was withdrawn from court by the second week of October.[12] Looking across other elections, one can see that Tarkhov's case was not exceptional and that it offers some sense of the obstacles facing any candidate or organization that opts to challenge an election. With the exception of a very few cases, such practices have come to be seen as nothing more than face-saving measures, with few prospects for yielding tangible outcomes.

The collision of federal law with historic events also compromised the effectiveness of federal normative acts in guaranteeing the competitiveness of regional elections. Of particular import was the initial creation of the regional election commissions that were responsible for the running and monitoring of elections for much of the remaining decade. According to every version of the Basic Guarantees, 50 percent of the members of regional election commissions are appointed by regional legislatures, and the other 50 percent by the acting regional executive. In theory, the separation of powers between these two governing bodies should provide the checks and balances necessary to prevent either from essentially "stacking the deck" in the regional election commission.

However, events conspired against such an arrangement. Following Yeltsin's "victory" against the parliamentary faction in October 1993, he disbanded all regional legislatures and ordered that elections for new bodies occur before March 1994. One of the more curious aspects of this decision is the fact that, as stated above, elections are to be implemented by regional election commissions staffed by equal proportions of regional legislature and regional executive appointees. With the legislatures disbanded, the executive was given full responsibility for the selection of election commission members and, thereby, the development of election institutions.

Given this chain of events, the first, post–October 1993 regional legislative elections occurred under circumstances that overwhelmingly favored candidates representing regional executives and their cliques.[13] As a result, relations between regional executives and regional legislatures were often more collusive than desirable for a properly working system of checks and balances. Among other indicators, the low number of executive vetoes, and the success of governors in receiving the types of term extensions, low election turnout limits, and single-tour elections described in further detail below, offer some indication of the actual independence of these two governing bodies in many of Russia's regions.[14] With this much collusion between the two branches, the two halves of the regional election commissions often represented the interests of the regional executive.[15]

Aside from the actual implementation of Russian election laws, a further threat to "free and fair" elections is what I call (for lack of a better term) Russia's "campaign culture." Simply put, a campaign culture is a set of institutionalized norms within a political system that guides the campaign behavior of individuals and organizations. In most advanced industrial democracies, this campaign culture includes unwritten norms that almost instinctively prevent the majority of political forces from pursuing the most unethical forms of campaigning. As an example, even in an established advanced industrial democracy, no method of enforcement exists that might prevent the printing of a small number of anonymous pamphlets threatening citizens with terrorist bombings in the event of a given candidate's election (to borrow an example from the Ul'ianovskaia Oblast case)—nonetheless, few candidates in these democracies would resort to such campaign tactics. For the Russian cases, such practices are nearly customary, with vicious rumors and threats of individual and mass violence and pure hooliganism marking nearly every single race. Clearly, the Russian political milieu continues to lack the self-enforcing mechanism of its counterparts in other democracies as political actors exhibit a willingness to pursue any form of campaign agitation they can get away with.

Having outlined the "rules of the game" for Russian regional executive elections and discussed some of the potential problems concerning their implementation, the following sections describe how the election system worked in practice by examining and comparing different election periods.

Incumbent Electoral Success in the Yeltsin and Early-Putin Eras

In his eight years as governor of Ul'ianovskaia Oblast, Iurii Goriachev took a number of measures typical of other executives throughout Russia to secure his position as head of the regional administration. Before the 1996 elections, the predominantly obedient regional legislature passed a law stipulating that outcomes of regional executive elections would be settled in a single-round, plurality-rule-based election. Ostensibly such a decision served the financial interests of the region, saving the public the expense of an extended election campaign, but most local critics recognized this decision as ploy to assure the governor's reelection in the upcoming contests. In the event, Goriachev won the 1996 election with 42.5 percent of the vote against five opponents. Had he been forced into a runoff with his main challenger, the outcome might have been very different.

During the interim between the 1996 and 2000 elections, another artifact of regional election legislation arose to threaten the governor's reign. According to the region's election law, governors were only permitted to serve two consecutive terms, and with the governor having been first appointed in 1992, 2000 would mark the end of his final term. The effort to "save the governor" resulted in another landmark piece of legislation. From this point forth, governors could only serve two consecutive *elected* terms— Goriachev's first term began with his *appointment* by President Yeltsin. The incumbent's reign was secure for now—he would stand in the 2000 elections.

Throughout the decade, similar legislative manipulation played out in other regions like Belgorodskaia, Murmanskaia, Pskovskaia, Brianskaia, Kirovskaia, and Volgogradskaia Oblasti. Furthermore, ample discussions in the media regarding incumbents' use of "administrative resources," control over regional media outlets, and their frequent resort to underhanded election tactics, helped foster a myth of entrenched regional executives largely invulnerable to their cowed electorates. Obviously, if such perceptions accurately represented Russia's regional executive elections, any search for electoral accountability would necessarily founder on the shoals of irreplaceable incumbents.

This next section directs a critical eye toward the conventional wisdom surrounding the issues of incumbent turnover and electoral competition by looking at trends and patterns of incumbent success throughout the decade. In the process, it indicates that, while election results by themselves offer limited insight into the ability of incumbents to maintain their posts in the face of popular opposition, factors like the success of challengers in elections and the increase in proincumbent election laws across first and second election contests suggest that incumbents were able to protect themselves from disgruntled elements in their societies and thereby lessen their level of accountability for policy outcomes. Aside from the intrinsic worth of these observations, this exploration yields a number of factors to include as controls in the quantitative models of chapter 5.

The decree titled Of Elections to State Organs in Russian Federal Subjects and Municipal Organs (September 18, 1995) functioned primarily as Yeltsin's effort to once and for all break the piecemeal cycle of pre-1995 regional executive elections and finally bring the institution of regional administrations into line with the requirements of the Russian Constitution—that is, elected executives at each post. Before this decree, while elections to Russia's "ethnic" republics proceeded more or less according to schedule, elections in Russia's oblasti, *kraia,* and autonomous *okruga* had occurred erratically (see table 3.1), in part because of the fact that nearly every set of regions that held elections during this period returned dismal results for Yeltsin's appointees. In 1993, elections held in seven oblasti and *kraia* resulted in the defeat of five appointees. In the same year, a federally unsanctioned election was declared by the Cheliabinskaia Oblast regional legislature that returned another defeat for a Yeltsin appointee (this was later annulled by the Yeltsin administration after the parliamentary crisis of October 1993, along with other elections in Brianskaia and Amurskaia Oblasti). The year 1994 saw oblast and *krai* elections nearly grind to a halt with only one contest occurring in Irkutskaia Oblast. In 1995, the pace once again increased with another "minicycle" of elections that resulted in better, but by no means encouraging, results for the Yeltsin administration. Nine out of fourteen incumbents won, but many of the incumbents' campaigns were characterized by marked efforts to distance themselves from Moscow.

Table 3.1. Russia's Regional Elections at a Glance, 1995–2001

Measure	1995	1996	1997	1998	1999	2000	2001
Number of elections	14	46	16	10	13	43	15
Number of elections with incumbent or "heir"	14	46	15	10	13	42	13
Incumbent success (percent)	71	48	63	40	77	67	60
Average incumbent vote share (percent)	55	47	52	52	57	53	61
Percentage of elections resolved in single round	71	65	81	70	69	70	60

Sources: Central Election Commission of the Russian Federation, *Vybory glav ispolnitel'noi vlasti sub'ektov Rossiiskoi Federatsii: Elektoral'naia statistika* (Moscow: Ves' Mir, 1997); Central Election Commission of the Russian Federation, *Vybory gosudarstvennoi vlasti sub'ektov Rossiiskoi Federatsii 1997–2000: Elektoralnaia statistika, tom 1–2* (Moscow: Ves' Mir, 2001); official Web site of the Central Election Commission of the Russian Federation, http://www.cikrf.ru.

Following this series of discouraging outcomes, the Yeltsin administration opted to forestall any further regional elections until after the upcoming 1996 presidential campaign.

Following his astonishing political rebirth and victory in the 1996 elections, Yeltsin stood at the start of at least another four years in office. With the risks associated with a poor showing by Yeltsin's regional executive appointees at their lowest point since the birth of the Russian Federation, the regime once again gave the green light for elections. Between September 1, 1996, and March 23, 1997, executives were elected in fifty-two of Russia's eighty-nine federal subjects, with thirty-five elections occurring in oblasti and *kraia,* six in republics, and eleven in autonomous *okruga.*

However, Yeltsin's 1996 victory meant little for the fortunes of his appointees in the regions. Whereas the elections permitted in 1995 were carefully selected by the Yeltsin administration, and therefore yielded relatively high rates of incumbent success, the fifty-two elections that occurred in 1996 exhibited higher rates of incumbent attrition than both the pre-1996 elections and the subsequent 1999–2001 election cycle. More than half the incumbents facing election in this first cycle were defeated.

Later elections exhibited much higher rates of incumbent success. By 1999, more than three-quarters of all incumbents survived elections. When examined in terms of "cycles," it is clear that incumbents in second-cycle elections (1999–2001), were markedly more successful than their counterparts in the first cycle (1996–97). As Dmitrii Oreshkin suggested, the numbers indicate a trend in Russia's regional elections from peculiarly high incumbent attrition rates, to aggregate outcomes that, at least in terms of raw numbers, looked increasingly like those in Western federations.[16]

What might account for this discernible change throughout the decade? In a study focused on economic accountability, one might first speculate that conditions within the regions had improved from the first to the second cycles, and that therefore incumbents faced less embittered electorates. However, a comparison of economic data across the two election cycles provides only mixed support for this contention. Though the overall economy improved during 2000, measures of average wages as a percentage of the subsistence wage indicated that the population entered 2000 with less purchasing power than they enjoyed in 1996.[17] Furthermore, as the figures for 1999 show, the marked increase in incumbent success rates appeared before the 2000 economic upturn indicating that regions recovering from the economic collapse of August 1998 were nonetheless returning high percentages of incumbents. Though these numbers say nothing about the effects of individual regional conditions (a subject to be dealt with in later chapters), they do caution against the argument that incumbent success increased in later years as a result of an all-Russia economic upturn.

A more plausible explanation might be that changes in the rate of incumbent success across these two cycles reflect the absence of Yeltsin appointees in the latter contests. Appointees are particularly vulnerable to a "referendum effect," whereby voters decide to support or oppose the candidate based on their assessments of the appointing president or other federal political entity. Despite his victory in the 1996 presidential election, Yeltsin remained an unpopular political figure throughout these initial regional executive elections and the perceived linkage between the president and his appointees carried a strong potential to depress support for the latter. One indicator of the relationship between an incumbent's status as an appointee and electoral fortunes can be found when one categorizes the elections into those in which Yeltsin appointees competed and those contests that immediately followed appointee-contested elections. Table 3.2 indicates a marked change in incumbent success rates across the two elections.

In many respects, the different logics involved in the presidential and regional executive contests are reminiscent of the "second-order election" literature discussed briefly in chapter 2. Voters might support Yeltsin for the simple fact that, for all the problems facing the country, they approve of the existing departure from the Soviet Union and would prefer Yeltsin to a potential return to Communism (as personified in Gennadii Ziuganov).[18] However, at the regional level, systemic change is no longer at stake (although,

Table 3.2. Appointed versus Elected Incumbents (percent)

Measure	Appointed Incumbents	Elected Incumbents
Mean incumbent vote	47	56
Success rate	51	70

Sources: Central Election Commission of the Russian Federation, *Vybory glav ispolnitel'noi vlasti sub'ektov Rossiiskoi Federatsii: Elektoral'naia statistika* (Moscow: Ves' Mir, 1997); Central Election Commission of the Russian Federation, *Vybory gosudarstvennoi vlasti sub'ektov Rossiiskoi Federatsii 1997–2000: Elektoralnaia statistika, tom 1–2* (Moscow: Ves' Mir, 2001); official Web site of the Central Election Commission of the Russian Federation, http://www.cikrf.ru.

certainly, some regional executives have carved out their own political and economic spaces, they are still subject to a great deal of influence from the federal center), and we might expect citizens to vote more "honestly"—and less strategically—by punishing or rewarding their regional administrators in part because of their linkage to the president that they so grudgingly voted for in 1996.[19]

The nature of the political processes surrounding the 1996–97 regional executive elections likely magnified the referendum voting effect. Two "proto-parties" (to borrow a term from Solnick) were created to contest the first cycle regional elections—the pro-Yeltsin All-Russian Coordinating Council (OKS) and the Communists' Popular-Patriotic Union of Russia (NPSR). Yeltsin clearly backed the OKS, and the two organizations were juxtaposed in the media as the alternative blocs in the upcoming elections. Both organizations endorsed candidates in each region, and kept an ongoing tally of "their" regions, as the elections progressed. Having lost to Yeltsin in the 1996 presidential elections, Ziuganov and the Communists were especially keen to once again prove their strength by demonstrating their support in the provinces.

As both Solnick and Golosov suggest, one should be wary of casting the OKS/NPSR rivalry in terms of alternative political and ideological programs.[20] In three instances, both the OKS and NPSR endorsed the same candidate, and discipline among constituent parties within the OKS was often lax with party organs "breaking ranks" to endorse other candidates. In some regions, the OKS altogether failed to support the incumbent. NPSR actions sometimes indicated that the protoparty was more interested in maximizing "its" winners rather than supporting like-minded candidates. As Solnick states, "Where possible the NPSR endorsed communist activists already registered as candidates; in general these candidates were not elected. In the remaining regions, the NPSR endorsed the candidate most likely to defeat the incumbent, regardless of ideological leanings."[21] In three regions, the NPSR shifted its endorsement to another candidate after the party's initial choice was eliminated in the first round. Despite the erratic nature of its election strategy (if it could indeed be called that), the NPSR publicly claimed any supported victor as notch in its "red belt."

But regardless of the somewhat arbitrary nature of OKS and NPSR support, the fact remains that later elections were clearly differentiated from the 1996–97 contests by the absence of a propresidential protoparty. This change severed any obvious linkage between certain governors and the president and provides support for the contention that "referendum voting" for or against the Yeltsin regime was an important factor distinguishing many regions' early elections from later contests.[22] The dominance of Yeltsin appointees offered a simple information shortcut for regional voters who, instead of making difficult assessments about relative regional conditions, could cast their votes according to their incumbents' apparent linkage to the president.

Following the 1996–97 cycle, the linkage between the president and regional executives became increasingly murky. The OKS faded from the scene and "opposition" governors who defeated Yeltsin appointees (and some appointees who underwent a political transformation into regime opponents) established their support by taking strong stands against the president. As a result of these changes, the voter going to the polls after 1997 no longer enjoyed the simple rule of thumb of previous elections, and assessments of incumbent loyalty gave way to the more complicated task of assessing performance.[23]

One final factor related to the appointment issue is that, regardless of the fairness of the 1996–97 election contests, the campaigns returned victors who more closely represented key elite groups and peculiar societal interests within their region. Yeltsin's appointment procedure often involved the placement of a locally unpopular but ostensibly pro-Yeltsin figure at the head of the regional government. To take the Ul'ianovskaia Oblast case as an example, Yeltsin's initial choice for governor, Valentin Malafeev, was a local businessman whose image as a "new Russian" earned him the approbation of a very "provincial" local power elite and society. The appointment immediately set off a wave of protest among deputies in the oblast soviet along with a number of public meetings, which culminated in an outpouring of support for the former chairman of the oblast soviet Iurii Goriachev. In this particular instance, popular pressure carried the day and resulted in Yeltsin removing his initial choice and replacing him with Goriachev.

The Ul'ianovsk case, however, proved to be an exception. In other regions like Brianskaia, Pskovskaia, Kurskaia Oblasti, regionally unpopular Yeltsin appointees remained in power until their regions' first elections (in Brianskaia Oblast, without the sanction of the federal government), when they lost to figures who enjoyed, if not mass-based, at least concentrated and organized elite support.

Hence, the greater margin of electoral success enjoyed by incumbents in each region's second election cycle, though in part reflecting the absence of the "referendum effect" described above, also stems from the somewhat mundane fact that these incumbents, regardless of their performance over the past four years, were backed by an actual local constituency.[24] This differentiated them from many of their appointed counterparts, who in 1992, were suddenly plucked from obscurity and entrusted with the highest political authority in the region. By itself, this observation takes some of the edge off arguments to the effect that increased incumbent success rates in later elections reflected the campaign maneuverings of an entrenched elite. To a limited extent, the system was performing its function as a means to regional governance that reflected the peculiar needs and interests of different geographical areas. As further evidence to this effect, public opinion polls conducted in January 1997 indicated that only 25 percent of the population was "unsatisfied" with the results of the fall and winter gubernatorial elections.[25]

Not Entrenched . . . but "Fortified"?

The figures on incumbent attrition across the past decade challenge some of the more strident claims that incumbent governors were somehow invulnerable to removal, and they suggest that the increase in the incumbent success rates in later elections reflects both the elimination of referendum voting and the fact that previous elections served at least some function as a means to replace poorly chosen presidential appointees with political figures more attuned to their particular region's political culture and elite constellations.

Nonetheless, do these benevolent processes fully account for the precipitous increase in incumbent success rates across the decade? A closer examination suggests the presence of other factors that secured certain executives against popular opposition and effectively undermined electoral processes' potential to return accountability-promoting outcomes.

The first of these factors, as suggested by the Ul'ianovskaia Oblast case described above, is the implementation of "incumbent-friendly" election laws between elections. In simple terms, changes in regional election legislation between the two rounds, though not necessarily "entrenching" incumbents, certainly provided a degree of protection against challengers. Among the many legal changes that could benefit incumbents in regional elections, changes from majority to plurality election rules and the lowering of turnout thresholds were most prevalent. Within policymaking circles and among election analysts, a shift from majority to plurality election rules was generally seen as benefiting incumbents by allowing them to maintain office in the face of popular opposition. Even an unpopular incumbent might survive an election challenge by dividing the opposition and squeaking by with less than a third of the popular vote.[26] Low-turnout barriers could serve similar purposes. Incumbents with concentrated and disciplined supporters could secure themselves by gaining low-turnout laws from regional legislatures and then undertaking various legal or illegal (rumors, threats, or disparagement of the election process itself) activities to drive down participation rates among the remaining eligible voters. For regions in which incumbents were particularly popular among pensioners, a low participation rate by itself may be sufficient for reelection, because turnout among the youth and the working-age population is consistently lower than among pensioners.

Events leading up to Brianskaia Oblast's 2000 election provide a telling example of this process. In the spring of 2000, the region's Duma legislated changes into the region's law on elections for head of administration that lowered the turnout barrier to 25 percent and established a simple plurality electoral rule eliminating the stipulation in the previous election law that, in the event that no candidate wins more than 50 percent of the vote in the first election, the contest must be settled in a runoff. As an exemplary "red governor," Lodkin's core supporters were found among Brianskaia Oblast's pensioners, veterans, and the rural population. The election laws, combined with the most flagrant use of the "clones" election strategy (at the end of the contest, the campaign included two Lodkins and two Denins), provided a means for the governor to win the election with a small, but loyal, progovernor electorate. In the event, the "real" Iurii Lodkin secured another four-year term in office with 29.4 percent of the vote. With turnout at 53.36 percent, only 16 percent of the region's eligible voters supported the incumbent.

The Brianskaia Oblast case clearly demonstrates the potential of proincumbent election laws, but how prevalent was such institutional manipulation

Table 3.3. Evolution of Regional Election Laws across First and Second
Elections (in percent, with raw numbers in parentheses)

Measure	First Election	Second Election
All elections		
Turnout thresholds (percent)		
0	6.67 (4)	5.41 (4)
25	58.33 (35)	75.68 (56)
33–35	6.67 (4)	2.70 (2)
50	28.33 (17)	16.22 (12)
Election rule		
Majority	73.44 (47)	53.33 (40)
Plurality	26.56 (17)	46.67 (35)
Changes between elections		
Turnout thresholds		
Lowered	20.75 (11)	
No change	75.47 (40)	
Increased	3.77 (2)	
Election rule		
Majority to plurality	26.42 (14)	
Plurality to majority	11.32 (6)	
Keep plurality	20.75 (11)	
Keep majority	41.51 (22)	

Source: Author's data. Much of the information was drawn from the collection of regional election laws on the "Panorama" Web site (http://www.panorama.ru). More recent information was drawn from press reports and election results for each of the regions in question.

in other regions? Looking first at electoral rules in a set of first and second elections for which data were available, table 3.3 indicates a marked decrease in the number of regions with majority-based election systems between the two contests.[27] If only one in four of regions' first elections occurred under plurality rules, nearly half were settled in this manner during their second. The bottom half of table 3.3 presents data on election rule changes for a subset of fifty-three regions for which data were available for both first and second elections.[28] These figures offer a better indication of the trend toward adopting plurality systems that accounts for the decrease in the number of majority-rule-based elections in the top half of the table. Clearly, many regional administrations recognized the benefits of plurality-rule-based systems as the decade wore on.

As table 3.3 suggests, there were five different turnout thresholds prevalent in the regions. Comparing first with second elections, one sees that the number of regions with fifty percent barriers decreased substantially and that more than three-quarters of second elections occurred under 25-percent-turnout thresholds. The bottom half of the table, again representing fifty-three regions that held two elections during this period, indicates that more than one-fifth of the regions in question lowered their turnout thresholds between elections.

However, though some analysts have been quick to attribute any lowering of participation barriers to incumbents' efforts to seek shelter from a disgruntled electorate, a number of factors warrant against making overly general statements about this issue. First, one must bear in mind the experimental nature of the early elections and the ongoing institutional learning process at work during this period. A number of elections that occurred during the first cycle were annulled after voter turnout fell below 50 percent thresholds. In the minds of administrators and election commission officials in some regions, the lowering of participation thresholds became a question of achieving *any* election outcome.

Second, as evidenced in the bottom half of table 3.3, a number of regions actually *increased* turnout requirements between elections. A combination of personal, historical, and ideological factors specific to certain regions and incumbents may also create conditions where the incumbent's popularity makes higher participation rates more amenable. Kurskaia Oblast, where the 25 percent participation barrier was raised to 50 percent after the 1996–97 election, provides one example. The oblast is a staunch red belt region that, even in the Unity-dominated 1999 Duma elections, cast 37 percent of its vote for the Communist Party. In 1996, Aleksandr Rutskoi, the former vice president of Russia and adversary of Boris Yeltsin in the events leading up to the October 1993 parliamentary crisis, defeated the Yeltsin appointee with 77 percent of the vote, compared with only 18 percent for the incumbent (with a respectable participation rate of 57 percent). The region's ideological characteristics combined with Rutskoi's leadership style and image as the arch-rogue governor made Rutskoi a remarkably popular regional executive. Under such circumstances, high participation requirements and an absolute majority election system minimize the possibility of defeat by a challenger with numerically small but disciplined supporters. Indeed, in 2000, Kurskaia Oblast's absolute majority election system and 50-percent-turnout requirement gave it one of the most exacting electoral requirements in the Russian Federation.[29] In the event, Rutskoi was defeated not by a challenger but by a legal infraction that disqualified him only hours before the election.

But regardless of these exceptions, the data on electoral rules appears to bear out the widely held contention that some incumbents took legislative measures to protect themselves from discontented voters within their regions. Another means to help secure one's hold on office is to eliminate competition before election campaigns, thus leaving voters with little choice but to support the incumbent, abstain, or vote "against all." How did Russia's regional executive elections rate in terms of competition?

The top half of table 3.4 presents data indicating the raw number of candidates participating in the decisive round of each regional executive election from 1995 to 2001. For the most part, the figures paint a heartening picture of regional electoral competition. Fewer than 3 percent of the elections undertaken during this period featured less than two candidates on the ballot, whereas 36 percent of the elections featured more than five candidates. Furthermore, the single-candidate elections appear to be an artifact of earlier elections, with none occurring since the Kabardino-Balkarskaia Republic's 1997 election. Looking at all the numbers for raw candidates, such figures suggest at least some element of electoral competition, with only a few worrisome exceptions of entirely uncontested elections.

However, these figures offer little insight into the actual viability of the candidates in question. The past decade of elections feature a number of cases in which incumbents gathered more than 70 percent of the popular vote, despite the fact that the election in question featured more than four candidates. Though record holders—in terms of total votes cast in their support—like Shaimiev in Tatarstan (97.14 percent in an uncontested 1995 election) and Valerii Kokov of the Kabardino-Balkarskaia Republic (99.35 percent in the uncontested 1997 elections—amid a turnout of 97.72 percent!) stood at the head of republics, Russia's oblasti, *kraia,* and autonomous *okruga* also featured lopsided contests. Among these, Murmanskaia Oblast's 2000 election resulted in the incumbent taking 87 percent of the popular vote while facing off against four opponents. Novgorod's Prusak took 92 percent of the vote against three opponents, and Vologodskaia Oblast's governor captured 81 percent of the vote on a ballot with six contenders. Such cases clearly indicate that competitiveness cannot be assessed by numbers of candidates alone.

Fortunately, Laakso and Taagepara's "effective number of parties" (here recast as the "effective number of candidates"; see the appendix for a formal description) measure provides a better means to assess the viability of candidates without resorting to detailed interpretive analyses of each case election.[30] To quote the originators of the concept, "The advantage of using the effective, rather than actual, number of parties (or actual number of parties above some arbitrary cutoff) is that it establishes a nonarbitrary way

Table 3.4. *Percentage of Elections Contested by a Given Number of Candidates by Election Year (in percent, with number of elections in parentheses and number of second-tour elections in square brackets)*

Raw Number of Candidates	1995	1996	1997	1998	1999	2000	2001	1995–2001
1	7 (1)	4 (2)	6 (1)	0 (0)	0 (0)	0 (0)	0 (0)	3 (4)
2	36 (5) [4]	41 (19) [15]	25 (4) [3]	50 (5) [3]	39 (5) [4]	33 (14) [12]	47 (7) [6]	38 (59) [49]
3	0 (0)	13 (6)	19 (3)	0 (0)	8 (1)	21 (9)	7 (1)	13 (20)
4	36 (5)	11 (5)	0 (0)	10 (1)	15 (2)	7 (3)	13 (2)	12 (18)
≥5	21 (3)	30 (14)	50 (8)	40 (4)	36 (5)	40 (17)	33 (5)	36 (56)
Effective Number of Candidates								
<2	14 (2)	23 (11)	24 (4)	40 (4)	31 (4)	28 (12)	27 (4)	12 (41)
Mean	3.11	2.95	2.62	2.31	3.09	3.15	3.20	3.02

Sources: Central Election Commission of the Russian Federation, *Vybory glav ispolnitel'noi vlasti sub'ektov Rossiiskoi Federatsii: Elektoral'naia statistika* (Moscow: Ves' Mir, 1997); Central Election Commission of the Russian Federation, *Vybory gosudarstvennoi vlasti sub'ektov Rossiiskoi Federatsii 1997–2000: Elektoralnaia statistika, tom 1–2* (Moscow: Ves' Mir, 2001); *Central Election Commission of the Russian Federation, 10 let izbiratel'noi sisteme Rossiiskoi Feder- atsii, Vybory v Rossiiskoi Federatsii 1993–2003: Elektoralnaia statistika,* CD-ROM (Moscow: Mercator Group).

to distinguish 'significant' from less significant ones."[31] In simple terms, this indicator takes candidate or party vote shares into account when assessing competitiveness and returns a coefficient indicating the number of "actual," viable candidates in each contest.

The effective number of candidate estimates in table 3.4 are calculated from first-tour election results, thus providing a clearer sense of the structure of regional competition before the elimination of candidates imposed by majoritarian election rules in some regions. Taken together, these results present a less optimistic picture of regional electoral competition. On the one hand, the average election during the six-year period under examination featured nearly three viable candidates. On the other hand, when one disaggregates these figures and focuses on the number of elections with less than one viable opponent (those elections with a coefficient less than 2), it becomes apparent that, on average, about 12 percent of the elections taking place between 1995 and 2001 were essentially unopposed. Numbers vary across each year, with 1998 featuring the most dismal record (mostly attributable to a higher number of republic elections in that year—see the discussion below).

In sum, these figures suggest that many voters going to the polls in Russia's regional elections faced the choice of supporting the incumbent or throwing their votes away on improbable challengers. Nonetheless, the fact that the mean effective number of candidates for a given election years has steadily increased since 1996 provides some grounds for optimism regarding electoral competition in Russia's regional executive elections.

Incumbent Success and Regional Status

To this point, the overview of Russia's regional executive elections has focused on comparisons across election years. However, aside from temporal differences, the collection of regional contests exhibits certain patterns across units. In fact, recent arguments by Stepan and Kahn suggest that elections in the so-called ethnic republics exhibit particularly low degrees of electoral competition due to the republican executives' control over regional election processes and institutions—itself a result of asymmetries within Russian federal structures that had authorities in Moscow looking the other way as Republican presidents established quasi-authoritarian forms of rule within their jurisdictions.[32] A brief comparison of electoral results across federal subjects provides some support for such arguments.

Table 3.5. Wins and Losses by Federal Subject, 1995–2001 (in percent, with number in parentheses)

Result	Cities of Federal Significance	Oblast/Kraia	Republics	Autonomous Okruga/Oblasti
Loss	25 (1)	41 (40)	38 (8)	35 (6)
Win	75 (3)	59 (58)	62 (13)	65 (11)

Sources: Central Election Commission of the Russian Federation, *Vybory glav ispolnitel'noi vlasti sub'ektov Rossiiskoi Federatsii: Elektoral'naia statistika* (Moscow: Ves' Mir, 1997); Central Election Commission of the Russian Federation, *Vybory gosudarstvennoi vlasti sub'ektov Rossiiskoi Federatsii 1997–2000: Elektoralnaia statistika, tom 1–2* (Moscow: Ves' Mir, 2001); official Web site of the Central Election Commission of the Russian Federation, http://www.cikrf.ru.

Table 3.5 presents win/loss data by type of federal subject, indicating that incumbents in the republics and autonomous *okruga* were slightly more successful than their counterparts in oblasti and *kraia*. Results for executives in the Cities of Federal Significance (Moscow and Saint Petersburg), represent only four elections and mostly reflect the reign of Mayor Iurii Luzhkov in Moscow. Comparing oblast and *krai* elections with their counterparts in republics and autonomous *okruga*, we find that incumbents in the latter two types of federal subject were only slightly more secure. Thus, the suggestion that executives in "ethnic" republics and autonomous *okruga*/oblasti are somehow "entrenched" is not strongly supported by the win/loss data.

However, looking at the number of candidates participating in each election, one gains some sense of the differences in electoral competition across federal subjects. Of particular interest are the uncontested election figures for republics where there occurred three of the four instances in the sample in which incumbents ran unopposed in the final election round. Furthermore, the data for the mean effective number of candidates presented in the last row of table 3.6 provide further insights into the level of electoral competition across federal subjects.[33] Once again, these measures were calculated from the results of first cycle elections (which, depending on the election law could also be "final" results) in order to present a clearer picture of the electoral field going into the election. As indicated, figures for republics and autonomous *okruga* were significantly smaller than those for oblasti and *kraia*. Taken together, both the raw and effective number of candidates indicators suggest that incumbents in republics and autonomous *okruga* faced significantly less competition than their counterparts in other regions.

Table 3.6. Number of Candidates in "Final" Election Round, 1995–2001 (in percent, with number of elections in parentheses and number of second-tour elections in square brackets)

Raw Number of Candidates	Cities of Federal Significance	Oblasti/Kraia	Republics	Autonomous Okruga/Oblasti
1	0 (0)	1 (1)	14 (3)	0 (0)
2	25 (1) [1]	41 (40) [36]	33 (7) [5]	21 (4) [1]
3	0 (0)	10 (10)	5 (1)	42 (8)
4	25 (1)	12 (12)	0 (0)	16 (3)
≥5	50 (2)	36 (35)	48 (10)	21 (4)
Effective Number of Candidates				
<2	75 (3)	18 (18)	38 (8)	42 (8)
Mean	2.63	3.12	2.72	2.51

Sources: Central Election Commission of the Russian Federation, *Vybory glav ispolnitel'noi vlasti sub'ektov Rossiiskoi Federatsii: Elektoral'naia statistika* (Moscow: Ves' Mir, 1997); Central Election Commission of the Russian Federation, *Vybory gosudarstvennoi vlasti sub'ektov Rossiiskoi Federatsii 1997–2000: Elektoralnaia statistika, tom 1–2* (Moscow: Ves' Mir, 2001); official Web site of the Central Election Commission of the Russian Federation, http://www.cikrf.ru.

The Elections through the Lens of the Accountability Criteria

In terms of the four accountability criteria, what does this discussion of Russia's election institutions and the events indicate? The data presented in this chapter offers little insight into the first criterion, whether voters possess the ability to assign responsibility for policy and policy outcomes. This particular issue will be dealt with in the next three chapters. However, the discussion above does provide some insights into whether incumbents face a real threat of removal (the second criterion), the extent of electoral competition, and whether or not incumbents have the proper incentives for maintaining office.

With regard to the second criterion, the 1996–97 and, to a lesser extent later elections, offer no conclusive evidence for the "entrenchment" of regional executive incumbents. High attrition rates amongst incumbents in the 1996–97 cycle clearly indicated that governors' "fiefdoms" were not unassailable, and it was not until later in Russia's regional election history that survival rates consistently exceeded attrition. But does this new survivability suggest entrenchment? The numbers alone provide little indication. As shown above, the 2000 survival rate approximates that of governors in recent American elections, and any claims of entrenchment based on quantitative data alone would thus have to apply to American state elections as well. Furthermore, though success rates increased over the course of the decade, the number of governors in office at the end of the decade who first took their post as Yeltsin appointees or elected republican officials in 1991–92 dwindled to thirty-five (fourteen of these "veterans" were found among the initially elected leaders of Russia's twenty-one ethnic republics).

However, the increase of "incumbent-friendly" legislation further complicates this story. By creating a set of election laws that, either by themselves or combined with other forms of election chicanery, allow incumbents to win elections with minuscule portions of the popular vote, regional governments may have disenfranchised a large portion of the electorate. Elections orchestrated under such proincumbent campaign legislation present certain barriers to discontented voters and lessen the accountability of executive incumbents. Theoretically, the electorate in such regions could still remove the incumbent, but only through an extremely strong show of opposition at the polls.

Nearly unanimous decisions to run for reelection in both election cycles satisfy the third criterion: Incumbents clearly have an incentive to run for reelection. Of all the elections that occurred up through 2001, incumbents voluntarily opted out of reelection bids in only six cases, and largely successful attempts to overcome existing but imperfect term limit laws indicate just how highly incumbents value their office. Nonetheless, changes under the Putin administration could have altered this picture.[34] If in fact term-limit laws had stiffened and incumbents had to actually surrender office without a campaign battle, would governors have shirked their final terms?

A number of different factors are involved in answering this question, but certain considerations warrant against the direst conclusions. First, tighter federal control in the form of the center's ability to remove rogue governors might have prevented final-term incumbents from plundering their regions.[35] However, more subtle "internal" mechanisms might also have rendered this more extreme measure unnecessary. The practice of choosing *preemniki* suggests that incumbents were concerned about life after office. Be this whether they sought protection for the crimes of their incumbency, or because they wished to see their vision for the region carried out beyond their term in office, the desire to hand over a solid base of support to a successor may have given incumbents an incentive to serve the electorate through their final term in office. One must keep in mind that, for better or worse, governors are often members of regional elites who will continue to exist in the region after elections. Ensuring that a friendly candidate follows a governor into office is a guarantee of at least a pleasant retirement and, at best, future enrichment in the nonpublic sector.

The figures for actual and effective numbers of candidates offer limited insight into the fourth criterion: stipulating that an opposition must exist. On the average, at least two viable candidates participated in each election and attracted a large enough portion of the vote to allay any accusations that most elections were staged. Nonetheless, the disaggregated figures for this measure suggest a more disturbing figure. As indicated above, with the exception of the contests that occurred in 1995, at least one-quarter of the elections in any given election year were undercontested. Ballots included more than one candidate, but election outcomes indicated that only one of the candidates had any real chance of actually winning the election. The voters faced a nonchoice: Vote for the incumbent or waste your vote.

Differences in incumbent success and levels of competition across oblasti, *kraia,* republics, and autonomous *okruga* suggest that elections are more competitive, freer, and fairer in some types of federal subjects than in others. For the most part, these figures support the evidence from numerous case studies indicating that democratic institutions are even weaker in the ethnic republics than in the rest of Russia's regions. Strong executive control and the center's apparent willingness to look the other way have given many republican presidents a certain degree of immunity from the effects of socioeconomic and political challenges within their jurisdictions.[36] This observation thereby warns against making overly general conclusions about the state of democracy in Russia's regions—some areas of Russia are more democratic than others by virtue of institutional asymmetries in the country's federal structure.

The Next Step

Having presented this guide to Russia's regional executive elections during the period under investigation, I now shift the focus from general questions to more focused analyses of accountability for economic conditions. The next chapter presents the results of the first stage of two analyses focusing on the role that economic factors played in the 1999–2001 election round. Looking at individual-level support calculi on the eve of elections in Ul'ianovskaia Oblast, we start with the individual building blocks of elections —the voters—asking whether and how these individuals took assessments of economic conditions into account when deciding whether to support or reject their incumbents. Following the results of this analysis, we will then shift back to the "bigger picture," looking at the outcomes of elections across Russia.

Notes

1. The phrase *sploshnie vybory* was often used in Russian media coverage of the 1999–2001 election round.

2. Conversations with Olga Shudra, a legal expert from the Middle Volga Academy of State Service, contributed to my understanding of Russian election law, especially with regard to the changes instituted in 1999. Other data in this chapter were drawn from the Web site of Russia's Central Election Commission (http://www.cikrf.ru) and from official Russian Central Election Commission publications, e.g., Central Election Commission of the Russian Federation, *Vybory glav ispolnitel'noi vlasti sub'ektov Rossiiskoi Federatsii: Elektoral'naia statistika* (Moscow: Ves' Mir, 1997); Central Election Commission of the Russian Federation, *Vybory gosudarstvennoi vlasti sub'ektov Rossiiskoi Federatsii 1997–2000: Elektoralnaia statistika, tom 1–2* (Moscow: Ves' Mir, 2001); Central Election Commission of the Russian Federation, *10 let izbiratel'noi sisteme Rossiiskoi Federatsii, Vybory v Rossiiskoi Federatsii 1993–2003: Elektoralnaia statistika,* CD-ROM (Moscow: Mercator Group); Grigoryi Belonuchkin's "Politika," http://www.cityline.ru/politica/vybory; the former *Regiony Rossii* Web site (this site is no longer functioning; files are available from the author upon request); telephone calls to regional election commissions; the "Panorama" Web site (http://www.panorama.ru/); and other mass media reports from both the central and the regional press.

3. Federal Law, Basic Guarantees of Citizens Electoral Rights and Rights to Participate in Referendums, October 16, 1994, December 19, 1997, and March 30, 1999.

4. The 1994 Basic Guarantees law allowed for length of residence requirements at the regional level, leaving the way open for some rather extreme instances like the ten-year-residency requirement in Bashkortostan. However, the 1999 amendments to the 1997 Basic Guarantees law prohibited any length of residency requirement.

5. The 1999 amendments to the 1997 Basic Guarantees law allow candidates for legislative positions to place a monetary deposit (*zalog*) upon registration in lieu of gathering signatures. During the 2000 elections, regional laws in only fourteen of the forty-four subjects that underwent elections allowed for candidates in regional executive contests to forgo signatures in favor of paying a deposit. See Central Election Commission of the Russian Federation, *Vybory gosudarstvennoi vlasti sub'ektov Rossiiskoi Federatsii 1997–2000: Elektoralnaia statistika, tom 1,* 19.

6. This restriction was added only in the final 1999 amendment to the 1997 "Guarantees." Before that, the "protest vote" was mainly symbolic. Hence, in the 1996–97 round of gubernatorial elections, even if the vote "against all" exceeded that of the votes of all other candidates, the candidate with the highest number of votes would be selected.

7. Before that, a number of regional laws specified a two-consecutive-term limit but were later circumvented by legislatures reinterpreting the law to state that executives could not be *elected* for more than two consecutive terms. Most governors were

appointed for the period from 1992–96 and, thanks to such changes, could run for a "second term" in 1999–2001.

8. For a further discussion of the ineffectiveness of federal government control in the regions before the Putin presidency see Vladimir Gelman and Olga Senatova, "Sub-National Politics in Russia in the Post-Communist Transition Period: A View from Moscow," *Regional and Federal Studies* 5 (Summer 1995): 211–23.

9. Robert Orttung and Peter Reddaway, "What Do the Okrug Reforms Add Up To? Some Conclusions," in *The Dynamics of Russian Politics: Putin's Reform of Federal Regional Relations, Volume 1,* ed. Peter Reddaway and Robert Orttung (Lanham, Md.: Rowman & Littlefield, 2004), 298.

10. Cases against the election commission or its members are handled by the election commission at the next federal level. All other cases are handled in court.

11. Such *dosrochnyi* votes are generally considered to be favorable to incumbents. First, they are very difficult to monitor and are hence subject to falsification. Second, the fact that they are cast before the election date naturally favors the incumbent. Incumbents have greater name recognition than challengers; hence, the less time opponents have to campaign, the more likely individuals are to simply cast their votes for the most familiar candidate. In the Samarskaia Oblast case, this last factor was especially relevant. In a tactical move, Titov had resigned from his post, forcing an early election, which inevitably cut into the timetables of challengers preparing for the regularly scheduled December elections.

12. Ol'ga Popova, "Tarkhov nachinaet i proigrivaet," *Samarskoe Obozrenie* 14 (October 2, 2000); Ol'ga Popova, "Tarkhov sdalsia, promeniav Samaru na Cheboksary," *Samarskoe Obozrenie* 14 (October 9, 2000).

13. Gelman and Senatova, "Sub-National Politics," 212–17; Grigorii Golosov, "Gubernatory and partiinaia politika," *Pro et Contra* 5, no.1 (Winter 2000): 96–108.

14. Thanks to Vladimir and Aleksandr Kazantsev for providing a brief analysis of this aspect of regional executive–legislature relations.

15. An examination of the changes in the regional election commissions in Samarskaia and Ul'ianovskaia Oblasti indicated that executives and legislatures frequently "exchanged appointees." Those individuals who were earlier appointed by one body were later appointed by the other in the course of creating a "new" body.

16. Gubernatorial elections in the United States also tend to follow a cyclical pattern with elections occurring in clusters. Thad Beyer provides two of the better-documented clusters, which include the 1982 elections where nineteen of twenty-five incumbents maintained office (an attrition rate of 24 percent), and the 1994 elections, where seventeen of twenty-three incumbents held onto office (an attrition rate of 26 percent). See Thad Beyle, "Gubernatorial Report Cards: Summer 1994," *Spectrum* (Spring 1995): 19; and Beyle, ed., *Governors and Hard Times* (Washington, D.C.: CQ Press, 1992). For an interesting comment on such international comparisons, see: I. B. Serkov, "Vlast Postroilas," *Literaturnaia Gazeta,* January 10–16, 2001; http://www.lgz.ru/archives/html_arch/lg01-022001/polit/art1.htm.

17. According to official data, the average worker's wage in 1996 was 176 percent of the subsistence wage; by 1999, this had decreased to 156 percent. Data were drawn from Goskomstat Rossii, *Regiony Rossii: 2000* (Moscow: Goskomstat, 2000).

18. And indeed, as McFaul, Colton, and others note, the 1996 election was couched in terms of a choice between Yeltsin or the Soviet Union (in its most totalitarian form). See Michael McFaul, *Russia's 1996 Presidential Election: The End of Polarized Politics*

(Stanford, Calif.: Hoover Institution Press, 1997); and Timothy Colton, *Transitional Citizens* (Cambridge, Mass.: Harvard University Press, 2000).

19. Mikhail Afanas'ev makes a similar point in his "Politicheskie partii v rossiiskoi regionakh," *Pro et Contra* 5, no. 4 (Autumn 2000): 164–83.

20. Steven Solnick, "Gubernatorial Elections in Russia, 1996–1997," *Post-Soviet Affairs* 14 (1998): 48–80; Grigorii Golosov, *Political Parties in the Regions of Russia: Democracy Unclaimed* (Boulder, Colo.: Lynne Rienner, 2004), 67–72.

21. Solnick, "Gubernatorial Elections in Russia, 1996–1997," 65.

22. The absence of the OKS, however, did not rule out the participation of other national parties. Reliable endorsement data for the entire set of elections is difficult to acquire, however, an examination of a subset of thirty-two regional and *krai* elections occurring during the 1999–2001 election cycle offers an acceptable representation of each political party's strategies and rates of success. The Communist Party and NPSR followed a course very similar to their 1996–97 strategy, supporting candidates in twenty-seven of the thirty-two elections under consideration. A few more than half of these candidates (fourteen in all) won. Two other parties also made concerted efforts to support candidates in the regions. Unity supported candidates in twenty-eight of the thirty-two elections, while the party "Fatherland" (Otechestvo), in turn, supported candidates in twenty-nine of thirty-two regions. In both instances, the parties "won" eighteen of the elections (with both being "center" parties, there was considerable overlap in the candidates that they supported). Nonetheless, though the positions of the parties in each election give a sense of a "left/right" contest in the regions, it should also be born in mind that, echoing the "competition" between the NPSR / Communist Party and the OKS in 1996–97, there were a number of instances in which candidates were endorsed by two or even all three parties. Hence, though an endorsement generally constituted recognition of a candidate's concurrence with a party's ideology, there were clear instances in which parties supported popular candidates for the instrumental purpose of increasing the tally of "their" leaders in the regions. See *Regiony Rossii: Politika i kadry,* February 5, 2001; and the Communist Party's Web site, http://www.kprf.ru.

23. Focused as he is on political parties in Russia's regions, Golosov gives a more extensive account of the NPSR and OKS rivalry in Golosov, *Political Parties in the Regions of Russia,* 67–72.

24. Vladimir Todres, "Marsh Gubernatorov," *Segodnia,* January 21, 1997.

25. The remaining figures were 45 percent "satisfied" and 30 percent "still undecided." The latter numbers probably represent individuals who wished to judge the election results by the subsequent performance of the victors. See Anna Petrova and Svetlana Klimova, "Izbirateli v osnovnom udovletvoreny rezultatami regional'nykh vyborov," *Baza Dannykh FOM* [Public Opinion Foundation, Fond Obshchestvennoe Mnenie, or FOM], January 23, 1997, http://bd.fom.ru/report/map/of19970305.

26. At the time of writing, Evgenii Mikhailev's November 2000 victory holds the record for the lowest percentage of the popular vote for a winning candidate. Running against twelve opponents (at least one of whom was likely supported by the governor himself), Mikhailev went on to a second term in office with 28 percent of the popular vote. For more on this election, see Andrei Morozov, "Izbiratel'nye tekhnologii i administrativnyi resurs: Pskovskii retsept sokhraneniia vlasti," in *Vybory i problemy grazhdanskogo obshchestva na severo-zapade Rossii* (Moscow: Carnegie Moscow Center, 2001).

27. It should be noted that this does not indicate exactly the number of regions that

changed rules between their first and second rounds. The first or second election of some of the regions in this sample fell outside the purview of the study. Nonetheless, this provides a relatively precise indication of the decrease in majority rule-based elections in this period.

28. These fifty-three regions are Belgorodskaia Oblast, Brianskaia Oblast, Vladimirskaia Oblast, Voronezhskaia Oblast, Ivanovskaia Oblast, Kaluzhskaia Oblast, Kostromskaia Oblast, Kurskaia Oblast, Moskovskaia Oblast, Riazanskaia Oblast, Tambovskaia Oblast, Tverskaia Oblast, Iaroslavskaia Oblast, Arkhangel'skaia Oblast, Kaliningradskaia Oblast, Leningradskaia Oblast, Murmanskaia Oblast, Pskovskaia Oblast, Saint Petersburg, Republic of Kalmykiia, Krasnodarskii Krai, Stavropol'skii Krai, Astrakhanskaia Oblast, Volgogradskaia Oblast, Republic of Marii-El, Kirovskaia Oblast, Permskaia Oblast, Komi-Permiatskii Autonomous Okrug, Samarskaia Oblast, Saratovskaia Oblast, Ul'ianovskaia Oblast, Kurganskaia Oblast, Sverdlovskaia Oblast, Tiumenskaia Oblast, Khanty-Mansiiskii Autonomous Okrug, Iamalo-Nenetskii Autonomous Okrug, Cheliabinskaia Oblast, Republic of Khakasiia, Altaiskii Krai, Ust-Ordynskii Buriatskii Autonomous Okrug, Omskaia Oblast, Tomskaia Oblast, Chitinskaia Oblast, Aginskii Buriatskii Autonomous Okrug, Primorskii Krai, Khabarovskii Krai, Amurskaia Oblast, Kamchatskaia Oblast, Koriaskii Autonomous Okrug, Magadanskaia Oblast, Sakhalinskaia Oblast, Evreiskaia Autonomous Oblast, and Chukiotskii Autonomous Okrug.

29. Astrakhanskaia Oblast was the only other oblast or *krai* in the 1999–2001 election round with similar requirements. Here, too, the governor was wildly popular, winning the 2000 election with the support of *every* party in the oblast and 82 percent of the vote (amid a participation rate of 55 percent).

30. Markku Laakso and Rein Taagepera, "Effective Number of Parties: A Measure with Application to West Europe," *Comparative Political Studies* 12 (1979): 3–27.

31. Laakso and Taagepera, "Effective Number of Parties," 455.

32. Alfred Stepan, "Russian Federalism in Comparative Perspective," *Post-Soviet Affairs* 16 (2000): 133–76; Jeffrey Kahn, *Federalism, Democratization, and the Rule of Law in Russia* (Oxford: Oxford University Press, 2002).

33. To remind the reader, this measure, using the equation $N = 1 \div \Sigma p_i^2$, provides an indication of the number of competitive contenders in each election. The use of this formula allows one to cut through the often large number of insignificant opponents in each contest and gain a better sense of which incumbents actually faced a strong challenge to their seat.

34. Nonetheless, as discussed in chapter 3, the Kremlin has made concessions on stiffening term limits that will allow executives to run for more than two terms. See Ivan Rodin, "Regional'naia politika Kremlia opiat' meniaetesia?" *Nezavisimaia Gazeta,* February 6, 2001, http://www.ng.ru/politics/2001-06-02/1_change.html.

35. Irina Skliarova, "Podpisei ne ponadobitsia: Pravitel'stvo nameleno uprostit' protseduru otstavki gubernatorov," *Vremia Novostei,* November 3, 2003.

36. In chapter 7 of his study, Kahn provides a detailed description of the various means through which republican presidents control opposition in their regions. See Kahn, *Federalism, Democratization, and the Rule of Law in Russia.*

Chapter 4

The Russian Jurisdictional Voter: Evidence from Ul'ianovskaia Oblast

Goriachev already had more than eight years to make things work. The economy only got worse. He was out of ideas and no one believed he had anything else to offer.

—Valentina Shuvalova

Right now there are rumors that I will withdraw my candidacy just before the elections. No! If I did that, the people of Ul'ianovskaia Oblast would never forgive me.

—Iurii Goriachev

This chapter opens the quantitative portion of the study with an analysis of those factors that influenced the decisions of citizens in a sample region to support or oppose their incumbent before the region's 2000 elections. In terms of Manin, Przeworski, and Stokes's four institutional/procedural criteria for accountability, this analysis essentially focuses on criterion one: whether or not citizens are able to assign responsibility for policy outcomes.[1] Once again, the focus is on accountability for economic issues—specifically, whether voters can discern areas of jurisdictional responsibility and punish or reward governors only for outcomes that fall within their policymaking jurisdiction.

The chapter begins with a brief history of the case region, Ul'ianovskaia Oblast, and continues with a discussion of the "ideal subnational jurisdictional voter"—indicating the type of behavior that would be necessary to meet Manin, Przeworksi, and Stokes's fourth criterion at the level of regional elections. Having laid out the criteria for the jurisdictional voter, I undertake an initial analysis to determine whether voters in Russia's regions exhibit

103

behavior similar to this ideal type. This analysis consists of an assortment of economic voting hypotheses tested against survey data drawn from Ul'ianovskaia Oblast before its 2000 regional executive election. The results are encouraging, and they suggest that respondents in the region closely approximated our ideal type, with their relative sociotropic considerations (i.e., assessments of the regional economy relative to that of other regions or Russia as a whole) ranking among the most influential factors determining incumbent support.

The Socioeconomic and Political History of Ul'ianovskaia Oblast

Ul'ianovskaia Oblast occupies a territory of 37,182 square kilometers in the European part of Russia. Its neighboring regions include Samarskaia, Saratovskaia, and Penzenskaia Oblasti, and the Republics of Tartarstan, Mordovia, and Chuvashia. Relatively mild temperatures and moderate rainfall make the region especially adapted for agricultural production. The Volga River is the predominant geographic feature of the region, and it continues to play a key role in local development.

Like other regions located along the middle and southern portions of the Volga, the city of Simbirsk (later Ul'ianovsk) was initially established as an outpost to protect the southern approaches and trade routes of the Russian Empire. For most of its history, the region surrounding this settlement was predominantly devoted to agricultural production, forestry, and fishing. Limited industrialization occurred in the region during the later half of the nineteenth century. But for the greater part of its history, the region remained a sleepy agricultural province remarkable primarily as the birthplace of Lenin and the site of a number of fierce struggles during the Civil War of 1918–21. Throughout the Soviet era, the oblast's former distinction made a strong impact on its subsequent economic and political cultural development as it became a sort of Mecca for Communist "pilgrims."

Only during and after World War II did Ul'ianovskaia Oblast experience marked growth as an industrialized region. Immediately following the Nazi invasion of the Soviet Union, the region witnessed a remarkable inflow of refugees as well as fifteen factories that were dismantled and shipped east in the face of the advancing Axis forces. These factories provided the basis for future growth in the region—perhaps the most relevant being the ZiS (Zavod imeni Stalina) automobile factory that later became the basis for the present-day UAZ (Ul'ianovskii avtomobil'nyi zavod). The late 1940s and 1950s witnessed continued growth in the region, as many of the relocated factories remained in place and a number of new enterprises sprang into existence as a result of the extensive reconstruction programs surrounding the building of the Kuibyshev hydroelectric plant.

In the mid-1960s, the USSR's Soviet of Ministers delivered two decrees: Of the General Plan for the City of Ul'ianovsk, and Of the Measures to Develop the City of Ul'ianovsk from 1966 to 1970. These decrees, partially motivated by the upcoming hundredth anniversary of Lenin's birth, laid the groundwork for a series of projects to redevelop large sections of the city and oblast. In addition to the construction of the Lenin Memorial (the largest and most extensive museum dedicated to his memory), a large hotel complex, and a teacher's university, the oblast witnessed a sharp increase in the number of educational and cultural institutions and the construction of almost 1.5 million square meters of housing. In terms of industrial development, a large aviation complex (Iskra, later Aviastar), the DAAS auto parts manufacturing plant in Dimitrovgrad and several other lesser firms were established during this period. The aviation complex was the largest of its kind in Russia, producing the gigantic cargo plane Ruslan. By itself, the construction of this complex attracted 200,000 people to Ul'ianovsk and spurred the construction of an entirely new and very contemporary section of the city (Novyi Gorod).[2]

These changes had a marked impact on the region's demography. By 1990, 35.4 percent of its working population was involved in some form of industrial activity; 15 percent worked in the agricultural sector and 11 percent in construction. Other important sectors for employment were education, culture, and the arts (9.7 percent); trade and retail (7.1 percent); and transport (6.2 percent). Within the industrial sector, the largest branch was machine production, which accounted for 47.9 percent of all industrial construction. Light manufacturing and food processing followed with 26.9 and 10.7 percent, respectively. Forms of manufacturing related to the Aviastar aircraft production complex and the UAZ auto plant dominated. In these respects, the region's economic structure was quite similar to that of other oblasti, *kraia,* and republics within the wider Volga region.[3]

In summary, by the end of the 1980s, this previously agricultural region was at the cutting edge of late Soviet development. A total of 72 percent of its population lived in urban settings, and firms like Aviastar boasted some of the newest and most advanced production facilities in the Soviet Union. According to Viktor Sidorenko of the Ul'ianovskaia Oblast Social and Business

Development Center, a study of the region by the European Bank for Reconstruction and Development in the early 1990s concluded that the combination of new capital, a strong agricultural base, and skilled workforce made Ul'ianovskaia Oblast one of the regions with the best prospects for development in the post-Soviet era.[4] Subsequent developments under the rule of Iurii Goriachev were to prove otherwise.

The Goriachev Administration

In March 1987, Iurii Frolovich Goriachev was elected chairman of the Ul'ianovskaia Oblast Executive Committee. Goriachev was born in 1938, received a degree as a veterinarian-bacteriologist from the Ul'ianovskaia Oblast Agricultural Institute, and slowly worked his way through various party and state organs in the oblast's agricultural *raions*. With his selection as chairman, he left his current position as head of Ul'ianovsk *raion* and entered oblast-level politics. In March 1990, he further expanded his power when he was simultaneously elected as a deputy of both the all-Russian and Ul'ianovskaia Oblast Soviets. In April of the same year, he took the position of first secretary of the oblast's Communist Party organs, which he held until the party was disbanded following the August 1991 putsch.

During and immediately following the putsch, Goriachev made a number of decisions that nearly cost him his political career but ultimately ended in his triumph over what was primarily an urban-based, democratic opposition. His actions during the putsch could be best characterized as "neutral," a stance for which he was later criticized and nearly censured by local democratic forces. However, his ability to organize and direct his supporters within the oblast party and state structures along with his skill at mobilizing a rather conservative public with populist slogans allowed him to prevail over both local opposition and an attempt by Boris Yeltsin to appoint a pro-reform industrialist, Valentin Malafeev, to the newly created post of governor in 1991–92.

In the course of a subsequent visit by the president to the region, "spontaneous" mass demonstrations of popular support and a carefully orchestrated itinerary led Yeltsin to sign a decree appointing Goriachev governor. This decision would have serious consequences for the future of the oblast because it both determined who would rule the region and where the major political fault lines would lay for the next ten years. To a very large extent, the maintenance of the Goriachev regime would hinge upon the maximum empowerment of the rural population and pensioners along with the simultaneous weakening of the financial and political strength of the cities.

The "Ul'ianovsk Phenomenon"

Immediately after his appointment, Goriachev set to work implementing a series of measures to "soften" the impact of the "shock therapy" efforts being undertaken at the time by the Yegor Gaidar government. Within a week of his appointment, decrees were issued to support prices on essential goods and maintain aspects of the Soviet-era coupon policy. Over time, these policies and others evolved into what came to be known as the "Ul'ianovsk model."

The core philosophy guiding this model (if indeed any actually existed) was that of the "gradual transition to the market." At base, this consisted of the retention of food coupons on certain goods, price supports for essential products and services, and limitations on the speed and extent of privatization. The immediate effect of these policies so sharply differentiated Ul'ianovskaia Oblast from other regions undergoing the full brunt of the wrenching economic dislocations of the early reform period that journalists and social scientists began to speak of an "Ul'ianovsk phenomenon." As just one example, during a December 3, 1993, television interview, the first vice head of administration, B. A. Saraevym, made the astounding comparisons for the period spanning 1990 to 1993, shown in table 4.1.[5] Such statistics became the norm in early 1990s discussions of Ul'ianovskaia Oblast, and many observers (as well as analysts, e.g., Robert McIntyre) treated Goriachev's policies as a real and viable alternative to the shock therapy being advocated by the Gaidar team.[6]

Table 4.1. Early Economic Indicators for Ul'ianovskaia Oblast (percent)

Indicator	Ul'ianovskaia Oblast	Russia
Volume of industrial production	−3	−34
Volume of food production	4	−35
Increase in income	147	172
Increase in prices	173	256
Decrease in living standard	−15	−33

Source: V. S. Shuvalova and Y. N. Shuvalov, *Sotsial'no-politicheskoe soznanie naseleniia Ul'ianovskoi Oblasti mezhdu vyborami v Rossiskii parlament 1990 i 1993 g.g* (Ul'ianovsk: Perspektiv, 1993), 4.

However, the program was not without its critics both within and outside the oblast, and once again members of the "democratic opposition" were quick to indicate a number of negative tendencies developing as a result of these policies. First, the administration was diverting funds from capital investment, targeted federal programs, and infrastructural development to finance food subsidies and other social programs. Though this would serve the purpose of "cushioning the blow" of Gaidar's reforms, its long-term effect would be seen in the gradual deterioration of local infrastructure and industrial capital. In many respects, Goriachev was mortgaging the oblast's future in the interest of a short-term deceleration of the effects of marketization.

For many analysts and critics, this deteriorating financial situation was simply the result of irresponsible, shortsighted, populist policies carried out by an administration whose background and leadership style precluded any other course. Other critics went a step further, claiming that rather than so-cially conscious policies, the administration's activities constituted pure patronage. Deals were being struck between key firms and the adminis-tration through which the firms would receive benefits in the form of tax breaks, subsidies, or monopolization of the market, in exchange for their fi-nancial, material, and administrative support of social programs. Firms like Prodovolstvo, Svyagina, and Ul'ianovskhlebtorg (the local bread monopoly) that played a key role in the provision of subsidized products were owned or directed by individuals close to Goriachev (in Prodovolstvo's case, Go-riachev's son).[7]

Regardless of the underlying causes, more objective budgetary data for this period provide a clear indication of the financial impact of Goriachev's social policies.[8] According to Russian Ministry of Finance data, between 1992 and 1997, Ul'ianovskaia Oblast's average budget deficit taken as a proportion of adjusted expenditures was 10.8 percent. In comparative terms, the average for Russia during this period was 4.2 percent, placing Ul'ianov-skaia Oblast well within the top quartile (Q3 = 5.5) of Russia's regions in the volume of its budget deficit. In fact, the only regions with higher average budget deficits were Komi-Permyatskii Autonomous Okrug, Kamchatk-skaia Oblast, the Republic of Chechnia, Sakha Republic, Koriakskii Au-tonomous Okrug, the Republic of Ingushetia, and Aginskii Buryiatskii Autonomous Okrug. Considering that two of these regions were the sites of intense armed conflict during this period and the remainder are far-east re-gions (with all the implied climactic and transportation difficulties), one can easily see the extent of the financial problems facing Ul'ianovskaia Oblast by the end of the first five years of reform.

To stave off a sort of oblast "bankruptcy," Goriachev was forced to turn to local and federal-level banks for loans (major loans were drawn from Sberbank, Alfa-Bank, and Inkombank). Moscow's cool and ambiguous relations with a market reform "laggard"—despite Goriachev's timely support for Yeltsin during such key moments as the 1993 parliamentary crisis and 1996 presidential election—precluded deficit-financing "free money" in the form of federal transfers.[9] As the 1990s progressed, such loans became even harder to come by, and the budget funds required to service loans with ever greater interest rates only contributed to the region's financial woes.

Furthermore, the "slow and steady" approach to market reforms took a heavy toll on an economy that was cast into a "limbo" that was neither a market nor a centralized economic system. Large production facilities like the UAZ auto plant, the Aviastar aircraft production complex, and a host of related firms like DAAZ in Dimitrovgrad remained the bulwarks of the economy. However, a combination of poor management, limited demand, and the severing of previous supply chains left UAZ in a perpetual crisis of wage and tax arrears.[10] Aviastar, despite its unique product, was hard pressed to attract and maintain orders, and like UAZ, was periodically forced to reduce workweeks, withhold wages, and lay off workers. Under such conditions, new forms of economic activity were necessary to provide both employment for the local population and budget revenues for the administration. Unfortunately—and this was the crux of the "slow and steady" approach—these new activities were either never fostered or grew too slowly to attenuate the difficulties that citizens faced once the bulk of the administration's social programs were removed in 1995–96.

Small business growth provides one example of the Ul'ianovsk model's failure to cultivate new forms of economic activity. It is now a widely accepted contention among economists that an active small business sector can provide the necessary alternatives to help regions survive the collapse of prior base production activities, and hence regional administrators are well advised to provide a system of incentives (tax breaks, limited regulation and licensing fees, etc.) to encourage small business growth.[11]

However, as shown by the author's interviews with local small and medium-sized business owners, business organizations, and economists, the Goriachev administration's small business policy (if indeed it could be called a *policy*) was a complete failure. Viktor Sidorenko, director of the

Ul'ianovskaia Oblast Business and Social Center (one of the few multi-national nongovernmental organizations in the region—a cooperative effort with the Canadian Chamber of Commerce) summarized the situation as such: "Small business in Ul'ianovskaia Oblast has grown *despite* the administration's policy . . . what we have today is one quarter of the oblast's full potential."[12] Iurii Lebedev, the director of the firm Pyramid, was even sterner: "The system is geared only toward self-destruction—no growth."[13]

Between 1991 and 1994, Ul'ianovskaia Oblast experienced a burst in the growth of small enterprises similar to that of other regions. The underlying factor for this general phenomenon was the federal-level "small privatization" program undertaken during this period, through which most of these businesses were established on the basis of preexisting state enterprise. However, after this brief, sharp increase, small business growth in Ul'ianovskaia Oblast leveled off at roughly 4,190 firms. In 1996, this rose to 4,877 firms, but by the next year, the number had actually shrunk back to 4,547. As the local economist Svetlana Kashkorova indicates, the optimal level of small business activity is one firm for every forty to fifty local residents, thereby placing a favorable level of small business activity in Ul'ianovskaia Oblast at nearly 30,000 to 50,000 firms.

The most prevalent explanations for this stunted growth were the policies of both local and oblast-level authorities. Small and medium-sized firms faced a tangle of bureaucratic procedures in the form of licensing, loan guarantees, and negotiations over the use of still proliferate municipal and oblast-owned property.[14] In addition, tax breaks for such firms were nearly nonexistent, and according to Lebedev, those organizations that oblast and municipal authorities had ostensibly set up to support small business growth were viewed by most local businesspeople as mere tools for the benefit of the administration's circle.

Finally, the governor occasionally made very public attacks on small entrepreneurs, spewing forth populist rhetoric about the greed and indolence of various small business owners. One particularly well-publicized example involved a private dental clinic in the center of Ul'ianovsk city. During the governor's weekly *Selektornoe soveshchanie* (call-in television program),[15] the head of the Oblast Department of Health presented a report regarding some suspicious and potentially illegal activities surrounding the clinic. Apparently dissatisfied with the report, Goriachev himself implored the head of department to "dig deeper" and went on to say that this clinic "for people with stuffed wallets" had received its property for a suspiciously low price (a jab both at the clinic and the city administration), acquired a great deal of "very expensive equipment," and seemed to work far shorter hours than "the rest of us."[16] Taken together, these factors created an environment in which those with enough capital and flexibility would simply invest their time and finances in other oblasti or set up businesses locally and conduct all activities beyond the bounds of the region.[17]

Given the administration's professed support for the rural population, the situation in the agricultural sector provides additional insights into the shortsighted nature of the Ul'ianovsk model. A work by Robert McIntyre, echoing similar assertions made in the administration-supported media, spoke of the benefits of Goriachev's policies for regional agricultural producers. McIntyre stated that "the Ul'ianovskaia Oblast authorities were successful in winning the loyalty (or at least respect) of local agricultural producers by close attention to ensuring the supply of agricultural inputs and services, especially fuel for farm equipment. . . . This helped to maintain agricultural production in what had long been an agricultural surplus area."[18] Unfortunately, other evidence points to a rather different story, which suggested that Goriachev's policies were oriented toward myopic supporters who would later feel the long-term effects of a degenerative process whereby farmers gradually gave up more and more of their output and existing capital stocks for progressively smaller amounts of inputs.

Contrary to McIntyre's assessment, agricultural production in the region was not actually maintained. According to official regional statistics, between 1990 and 1999, the number of agricultural enterprises remained relatively steady, at 390 in 1990 and 395 in 1999. However, employment was cut by more than half, from 130,100 to 63,500. Cattle herds were decimated, from 579,700 to 201,300 head. Grain production fell from 1,896,400 to 858,500 tons; beets, from 326,300 to 158,400 tons; and potatoes, from 93,200 to 4,600 tons. Milk and egg production also suffered, dropping from 498,200 to 173,100 liters and 344,100 to 271,900 eggs, respectively. Wool production was completely devastated, dropping from 1,626 to 34 tons. Production also became highly erratic, with grain harvests varying from 5.4 to 19.8 quintals per hectare. In terms of inputs, the number of tractors fell from 17,600 to 11,600, and combines from 7,100 to 3,600.[19]

The root causes of this collapse were the exact mechanisms that McIntyre claims had helped ensure sources of supplies and markets. As he notes, the administration developed a system whereby farmers received "credit" in the form of parts, fuel, and seed (*tovarnyi kredit*). At the end of the harvest, the farmers were then indebted to repay this credit (plus any unpaid debts from previous years) by selling their products to the administration at prices lower than the market. This "vicious credit circle" gradually demonetized the rural economy, depleted the already inadequate rural infrastructure and capital supply, and resulted in the near pauperization of the rural population. By 2000, the average agricultural wage was 450 rubles a month —two times lower than that of the oblast average and three times lower than that of the Russian average.[20] To make matters worse, agricultural workers— like their counterparts in Ul'ianovskaia Oblast's large enterprises and the public sector—suffered from wage arrears and payments in kind.

Taking all these points in mind, it becomes apparent that the Ul'ianovsk phenomenon was largely a Potemkin village. Though these policies were able to stave off the immediate shocks of the Gaidar-era reforms and thus gain a measure of popularity for the Goriachev administration, their long-term impact was the steady degradation of the region's economic potential and the stagnation of wage growth. When social programs were gradually and inevitably scaled back, the local population found its spending power dramatically reduced. As the 1990s continued, to quote Igor Egorev, it remained "easier to survive in Ul'ianovsk, but more difficult to live."[21]

Political Control and Adaptation

Despite the increasingly difficult economic conditions in the region, the Goriachev administration, along with its supporters in *raion* administrations and the oblast legislature, survived nearly thirteen years in a system that (at least on paper) was increasingly based on free elections. The negative figures cited above combined with the fact that the bulk of the region's social policies were removed by 1995–96 prevents one from relying exclusively on the regime's populism as an explanation for its sustainability. A brief examination of several key moments in the regime's political history points to a number of factors that allowed the administration to control the political discourse in the region and, as Vladimir Kazantsev has put it, create the "myth" of the Ul'ianovsk phenomenon.

The 1992–1996 Institutional Vacuum and the Consolidation of the Administrations' Control

From 1992 to 1995, the administration operated in a literal institutional vacuum that allowed it to rule nearly unchallenged and provided it with the means to control the shape of future institutions. Though Goriachev's popularity was initially fueled by the apparent success of the Ul'ianovsk model,[22] the consolidation of control over the region's media, judicial organs, and legislative bodies—as well as the institutionalization of the governor's rule in laws geared toward its perpetuation—allowed the administration to smother potential sources of opposition as the cracks began to show in the Ul'ianovsk phenomenon.

Following Yeltsin's dismissal of all regional soviets in 1993, the Ul'ianovskaia Oblast administration, with the help of the administration-appointed and -supervised regional election commission,[23] set about creating a two-chamber legislature that overrepresented rural interests and whose very structure conflicted with the tenets set out in both the Russian Constitution and the presidential decree titled Basic Conditions for the Elections to Representative Organs of the State Authorities in Kraia, Oblasti, Cities of Federal Significance, Autonomous Oblasti, and Autonomous Okrugi.[24] Attempts to challenge the election law were drawn out in long hearings with the local prosecutor, and only after intervention by the then-chairman of the Central Election Commission, A. V. Ivanchenko, and separate rulings in the federal Duma was the election canceled—merely two days before its scheduled date.[25]

Although the prosecutor's ruling appeared to be a defeat for the Goriachev administration, it actually worked to its long-term advantage. Elections were rescheduled for December 1995, and in the interim, the administration enjoyed another year and a half of nearly unchecked rule. This period was put to good use strengthening the administration's control over economic and political resources and laying the groundwork for a stronger finish in the next Assembly elections. Also, one should not underestimate the importance of the timing of the 1994 campaign's cancellation. Having occurred merely two days before the scheduled date, less well-financed opposition candidates wasted valuable—and in several cases irreplaceable—resources on an election that never occurred. The end result was the further strengthening of the administration's position and, in turn, the weakening of the basis for a strong opposition.

Another aspect of the oblast's institutional vacuum was the long absence of a city council in Ul'ianovsk. In this respect, the oblast administration's attempt to weaken the political representation of urban voters was again manifest. As long as Mayor Sergei Yermakov maintained his post at the head of the city administration, Goriachev could continue to rule comfortably with the support he enjoyed in the countryside. An election to a newly formed city council was an understandably undesirable outcome for a politician who had nearly been dismissed from his post by the Soviet-era city council. In response to questions regarding the absence of a city council, city and oblast administration officials explained that it was too "burdensome" for the city of Ul'ianovsk to have two legislative organs, or stated that a referendum needed to be held to determine whether the city actually needed such an organ.[26] Nonetheless, events at the center again pushed the administration into compliance with the federal law titled Of General Principals for the Organization of Local Administration in Subjects of the Russian Federation (issued in August 1995), and on September 17, 1996, elections were scheduled in December for the city council.

Hence, one can argue that the period from 1992 to 1995–96 was one in which, with Yermakov as mayor of Ul'ianovsk city and no sitting legislatures to contend with (until the election of the Oblast Legislative Assembly on December 17, 1995), the oblast administration ruled in the absence of local checks on its power. Furthermore, strong support in the rural districts combined with the financial losses by opposition candidates in the aborted April 1994 elections ensured that even the Oblast Legislative Assembly would not pose a serious threat. In fact, the timid and even loyal nature of the Assembly over the next four years would actually provide a new basis of legitimacy for the governor's rule.[27]

The Year 1996: The Rise of a Viable Opposition

In retrospect, the 1996 gubernatorial elections marked the beginning of a downward spiral for Goriachev's political trajectory. Most of the social guarantees that had attracted the support of the rural, elderly, and poor had been eliminated nearly a year before the December elections. Furthermore, the oblast's growing budgetary problems were beginning to have a more direct impact on the citizenry—one of the major themes of the 1996 election was the prospect of heating and energy shortages in the upcoming winter.

Perhaps more on account of the weakness of his main opponent—the first secretary of the Ul'ianovskaia Oblast Communist Party, A. Kruglikov—than on account of his own political strength, Goriachev nonetheless survived the 1996 elections and went on to rule for another four years. As first secretary of the regional Communist Party organs, Kruglikov proved a difficult figure around which to unite the diverse interests set against the Goriachev administration—especially local entrepreneurs and the remnants of the "democratic opposition." Furthermore, the standoff between a Communist Party member and an incumbent who, though not a member of the party, followed policies very close to the spirit of its platform, resulted in a

Figure 4.1. Electoral Geography of Ul'ianovskaia Oblast's 1996 Regional Executive Elections (percentage for incumbent/percentage for main challenger)

Source: Map provided by Vladimir Kazantsev, from his essay "Rezul'taty vyborov glavy administratsii Ul'ianovskoi Oblasti 22.12.96" (unpublished manuscript).

split within Kruglikov's electoral base, with many of these potential voters opting for the more familiar incumbent. Nonetheless, the results of the mayoral election in the city of Ul'ianovsk, where Goriachev's political ally Yermakov lost to Vitalii Marusin, opened up a new stage in oblast politics in which, for the first time since the August putsch, opponents of the oblast administration had an administrative pole around which to consolidate.

The political geography of the elections provides a remarkable indicator of Goriachev's core political support in 1996 (see figure 4.1). His support was strongest in the rural regions where information was limited to state-sponsored television, radio, and printed media and where the governor had focused his most visible, hands-on political tactics (school building, gas pipeline construction, roads). A comparison of regional results indicates a general pattern of stronger support for Goriachev as one moves further into the agricultural regions from the capital city.[28] Some of the peripheral *raions* returned as much as 60 percent of the vote for Goriachev. Turnout in these regions was also higher and generally increased as one moved further from the capital. The average turnout for the rural regions (minus the two regions adjacent to the city of Ul'ianovsk, which exhibited outcomes similar to the capital) was 65.0 percent, with minimum and maximum values of 53.7 and 80.1 percent, respectively. These outcomes stand in marked contrast to the urban figures to which we now turn.

For the oblast administration, results in the cities were cause for serious concern. In Dimitrovgrad, Goriachev handily defeated Kruglikov, but outcomes on other variables indicated a degree of political estrangement in the city. First, at 33 percent, Dimitrovgrad exhibited the lowest turnout of any area in the oblast. Second, Dimitrovgrad was also the apex of an otherwise unremarkable electoral map for the opposition candidate Nikolai Semashin. Third, Dimitrovgrad exhibited one of the higher proportions of voters voting "against all" candidates—5.6 percent, as opposed to the oblast's 4.6 percent. The results in Ul'ianovsk city indicated the growing discontent of the oblast center's administrative citizens with the course of regional politics. Kruglikov defeated Goriachev in two of four urban districts and carried the city as a whole with 36 percent of the vote, as opposed to Goriachev's 32 percent. However, as in Dimitrovgrad, perhaps the most interesting results were those related to participation and votes cast "against all candidates." Of the six districts in the city, the average vote against all candidates was 9.1 percent. Results ranged from 5.5 percent in the Zheleznodorozhnaia district to 23.9 percent (!) in Zavolzhkaia No. 2 (this region includes the Aviastar production complex and the Novyi Gorod region). Across the city, turnout was also low, with an average of 43.9 percent and maximum and minimum outcomes of 48.2 and 36.7 percent, respectively. Zavolzhkaia No. 2 again constituted a "protest region," registering the lowest turnout of all the city's districts.

Again, perhaps the most significant long-term result of the 1996 election was the election of an opposition mayor in the city of Ul'ianovsk. Vitalii Marusin, running with the support of the local committee of the Communist Party, beat incumbent Sergei Yermakov by 39 to 30 percent. Whether or not it was perceived as such at the time, this constituted the first major break in the monopoly on local power that the Goriachev administration had held since 1992. Up to this point, despite the troubles with the largely disorganized city-based opposition in the past, the oblast and municipal administrations had enjoyed a comfortable and mutually supportive relationship. With the arrival of an opposition mayor, this situation would change dramatically. Within a year, the two sides were locked in political conflict, as each side's respective media organs became the platform for ever more vicious attacks and the oblast administration began to starve the city of budget funds.

Between Elections

The period between the 1996 and 2000 elections was marked by the accelerating decline of economic conditions in the oblast. Each of the negative dynamics outlined in the "Ul'ianovsk Phenomenon" section above reached a critical stage during this period. To make matters worse, the administration waged a budget war with the Ul'ianovsk city authorities that substantially worsened conditions within the city itself. Following Marusin's victory in December 1996, the city began receiving a smaller and smaller portion of consolidated budget expenditures. The result was a steady decline of the already weakened city infrastructure and a breakdown of municipal services, including the supply of heat and electricity.

Other problems were evident throughout the oblast. Wage arrears for federal and private employees rose, and child welfare payments were either absent or late. Partly to blame were the growing budget deficit combined with the ever-growing portion of the budget dedicated to paying interest on previous loans. However, there were increasing accusations that funds were also simply "disappearing" and that transfers for federal employees' wages were being temporarily invested in high-yield funds.

Wages also became an increasingly poignant issue as the last remnants of Goriachev's social programs gave way. In this respect, it is useful to compare Ul'ianovskaia Oblast with neighboring Samarskaia Oblast, which experienced similar 1991 starting conditions in terms of economic structure and performance. In 1995, the average wage as a proportion of the regional minimum living standard was 203 percent in Ul'ianovskaia Oblast and 185 percent in Samarskaia Oblast. By 1998, Samarskaia Oblast had jumped ahead to 265 percent, while Ul'ianovskaia Oblast remained at 203 percent. Preliminary figures for 2000 indicated that this gap had only widened. As discussed briefly above, the Ul'ianovsk model had been oriented toward the preservation of existing costs of living, but the flip side of preservation was the flight of new capital. Without the growth of new forms of economic activity, wages stagnated; and when social programs were removed, local living standards suffered. Samarskaia Oblast had opted for a more growth-oriented marketization approach. Though its citizens initially suffered a painful drop in their standard of living as prices rose faster than wages, this was eventually overcome as wages rose in the middle 1990s. Even by 1996, the citizens of Ul'ianovskaia Oblast could look over at their neighbors in Samarskaia Oblast and see that the standard of living there was accelerating past their own.

These and other problems gradually culminated in near-crisis conditions by 2000—even though an improving economy was leading to growth in nearly 90 percent of Russia's regions. By the autumn of 2000, it had become clearer that the oblast would face another energy crisis in the upcoming months. In October, the residents of Nizhnyi Terras, a region on the left bank of the Volga, cut access to the only bridge connecting the two portions of the capital to protest shortages of electricity, telephone service, and gas in their apartments. Workers at the UAZ auto plant were still suffering from wage arrears, and conditions at Aviastar were little better. In an article published in *Ul'ianovsk Segodnia* on October 17, Deputy of the Legislative Assembly Pavel Romanenko (who himself would later run for mayor of Ul'ianovsk city) announced that the oblast was bankrupt. The appropriate preparations had not been made for the heating season, and no advanced measures had been taken to deal with the rising cost of heating fuel. As a result, the fourth-quarter budget for 2000 was insufficient to cover the costs of the upcoming winter months.[29] Though Romanenko was clearly an opponent of the oblast administration, most observers agreed that the oblast budget was in crisis and that the struggle between the regional administration and city of Ul'ianovsk government struck a particularly heavy blow to the oblast center. The funds allocated by the regional administration for the city's budget were to be the leanest yet—800 million rubles.[30]

The continuing decline of Ul'ianovskaia Oblast's regional economy was certainly not lost on its citizens. Drawing on data from the Perspektiva survey, table 4.2 indicates attitudes toward the local economic situation in Ul'ianovskaia Oblast as measured during the summer of 2000.[31] The results offer some indication of the level of dissatisfaction with the regional economic situation, particularly when respondents compared conditions with those of other regions. Well over half of the respondents in Ul'ianovskaia Oblast evaluated their oblast's level of socioeconomic development as "much lower than others'." Clearly, the citizens of Ul'ianovskaia Oblast were cognizant of their region's relative stagnation, and most were dissatisfied with

Table 4.2. Responses to Economic Evaluation Questions, Ul'ianovskaia Oblast, September 2000

Question	Response	Percent
How would you evaluate the level of socioeconomic development and lives of the population in our oblast in comparison with other regions?	Much better than in others	2.3
	About the same as in others	20.0
	Much lower than others	65.3
	Difficult to say	11.3
	Refused to answer	0.1
How would you evaluate the level of your income?	Very high	0.1
	Higher than average	0.4
	Average	24.8
	Lower than average	30.9
	Very low	42.9
	Difficult to say	0.4
	Refused to answer	0.1

Source: Ul'ianovsk State Technical University, "Perspektiva" Sociological Laboratory, "Vybory gubernatora Ul'ianovskoi Oblasti v 2000g."

their personal living conditions. The question remained as to whether and how they would lay the blame at the feet of their incumbent.

The 2000 Election Campaign

By 2000, the budgetary and political struggle between the Ul'ianovsk municipal and oblast administrations, continued economic woes (made particularly sharp when considered against the background of the growth experienced in the majority of other regions during 2000) and mounting criticism of the administration's policies gave almost any observer the sense that a crisis was mounting in the region. Every conversation with a local political analysts or journalist contained a common theme: "No matter who wins, things will change here after the election." However, at the beginning of 2000, it was not clear whether a viable challenger would arise to contest the election. This situation changed in March with the first rumors of General Vladimir Shamanov's intention to run in the December election.

Shamanov—decorated the "hero of Russia" and former commander of the 58th Army—participated in both Chechen campaigns, gaining fame throughout Russia as one of its top military leaders. It was well known that the general possessed extensive financial means, and it was rumored that he would bring a team of expert campaign advisers to the oblast (this was later questioned as the details of his campaign became known). His image as a military hero had the potential to attract the support of a wide number of social groups in what was still considered to be a traditionally minded (economically, politically, and socially) region. Furthermore, these and other qualities allowed him to create a coalition of key local elites, including the rector of the State University; the Oblast Committee of the Communist Party; directors of large enterprises such as UAZ and Aviastar; the Ul'ianovsk city administration; and regional and municipal media outlets like *Simbirskii Kur'er, Simbirskie Gubernskie Vedomosti,* and *Ul'ianovsk Segodnia.*

With such a wide diversity of interests backing Shamanov (it is sufficient to point at that both the regional business daily, *Simbirskii Kur'er, and* the regional Communist Party organs backed the same candidate), the basis for this broad coalition was anything but ideological. First, the very diversity of the group is a ready indicator that other factors were coming into play. Second, the erratic nature of Shamanov's economic and political program (or perhaps, simply the *lack* of a defined economic and political program) also ruled against a strong policy-based coalition. From news articles and public statements, there appeared to be a general understanding that Shamanov would somehow attract investment to the region. However, what type of investment was not entirely clear. A look at Shamanov's "official" economic program indicated that he was in favor of *strengthening* the state's control over land and that he supported a program of *reprivatization* of property privatized through illegal means.

In any case, few in the oblast would even know that Shamanov's platform included such planks. Despite the fact that this was *the* dominant issue of the election—at public meetings, during television debates, and in newspaper interviews—he rarely discussed economic policy, and the above-mentioned brochure had a pressrun of only 1,000 copies.[32] Given these facts, the impetus for the coalition that eventually supported him was most likely the popular slogan "Anyone but Goriachev."

Nonetheless, despite the problems facing the oblast and the apparent strength of Goriachev's future challenger, observers were far from confident in Shamanov's victory. Two factors were particularly in question: What role would Moscow play in the elections and to what extent were the Goriachev administration's "administrative resources" still intact (and to what lengths would the administration go, or be allowed by the federal center, to employ them)?

With regard to the first issue, both Shamanov and Goriachev would benefit from an endorsement from the Russian president. The issue of regional transfers noted above had already been discussed in the local press by 2000 and had thus entered the public consciousness as a key factor in choosing a candidate. According to this discourse, the candidate whom the president endorsed would have the key to the federal funds necessary to renew the oblast's economy, pay for energy, and reduce wage arrears. Shamanov's image as an outsider with strong ties to the military brought with it a certain expectation of central government endorsement. An official announcement by President Vladimir Putin would only reinforce this expectation. For Goriachev, however, an endorsement would assist him in undermining Shamanov's image as a resource-rich outsider and create the perception that, after ten years of indifference (bordering on hostility), the central government had finally come to see Iurii Goriachev for the good caretaker that he was.

In the end, no concrete endorsements were forthcoming. One can identify two critical moments regarding the central government's ambivalent role in the 2000 Ul'ianovskaia Oblast election. The first was related to the energy crisis in the region and centered primarily on the November 14 visit of Sergei Kirienko, the Volga Federal District presidential envoy, to Ul'ianovskaia Oblast. Accounts of this visit were varied as the different press organs put their own spin on the events. Opposition papers attempted to paint the visit as negatively as possible. In their accounts, Kirienko played the role of a reprimanding parent visiting an errant offspring's home in an attempt to "set things in order." Such quotes as "the worst disorder I've ever seen" (with regard to the local energy system), and references to the contention that all the oblast's problems were the work of vaguely defined "local individuals" featured prominently.[33]

As expected, proadministration media put the most positive spin on events. *Vesti* ran a headline across a picture of Kirienko and the governor embracing that read "Kirienko: 'Impression of the Oblast? Good!'" Reports in both *Vesti* and *Molodezhnaia Gazeta* seemed to suggest that, though Kirienko was correct in placing part of the blame for the heating crisis on the city/oblast rift, the municipal authorities played a more malicious role.[34] *Narodnaia Gazeta,* the official oblast administration publication, ran an interview with the oblast's federal inspector, Valerii Sychev, which briefly spoke of the energy crisis and than moved on to issues like Kirienko's cool reaction to Shamanov's alleged attempt to gain his endorsement; the presidential envoy's overall positive impression of the oblast (along with "evidence" in the form of "unexpected additional stops"); and, finally, "unexpected" birthday wishes for Goriachev from the president himself. ("According to protocol, the president congratulates a governor only on his jubilee.")[35]

Regardless of the visit's tone, a number of objective factors (i.e., those upon which all press accounts agreed) cast more doubt upon the president's stance in relation to Goriachev. Kirienko stated that he saw two basic causes behind the current energy crisis. First, 130 million rubles had disappeared as consumers' payments entered the hands of energy "middlemen." Second, at 12 to 13 percent of actual energy costs (as set by the regional energy commission), consumers' energy payments were too low; and to make matters worse, it was not clear who was responsible for providing the additional 87 percent subsidy. The rift between the city and the oblast only exacerbated this problem. At the conclusion of the visit, Kirienko supervised an agreement among the oblast administration, city administration, and energy suppliers; instructed regional and local authorities to raise the energy tariff; and then offered a government loan in the sum of 70 million rubles.[36]

The center's unpredictable reaction to events in Ul'ianovskaia Oblast did not stop with Kirienko's visit. On December 6, only two weeks before the election, Putin and Goriachev met together in Moscow. During this meeting, Goriachev submitted a letter in which he briefly described the course and successes of the region's "gradualist reforms" and asked for administrative and financial support for his 2001–4 regional development program. In the course of the executives' meeting—details from which were later recounted ad infinitum by Goriachev through *Narodnaia Gazeta,* GTRK Volga, and elsewhere—Putin wrote a brief memo across the letter addressed to Prime Minister Mikhail Kas'ianov and Kirienko. The memo read: "I ask that you consider supporting the governor and to take into account the proposals of the oblast as regards the regional development program."[37] The proadministration media repeatedly ran articles featuring images of the letter with "I Ask You to Support the Governor" and similar headlines (sometimes adding "Goriachev" after "governor"), claiming that the governor had Putin's blessing and implying that, if Goriachev was elected, the center would provide the financial and administrative support necessary to develop the region.[38]

Aside from the memo to Kirienko, Putin also offered the oblast 70 million rubles to deal with the regional energy crisis and to cancel a portion of the arrears to regional federal workers (much debate remained as to whether this was *the same* 70-million-ruble loan that Kirienko had offered in late November). Returning again to the public relations aspect, the timing of this federal "gift" was perfect for a governor who had built his popularity upon his image as the regional patron. However, in broader terms, it also called into question the administrations' commitment to "rein in" the governors. To satirize the situation, Iurii Goriachev, populist spendthrift, who had thumbed his nose at Moscow's official market reform policies for ten years, once again received finances to cover a gaping budget deficit and extract his oblast from an administration-induced crisis (again, just in time for elections). For all supporters of tighter budget constraints who had placed their hope in the prospect of Putin strong-arming the regional political elite, this outcome could be nothing but a disappointment.

However, it could also be argued that the federal center, having demonstrated its strength and resolve in the Kurskaia Oblast election campaign, asserted all the control over remaining regional elections that was necessary.[39] During Kurskaia Oblast's 2000 contest, the incumbent governor, Aleksandr Rutskoi, was removed from the ballot a mere thirteen hours before the polls opened on October 22. The oblast court ruled that Rutskoi had failed to include one of his automobiles, a 1994 GAZ Volga, in the property declaration that all candidates in the oblast were required to submit during their registration process. Rutskoi was an arch-opponent of the Yeltsin administration, maintained his opposition to the central government under Vladimir Putin, and was widely acknowledged as a person on Putin's gubernatorial blacklist. The timing of the ruling, for an infraction that should have been identified as early as a month before the election, suggested very strongly that the court acted on behalf of the Kremlin. In the aftermath, the threat of a repetition of the "Kursk variant" was a persistent theme in the Ul'ianovskaia Oblast press, and visits and statements by the chairman of the Central Election Commission, Aleksandr Veshniakov, clearly defined the bounds within which Goriachev would have to operate. This factor had a strong impact on the second area where Goriachev's strength was still uncertain—so-called administrative resources.

Here, it could be said that, even barring consideration of the Kursk factor, the administration's ability to control the regional dialogue had been weakened as compared with earlier elections. First, in terms of the media, a simple look at the numbers indicates the degree to which the administration's control over information had changed since 1996. Whereas in 1996, *Simbirskii Kur'er* constituted the only major opposition newspaper in the oblast, by 2000, *Ul'ianovsk Segodnia* and *Simbirskie Gubernskie Vedomosti* (previously a pro-Goriachev newspaper whose stance had changed with the introduction of a new head editor in 1998) had been added to the ranks. With the administration supported by *Narodnaia Gazeta, Ul'ianovskaia Pravda,* and *Vesti* (an essentially "yellow" paper created in response to the new editor at *Simbirskie Gubernskie Vedomosti*), by 2000, the playing field had nearly been leveled for printed media.

However, broadcast media continued to be dominated by the oblast administration. GTRK Volga, the regional affiliate of RTR, consistently produced news programs and political commentaries that coincided with the views and policies of the governor. At times, these practices even interfered with broadcasts from the federal authorities in Moscow. Two examples of such interference arose regarding attempts by the chairman of the Central Election Commission to broadcast a press conference within the region. [40] In the first case, GTRK Volga failed to broadcast the presentation and replaced it with a half-hour program in which Goriachev's older son promoted his company Prodovolstvo. In the second instance, the broadcast was again canceled and replaced by a short program featuring the governor himself visiting the twice-yearly farmers' fair, where grateful citizens heaped praise upon him for his agricultural policies.[41]

The weekly broadcast of the governors, *Selektornoe soveshchanie,* a nearly-two-hour program on which the governor and his staff answered letters and telephone calls for assistance with individual problems (leaking roofs, dirty apartment landings, etc.), was also one of GTRK Volga's hallmarks. The *selektornoe* continued throughout the campaign, showing the governor in the role of the good *khoziain* taking care of the needs of his citizens.In the second week of October, as the elections drew nearer, GTRK Volga also added another program called "Without an Orchestra," on which a local political "expert" praised the governor and berated local administrators as he "objectively" discussed issues of regional import.

Finally, even television debates between candidates were not free from the meddling of GTRK Volga's programmers and staff. At the end of the first debate between the candidates (at which Goriachev and Shamanov were absent), the station presented an unannounced "news program" detailing Goriachev's visit to Putin and his success in gaining the president's endorsement of his program (and by implication, his candidacy). In the final debate, an attempt was made to bring a team of proadministration journalists to the studio to ask questions, and a microphone was set up outside the studio so that selected "bystanders" could offer questions. In the first case, the debaters refused to allow the journalists into the studio (as evidence, television viewers were treated to a row of empty seats at the beginning of the debate); and in the second case, the "bystanders" were shouted down as they attempted to present their questions.

In summary, on the eve of the elections, the following factors (and *non-factors*) may be identified. First, the Shamanov campaign team commanded the resources and personnel to mount a strong, if poorly targeted, campaign. In addition to the groups of "experts" that accompanied him from Moscow, he could rely on an already-developed network of local elites and well-developed opposition media organs in the form of *Simbirskii Kur'er, Simbirskie Gubernskie Vedomosti,* and *Ul'ianovsk Segodnia.* Provided the appropriate stimulus and support, these could unite into a strong opposition and present a significant challenge to the incumbent governor.

As for Moscow's direct role in the election and the impact of the still-developing new presidential order in the regions (signified at this point primarily by new laws for the organization of the Federal Assembly, new powers to remove elected governors, presidential envoys in the recently established seven federal districts, and the threat of the "Kursk variant"), one can see little *direct* evidence that these factors had any influence on the course of the election. In the eyes of the voter, Putin as well as his district envoy Kirienko did very little to weaken *or* support either candidate. Finally, with regard to "administrative resources," it is clear that, while the governor still commanded substantial resources (especially in the rural regions), the presence of a hostile city administration in Ul'ianovsk had seriously weakened his control over the regional political discourse. Though he could and did starve this administration and ultimately drive its mayor away from another election bid, the fact remained that the "Ul'ianovsk myth" would no longer be propagated among a captive audience.

In the end, Goriachev lost his post to General Shamanov, with the challenger gathering 56.2 percent of the vote to the incumbent's 23.6 percent (see figure 4.2). In only one district (an agricultural district in the oblast's southern extreme), did Goriachev gain more votes than Shamanov. As another indicator of the administration's overall loss of popularity, sixteen of twenty-three heads of regional and city administrations lost their posts in parallel elections. The 2000 election was a rejection not just of the governor but also of the entire administrative apparatus that had ruled the region for the past decade.

A First Look at Jurisdictional Support in Russia's Regions

The voters who went to the polls during Ul'ianovskaia Oblast's 2000 gubernatorial elections faced the whole array of obstacles with which their

Figure 4.2. Electoral Geography of Ul'ianovskaia Oblast's 2000 Regional Executive Elections (percentage for incumbent / percentage for main challenger)

Source: Map provided by Vladimir Kazantsev. Election results drawn from Regional Election Commission, Ul'ianovsk Oblast.

counterparts in most of Russia's eighty-nine federal subjects struggled throughout the 1990s: poorly defined policy jurisdictions, a biased and controlled media, challengers with vague platforms and biographies, and none of the informational shortcuts commonly made available by political parties. Yet the role of "third parties" like the federal center was still sufficiently ill defined that voters and candidates were essentially alone together in the political arena, with candidates attempting to prove to voters that they possessed the means to improve regional conditions and voters deciding through a haze of disinformation which candidate would best lead the region through the next four years.

Nonetheless, voters understood that the region was performing poorly, and even pro-oblast administration media were hard pressed to put an entirely positive face on affairs—most of their statements about regional conditions argued that conditions were "not *that* bad." The key question then came down to assigning blame and determining whether the "devil you know" was preferable to the unproven challenger. Would regional voters cut through this mass of contradictory information and deliver the type of outcome predicted by Fiorina's retrospective voter? The results of this analysis suggest so. The region's voters delivered a remarkable display of subnational economic voting; eliminating an incumbent whose policies had slowly driven the region into crisis.

Aside from the practical consideration of data availability, a number of factors make the Ul'ianovskaia Oblast case an interesting opportunity to explore whether regional voters exhibit jurisdictional voting behavior. Occurring during Russia's 1999–2001 election cycle, the election was free of the presidential referendum effect that accompanied the 1996–97 rounds, in which sitting incumbents held their offices almost exclusively by presidential appointment.[42] Therefore, one can expect that voters in this round were more likely to cast votes based upon considerations of regional factors rather than as a means to punish an unpopular President Yeltsin.[43] Additionally, Goriachev had held the governor's office for at least eight years before the election date, providing ample time for him to make his mark on the region's development.[44]

Furthermore, as one of the handful of oblast and *krai* elections that occurred during the 1999–2001 cycle in which an incumbent was defeated, this election provided an opportunity to examine the type of voting behavior that accompanies an incumbent's removal from office. Finally, Ul'ianovskaia Oblast's economic downturn and a host of other woes provided the conditions under which voters are most likely to "throw the rascal out" in response to poor regional socioeconomic conditions. If voters exhibited jurisdictional economic voting behavior in the Ul'ianovskaia case, then there are grounds for optimism in other cases where well-fortified governors ruled over ailing regional economies.[45] In light of these considerations, the remainder of this study presents a single-case plausibility probe for applying the jurisdictional voting model to Russian regional executive elections.

Based as it is on cases from one region, the following analysis is not an attempt to present the first and final word on economic voting behavior across all of Russia's regions. What it does offer is an initial examination of whether voters in the case region exhibited behavior that approximated the ideal jurisdictional voter described in chapter 3 and again in the following section. Nonetheless, the results of the study provide the most detailed insights into this understudied issue and are sufficiently intriguing to encourage scholars to further examine whether similar dynamics are present in a broader number of cases. As a first step in the examination of regional-level economic voting behavior, the "value added" of this study exceeds some of the methodological problems resulting from a single case study and the nature of the survey data.

The Ideal Subnational Jurisdictional Voter

Given the previous discussions of accountability throughout this study, what might the ideal "jurisdictional voter" look like? Generally speaking, such voters would recognize the limited jurisdiction of their regional executives and representatives and "punish or reward" incumbents only for those outcomes for which they are (at least conceivably) responsible.[46] Faced with a region of jurisdictional voters, gubernatorial incumbents would have an incentive to maximize the well-being of their citizens because voters will assess their performance and choose to vote for them based solely (or at least primarily) on those outcomes for which they are perceived to be responsible.

This entails two things for the study of economic voting behavior at the regional level. First, one would expect voters to discern between the effects of external factors and the effects of incumbent's policies. For example, if the entire nation is suffering an economic downturn, the jurisdictionally minded voter would not automatically go to the polls during a gubernatorial election to "turn the rascal" out. Instead, this ideal type would apply some method to assess whether or not the incumbent governor has done all in his or her power to reverse or at least soften the effect of the general downturn in the region under his or her policy jurisdiction. One of the simplest assessment mechanisms would be to compare the downturn in the voter's region with the downturn in other regions. Seeing that conditions in the voter's region are deteriorating faster than in other regions (they have heat, we do not; our streets are filled with striking public servants, theirs are not), the voter might reasonably conclude that the incumbent is shirking and vote for the incumbent's opponent. If voters fail to apply any type of mechanism to discern between regional and external factors, then incumbents have little incentive to work for the voters' welfare maximization— amid a national economic upturn, all governors would win (and in a downturn, lose), regardless of the policies that they implemented in the course of their terms.

The second implication of the jurisdictional voter definition is that voters should give salience to sociotropic over pocketbook considerations. Though pocketbook voting in the case of a broad upswing or downturn could yield a certain degree of accountability, such behavior is far less efficient than when sociotropic concerns dominate. Sociotropic assessments focus more closely on that issue for which incumbents are responsible—the general well-being of the society within their policy jurisdictions. Voters focused primarily on pocketbook issues introduce a great deal of noise into the accountability relationship. Not only would votes be responses to those personal fortunes resulting from incumbents' policies, but they would also be responses to personal mishaps, sudden windfalls, and criminal activities. On a more speculative note, sociotropic concerns may also indicate a less "myopic" voter.[47] To continue with Manin, Przeworski, and Stokes's analogy, regional-level pocketbook voters may by perfectly happy sipping champagne as the incumbent cuts down all the trees. Sociotropic voters, by focusing on society-level conditions, may be more discerning about the long-term effects on societal welfare of such shortsighted policies as clear-cutting the oblast.

Hypotheses

The above discussion of the ideal jurisdictional economic voter yields three test hypotheses. Hypothesis one (H1) states that *support for the incumbent is positively related to the respondent's evaluation of his or her personal economic situation (pocketbook effect).* This represents a classic pocketbook hypothesis to determine whether regional voters evaluate their regional executives based upon their recent *personal* economic fortunes. As indicated above, a strong showing for the pocketbook hypotheses would not necessarily indicate that a basis exists for jurisdictional economic voting in these regions. An individual's economic situation is the result of a combination of both external and personal factors. Individuals may lose their job or become fabulously rich regardless of the actions of governing officials. Hence, if respondents appear to be "punishing and rewarding" incumbents on the basis of personal economic assessments, this could actually create a situation in which incumbents remain unaccountable for the results of those policies within their jurisdiction.

This consideration leads to a second hypothesis (H2), which states that *support for the incumbent is positively related to the respondent's evaluation of the regional economy.* This hypothesis addresses so-called absolute sociotropic effects, seeking to determine whether the respondent focuses on the economic situation in his or her region *independent* of the situation in other regions. Support for this hypothesis would suggest that, though regional economic conditions have an impact on regional executive assessments, they are not consciously determined by comparisons with other regions. Should such absolute assessments take precedence, any regional executive risks punishment under conditions of poor *national* performance.[48] As with the pocketbook hypothesis, the salience of absolute sociotropic support calculi would effectively reduce the accountability of regional executive incumbents for those policies that lie within their jurisdiction.

In light of this argument, further refinement is necessary. Hypothesis three (H3) states that *support for the incumbent is positively related to the respondent's evaluation of his or her region's performance relative to other regions.* This hypothesis focuses upon whether respondents construct opinions based upon the economic situation in their region *as compared with* the economic performance in other regions. Support for this hypothesis would indicate that *relative* regional performance matters, rather than *absolute* evaluations of national performance as a whole. Relative assessments imply that respondents recognize "winners and losers" among regions rather than merely projecting national assessments of the economy upon their regional executives.[49] If relative economic assessments are important in evaluating regional executives, then elections could act not only as a mechanism to hold executives accountable for economic outcomes but also as a means to compel administrations in low-performing regions to imitate and hopefully converge upon the policies of more successful regions.[50]

The Survey

To test these hypotheses, the following sections analyze survey data drawn from Ul'ianovsk Oblast before the region's 2000 gubernatorial election. Data for the survey was drawn from an oblast-wide 1,630-respondent survey undertaken in September 2000 by the Ul'ianovsk State Technical University's Perspektiv Sociological Laboratory (Valentina Shuvalova, director). Perspektiv initially conducted the survey by order of one of the candidate's staff as a means to sample public opinion before developing the candidate's campaign strategy. This factor has been the source of some criticism following earlier presentations of this study. In response to this, I note that Perspektiva is a reputable survey organization that worked in the region for roughly ten years, conducting studies for both VtSIOM and a number of Western agencies and research teams. I met with members of the Perspektiva research team to discuss in detail the methodology used for the study, and it conformed to strict survey research standards.

Furthermore, given the initial intended use of these surveys as a means to canvas the population and provide information for the development of the candidate's campaign, there is little logical reason for either the agency or the client to desire anything but the most objective results. These surveys were provided only for the candidate's campaign staff before the author acquired them for his own exclusive use. No portion of this survey was released to the media or ever used for campaign agitation.

With regard to the methodology, the survey organization employed multistage sampling techniques to draw 1,630 respondents from all regions of the oblast. Districts were defined, and interviewers were sent to randomly drawn locations within the districts to question respondents in interviews of 35 to 50 minutes in duration. The demographic structure of each district's sample was then compared with the district's population demographics. As a follow-up, project coordinators later contacted 10 percent of the respondents to confirm their responses. The survey had a 3 percent margin of error.

A Preview and Summary of Results

The analyses presented in the remainder of this chapter paint an encouraging picture of the decisionmaking process that guided Ul'ianovskaia Oblast's voters in voting for or against the incumbent regional executive. For the most part, they focused on the executive's jurisdiction, punishing or rewarding him for the region's performance relative to other regions and paying less attention both to their own personal misfortunes and to national issues lying beyond the control of the executive. Decisions were less driven by partisan leanings, and individuals frequently "broke ranks" with their particular socioeconomic groups to cast votes based on rational assessments of regional conditions rather than marching in lockstep to vote for the "pensioners' candidate." Contrary to the casual observations of analysts and pundits—both East and West—they were also less susceptible to a biased media. Voters were little persuaded by outlets that did not already reflect their preconceived notions of various political actors, and newspapers in particular exhibited little persuasive effect. The main exception in this case

Figure 4.3. Support Calculi, Ul'ianovsk Oblast, 2000

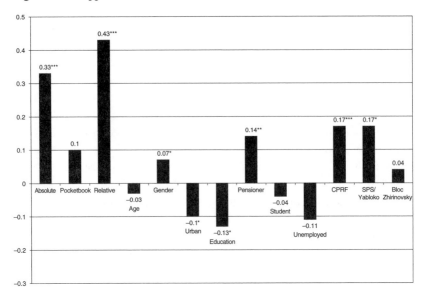

* $p \leq .05$, ** $p \leq .01$; ***$p \leq .001$.
Note: CPRF = Communist Party; SPS = Union of Right Forces.

was the regional television station, whose monopoly on regional news provided it with a degree of propaganda power.

Figure 4.3 provides a graphical summary of the results discussed in further detail throughout the remainder of this chapter. Each bar on the histogram represents the strength and direction of the relationship between the independent variable in question and the voter's decision to support or oppose the incumbent. By comparing the strength and directions of each relationship, one can gain a sense of which issues were more important to the voter relative to all the other possible considerations included in the model.

A perusal of the results clearly indicates the comparative strength of the relative sociotropic assessment (see the figure bar labeled "relative") that represented the voter's perception of overall regional conditions relative to conditions in other regions. Voters made distinctions between different types of economic assessments (absolute sociotropic, relative sociotropic, and pocketbook) and held the governor most accountable for the relative performance of their region. To recap our discussion of jurisdictional voting, had pocketbook or absolute sociotropic considerations figured more heavily into their decision, governors may have been held responsible for personal misfortune or national level decisions over which they exercised little control.

Furthermore, other factors like media consumption, party support, and socioeconomic status played a lesser role in voters' decisions to support or oppose the incumbent. As further described in the following sections, only viewers of the local television station GTRK Volga (the variable for which was omitted from figure 4.3) had an appreciable persuasive effect on viewers, but this fell far short of the impact of relative sociotropic assessments. Party support, though significant, once again exhibited a much smaller effect on decisions to support the incumbent than the respondents' perception of the region's performance relative to the rest of Russia.

The same could be said for socioeconomic standing. Levels of education, gender, age, and other factors played some role in respondents' decisions to support or oppose the incumbent, but the strength of the relative sociotropic assessment again indicates that respondents made assessments independent of their placement within the region's social structures. In short, these survey results suggest very strongly that Russia's regional voters "voted correctly," taking jurisdictional considerations into account and sanctioning and rewarding governors for the perceived relative state of the region.

Measures

Delving further into the details of the analyses, we turn first to issues of measurement. This study utilizes a dichotomous dependent variable measuring support/nonsupport for the oblast's current incumbent. This measure is recoded from the survey question, "If the gubernatorial election was held next Sunday, for which candidate would you be most likely to vote for?" Respondents were given the option to choose from a list of all possible candidates, "against all candidates," to not vote, or "difficult to say." For the purposes of this measure, all responses other than "Iurii Goriachev" are coded as a vote "against the incumbent."

Turning to the independent variables, ABSOLUTE measures the absolute sociotropic effect and is derived from responses to the question, "In your opinion, is the oblast socioeconomic situation currently moving in the right direction?" Respondents were given a list of possible responses, including (1) yes, in the right direction; (2) generally speaking, in the right direction; (3) no development at all; (4) not in the entirely right direction; or (5) in the completely wrong direction. The coding reversed the order of evaluations found on the questionnaire (to reflect movement from worse to better evaluations), with "difficult to say" and nonresponses coded as "missing." To standardize the three economic variables (both ABSOLUTE and POCKET-BOOK have ranges of five, while RELATIVE has a range of three), the upper and lower two categories were collapsed into "right direction" and "wrong direction" categories.

The RELATIVE variable taps into the comparative sociotropic concept captured in hypothesis H3. Respondents were asked, "How do you evaluate the level of socioeconomic development and life of the population in our region as compared to other regions?" Each respondent had the option of answering (1) much higher than in others, (2) same as in others, (3) much worse than in others, (4) difficult to answer, or (5) no answer. During the coding process, the order of options one to three was reversed (creating a worse to better scale), and nonanswers were coded as missing.

The variable POCKETBOOK measures respondents' evaluation of their personal "pocketbook" economic situations. The respondent was asked: "How do you evaluate your current level of income?" and given a list of possible responses: (1) high, (2) higher than average, (3) average, (4) lower than average, or (5) low. Once again, the coding reversed the order of evaluations found on the questionnaire (to reflect movement from worse to better evaluations), with "difficult to say" and nonresponses coded as "missing." As with the ABSOLUTE measure, the upper and lower two categories were collapsed into "high" and "low" categories.

Before moving on, some discussion is necessary regarding the potential for high correlations between these three measures. Each measure is differentiated by a particular nuance that might be overlooked by the respondent, and one could easily imagine that individually unfortunate respondents might simply apply negative assessments across all three measures. This would increase the danger of multicollinearity and thus undermine the logistic regression results. However, a correlation matrix indicated surprisingly weak relationships between the three measures. Of all the possible combinations, the highest correlation was between the comparative and absolute sociotropic evaluations. At −0.23, one could hardly consider this a strong relationship, and hence, the risk of multicollinearity appears quite low. The remaining correlations are close to or smaller than plus or minus 0.20. By itself, this is a significant finding, because it indicates that respondents make rather sophisticated decisions about the economic situation in their regions, differentiating among personal, absolutely sociotropic, and relatively sociotropic conditions.

Moving on from the hypotheses-testing measures described above, the analysis also controls for a number of "noneconomic" variables in each region. These include measures indicating from where the respondent receives most of his or her information, as well as the respondents' age, ideological inclination, education, gender, employment status, attitude toward candidates from security organs, and whether he or she lives in a rural or urban setting.

The addition of the age, urbanization, gender, and education controls are more or less de rigueur for survey analyses and do not warrant a great deal of discussion. Measures for employment status (EMPLOYMENT) and party and ideological preference (DUMA99) require at least some explanation to assist with the interpretation of the logistic regression results. The employment variable indicates whether the respondent is employed, a pensioner, a student, or unemployed and seeking work. In the logistic regression below, "employed" is the baseline measure for this categorical variable.[51] Party support and ideology are determined by which major party the respondent supported in the 1999 Duma elections. For the purposes of this model, the responses are grouped into four categories: Communist Party voters have their own category, voters for Unity and Fatherland are grouped into a "center" category, SPS (Union of Right Forces) and Yabloko voters are grouped into a "liberal" category, and supporters of "Bloc Zhirinovsky" (a reincarnation of the Liberal Democratic Party after it was denied registration for the 1999 Duma elections) constitute the final category. In introducing the party measure into the model as a classification variable, the "center" group acts as the baseline.[52]

The information controls tap into questions as to how information affects voters' behavior and influences their assessments of political figures and institutions.[53] Depending upon the business environment, the orientation of regional governing bodies, and a number of other factors, the major players in a "typical" regional media environment generally consist of the oblast-controlled television-radio station (GTRK), perhaps one or two independent stations with varying political loyalties, one or more oblasti and/or major municipality controlled-newspapers (including publications specific to various departments of the oblast and city administrations—i.e., social services), a "business daily/weekly," and the regional Communist Party's newspaper.[54]

Each of these outlets usually exhibits a clear agenda in reporting on regional conditions and supporting or opposing the regional administration. Oblast publications and broadcast media will naturally put the best face on the regional administration's activities and place the blame for the most obvious regional problems on either other levels of government or some other outside force. Business publications are often comparatively well financed, hire more professional journalists, and have at least a "look" of objectivity (i.e., few sensationalist headlines, shocking photographs, or eye-catching text). Their loyalties will vary depending on their ties to regional business tycoons and these tycoons' relations to the regional administration. The local communist publication will generally vary in its stance depending upon both the ideological orientation of the regional administration in question and the administration's relationship to the local party organs (the latter not necessarily being determined by the first).

Uncovering the general orientation of any of the above-listed media outlets does not require sophisticated content analyses. A simple comparison of the handling of a number of important and contentious issues is sufficient to indicate that subtlety is not a prerequisite for joining a Russian regional news staff. Having said this, one must consider these factors when examining how citizens formulate their understandings of political figures and regional socioeconomic conditions. To take a simple example, a citizen living in an oblast's administrative center knows whether or not her house is heated. By talking with her neighbors or walking to the store four blocks away, she can also investigate whether or not a substantial portion of her city has heat. However, if the oblast-controlled news station reports that the regional center is the only area without heat and that citizens in other places throughout the oblast are walking around their apartments in shorts and tank tops (cut to images of happy citizens doing just that), the viewer may well believe that this is a local (i.e., the mayor's) problem. With this example in mind, these controls are included to account for the regional media's potential power to create (or at least obfuscate) political and economic realities and persuade voters to cast their votes for one or another candidate.[55]

To explore this nexus between information and incumbent support, the model uses a measure based on the question, "Which of the following local media sources do you or your family use?" Respondents chose from a list of specific newspapers and television stations. On the basis of information from interviews with local media representatives, scholars, and other observers, each media outlet was classified as progubernatorial, antigubernatorial, or "central" (those newspapers that were essentially federal-level publications with regional inserts).[56] Dummy variables were created for each news source, indicating whether the respondents read that particular paper or watched a particular station (no = 0, yes = 1).

Each variable was then included in the general model.[57] Though the survey instrument admittedly does not contain a question asking respondents *how often* they watched/listened to the news or read a newspaper, interviewers did ask them from which sources they received their information. Hence, although the study presents little information about the amount of information received (except in the cases where respondents said they never read a newspaper, listened to the radio, or watched television), it nonetheless contains the data necessary to explore the effects of the *type* of information received.

Finally, because it constitutes a somewhat unorthodox indicator (at least in terms of economic voting studies), a few words are necessary regarding the security opponent control (SECURE). This measure taps into the respondents' attitude toward candidates from security organs and is included to determine whether a particular preference for candidates from these organs played a role in citizens' decisions to oppose the incumbent.[58] After the election of General Vladimir Shamanov to the governor's post in December 2000, a number of commentators attributed the incumbent's loss to a particular type of conservatism in the region that had shifted preferences from conservative communist leaders to another traditional institution—the military.[59] Furthermore, at the time of the 1999–2001 round of gubernatorial elections, the idea that regional executives would be "overrun" by Putin-backed military and security candidates was popular among in Russian and Western press. The inclusion of this variable permits one to assess whether there was sufficient observable evidence for this contention.

Model Specification and Results

To remind the reader of the method described in the appendix, the fact that INCUMBENT is a dichotomous variable measuring support/nonsupport for the incumbent precludes the use of linear regression techniques. Hence, this analysis utilizes binomial logistic regression models that allow one to determine the net effects of a number of predictors on a dichotomous dependent variable.[60] Whereas linear regression indicates the linear relationship between a set of predictors and a continuous dependent variable, logistic regression allows us to measure the change in odds that a certain outcome will occur in a categorical variable given changes in a set of categorical, continuous, or binomial predictors. The values in the table are total effects, which in this case indicate the change in the odds of supporting the incumbent governor as one moves from the particular indicator's minimum value to its maximum value. To anticipate the discussion of the results, if "relative regional" has a value of 0.43, then this indicates that those individuals with the highest assessment of their region's comparative economic situation are more likely by a factor of 0.43 to support their governor than those with the lowest assessment.

Moving onto the analysis, after experimenting with numerous iterations (omitted from this chapter), a final model was tested that included each of the above-discussed indicators as predictors of incumbent support. Table 4.3 presents the results.

Focusing first on the coefficients, table 4.3 presents the total-effects estimates indicating the change in the probability of supporting the candidate across the range of the indicator. In terms of the economic assessment hypotheses, the table presents encouraging results from the standpoint of jurisdictional voting. Both the absolute and comparative economic assessments are highly significant, with the latter exhibiting a stronger relationship to incumbent support than the former. Pocketbook effects, though positively related to incumbent support, fail to meet the lowest significance criteria. In sum, these results suggest that voters in this case election placed the greatest emphasis on the comparative assessment of the regional economy, thus holding the incumbent responsible for the perceived economic situation in the region *relative* to those of other regions. The respondents were clearly "jurisdictionally oriented."

The fates of the control variables are also instructive. As in Solnick's aggregate level analyses of the 1996–97 elections, ideology and partisanship appear to affect respondents' tendency to support the incumbent—perhaps not surprising, considering Goriachev's reputation as a "red" governor. However, returning to the present chapter's earlier discussion regarding the rift between the local Communist Party organs and Governor Goriachev (see note 51), one should note that in this particular case this relationship probably represents an affinity between the governor's and respondents' ideological and policy preferences rather than an expression of partisanship in the sense often employed in studies of Western voting behavior.[61] Furthermore, the relationship is less stable than the economic indicators, and the indicator's overall significance level is lower than both sociotropic measures.

Coefficients for the pensioner, gender, education, and urbanization measures yielded few surprises. Goriachev built his political support upon his image as the champion of the elderly and other vulnerable groups in society. This image probably accounts for the greater likelihood of pensioners to support the incumbent, and it may have gained the governor an albeit unstable (as evinced by the standard error) advantage among women ("male"

Table 4.3. Logistic Regression Model for Incumbent Support

Measure	Min → Max[a]
Absolute regional (ABSOLUTE)	0.33***
Personal pocketbook (POCKETBOOK)	0.10
Relative regional (RELATIVE)	0.43***
Attitudes toward security candidates (SECURE)	0.35***
1999 Duma vote (DUMA99)	
Communist Party	0.17***
SPS (Union of Right Forces), Yabloko	0.17*
Bloc Zhirinovsky	0.04
Age (AGE)	−0.03
Gender (GENDER)	0.07*
Urbanization (URBANIZATION)	−0.10*
Level of education (EDUCATION)	−0.13*
Employment status (EMPLOYMENT)	
Pensioner	0.14**
Student	−0.04
Unemployed	−0.11
Media indicators	
Ul'ianovskaia Pravda	0.05
Simbirskie Gubernskie Vedomosti	0.02
Narodnaia Gazeta	0.04
Simbirskii Kur'er	−0.03
Ul'ianovsk Segodnia	0.19
Zhizn' i Ekonomika	−0.05
Molodezhnaia Gazeta	0.17
Komsomol'skaia Pravda (regional insert)	0.01
Other newspapers	−0.17*
GTRK Volga	0.12***
TNT	0.03
Reporter	−0.09
2 X 2	0.03
Model χ^2	296.22***
Pseudo R^2	0.27
N[b]	881.00

* $p \leq .05$, ** $p \leq .01$; *** $p \leq .001$.

[a] Total effects derived using CLARIFY; 1,000 simulations drawn. For more information, see Gary King, Michael Tomz, and Jason Wittenberg, "Making the Most of Statistical Analyses: Improving Interpretation and Presentation," *American Journal of Political Science* 44, no. 2 (April 2000): 347–61; and Michael Tomz, Jason Wittenberg, and Gary King, "CLARIFY: Software for Interpreting and Presenting Statistical Results, Version 2.1," Stanford University, University of Wisconsin, and Harvard University; available at http://gking.harvard.edu.

[b] Most of the missing cases resulted from lower response rates to the 1999 Duma vote measure. Results from separate logits with the 1999 vote measure removed exhibited no significant change in the relative magnitude and significance of the coefficients of interest.

is the base value for this dichotomous measure).[62] The rural/urban control exhibited a weak yet significant relationship with incumbent support. However, though rural respondents ("rural" is the base measure for this dichotomous variable) were more likely to support the incumbent, the standard error indicates that it was not a particularly stable relationship. Given the fact that rural residents were often seen as part of Goriachev's core political support, this particular result indicates a significant erosion of the incumbent's political base. Indeed, as indicated above, Shamanov won the votes of a larger portion of the electorate in virtually every rural area of the oblast.

The security variable's performance also deserves note. Its coefficient indicates that the probability of supporting the incumbent governor increased by a factor of 0.34 as respondents moved from the most positive to the most negative attitudes toward security organ-based governors.[63] Hence, there is some indication that a desire for an ex-military leader (with all the assumptions of order, traditional values, and strength that this status implies) in the governor's seat may have also played some role in respondents' decisions to oppose Goriachev.

The results for the informational predictors suggest some additional interesting relationships. Overall, with the exception of the progubernatorial *Molodezhnaia Gazeta,*[64] the oblast-administration-controlled (and therefore strongly progubernatorial) television-radio company GTRK Volga and the "other newspapers" category, all other media variables exhibited weak and statistically insignificant relationships with incumbent support.

What might account for the overall poor performance of the media variables? Much of the discourse surrounding regional elections and the "feudalization" of regional politics speaks of incumbent administrations' control of the media as a major impediment to regional-level democracy.[65] The implicit assumption behind these arguments is that the governor-controlled media influences voters to see the region in a positive light and attribute positive developments to the incumbent governor. However, the logistic regression results in table 4.3 suggest that, for the most part, this relationship failed to hold in the Ul'ianovskaia Oblast case. Such results imply that there is something faulty in the causality posited by explanations focusing on the media as an instrument of persuasion. Specifically, instead of the media pouring ideas into the heads of voters and persuading them to perceive the region or incumbent in a specific way, perhaps voters choose media sources on the basis of certain predispositions, primarily exposing themselves to those sources that best reflect their existing attitudes and beliefs.

Support for this explanation comes from the overall weakness of the newspaper indicators as opposed to GTRK Volga.[66] Unlike television viewing, the nature of newspaper reading is conducive to *selective exposure,* because individuals incur certain costs (paying for a subscription, or walking to the nearest kiosk where the newspaper is sold) when choosing their preferred source.[67] Given these costs, one might expect that respondents are more likely to pay for and read those newspapers that best reflect their particular predispositions. Television exposure, particularly in a region dominated by one station, is less selective. Individuals incur few costs from tuning in to a particular station, and therefore a broader range of individuals receives the station's message.[68] In light of these observations, one might argue that newspapers play a primarily *mobilizational* or *reinforcement* function among individuals with views already quite similar to the given paper of their choice. Television, having a much broader audience due to the low-cost nature of exposure, might exhibit mobilizational and reinforcement effects as well as a certain degree of *persuasive* power.

To explore this issue further, separate logistic regression models of incumbent support were run, using first only the media variables and then both media and demographic indicators as predictors. The results from these analyses provide additional support for the selectivity explanation described above. When all other economic evaluations and socioeconomic variables are removed, five of the fourteen media outlet variables exhibit significant relationships to incumbent support, with the direction of the relationship coinciding with expectations based upon the particular media outlet's bias (consumers of progubernatorial news tended to support the governor and vice versa).

However, with the addition of demographic variables to the model, most of the media variables lose their predictive power. Because respondents' age, gender, education, place of residence, or employment are stable social attributes whose status is highly unlikely to be determined by their choice of media, this observation further challenges common assumptions regarding the persuasive effect of the media on voters' decisions. If the media variables lose their predictive power when the demographic measures are included, one can conclude that a respondent's placement within the web of regional social cleavages has a greater impact on support for the incumbent than any information that he or she is receiving from the media. Due to selective exposure, newspapers are not persuading significant numbers of individuals to vote for a specific candidate. Voters with specific predispositions "self-select" their information and primarily consume those media that reflect their preferences.

GTRK Volga's dominance of the regional broadcast media market likely intensified the broadcast media effect. As the regional television station with the strongest signal, GTRK Volga offered many respondents the only option for regional-level news broadcasts. Furthermore, GTRK Volga's viewing area extended into parts of the oblast with few broadcast *or* print media alternatives. The highest proportions of GTRK Volga viewers appeared in the rural regions where audience rates in *raion* centers, towns, and villages reached 64.1, 60.9, and 63 percent, respectively, as compared with audiences of 48.3 percent in Ul'ianovsk city and 55.9 percent in other major urban settlements like Dmitrovgrad (after the city of Ul'ianovsk, the second largest city in the region). Among the portion of GTRK Volga's audience living outside Ul'ianovsk city and Dimitrovgrad, 20.2 percent claimed that they read no newspaper and 61.2 percent claimed that they read only one. Of the audience members reading only one paper, 26.8 percent read the progubernatorial *Narodnaia Gazeta*. Such figures suggest that much of GTRK Volga's broadcast area included a "captive audience" with little or no access to opposing viewpoints.

Figure 4.4 offers a clear graphical representation of the effect on respondents of exposure to GTRK Volga's news coverage. The figure indicates the change in the probability of supporting the incumbent across varying comparative assessments of the regional economy for both viewers and nonviewers holding all other variables in the full logit regression model (table 4.3) at their means. Across all categories, GTRK Volga viewers were more likely to support the incumbent with only slight convergence among respondents who saw the socioeconomic situation as being "much worse" than in other regions. Exposure to the administration's broadcast media effectively softened the impact of economic assessments on support for the governor, and as evidenced by the predictor's resilience within the fully specified logistic model, exhibited some persuasive effect on respondents.

Casting Stones within a Federal Context

The above analyses demonstrate quite clearly that voters in the case election held their governor responsible for perceived conditions within the region and that these effects retained their strength even after controlling for media effects and other sociological factors. However, the results tell us very little about the possibility that voters might apply the same logic across other levels and branches of government, "punishing and rewarding" any

Figure 4.4. Support for Incumbent by GTRK Volga Viewership

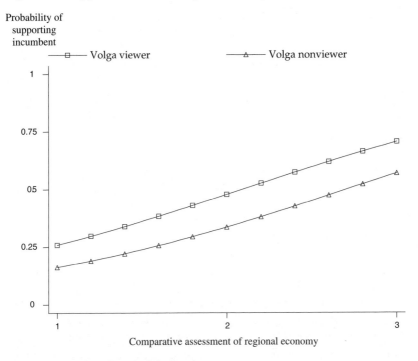

Source: Estimated from the author's logit analyses.

incumbent who appears on a ballot in the region. A comparison of respondents' behavior in gubernatorial elections with their behavior in presidential and federal legislature elections might provide a more convincing view of the "jurisdictional" nature of their support calculi.

Fortunately, the survey also includes questions concerning the assignment of responsibility for regional conditions and the respondents' vote in the most recent presidential and parliamentary elections. Table 4.4 presents respondents' answers to a battery of questions asking them to rate the degree to which various political figures effect conditions within the region.

In light of the literature on multilevel government and accountability in other contexts, the data given in table 4.4 show some rather startling results. Federal-level actors were predominantly given ratings below the midpoint. When assessing the governor's influence, well over three-quarters of the respondents gave the incumbent a score of four or higher. This rather strongly

Table 4.4. Responses to the Question "Please rate who, in your view, most affects conditions within our oblast" (percent)

Rating of Effect	President	Russian Parliament	Single-Mandate-District Representative	Governor
0 (completely no effect)	0.23	0.91	0.79	0.68
1	30.31	33.03	36.66	4.20
2	12.37	16.57	15.32	2.50
3	15.21	16.91	15.55	7.26
4	9.08	8.29	7.38	12.83
5 (greatest effect)	18.62	7.95	8.06	68.10
Hard to say	13.51	15.32	15.44	3.86
Refused	0.68	1.02	0.79	0.57

Source: Ul'ianovsk State Technical University, "Perspektiva" Sociological Laboratory, "Vybory gubernatora Ul'ianovskoi Oblasti v 2000g."

indicates the voters' sense of jurisdictional responsibilities in the Russian context. Respondents clearly see the main onus of regional development resting squarely on the shoulders of the regional executive.

But do the data in table 4.4 translate into electoral behavior? Comparisons of behavior in the December 1999 Duma elections and in the March 2000 presidential elections with support for the governor in September 2000 provide further evidence of the jurisdictional nature of regional voting decisions. Table 4.5 compares voting behavior in the presidential elections and support for the governor using a reduced version of the model (essentially removing the media variables) presented in table 4.3. Before examining the tables, however, the reader must bear in mind that this poll was taken in September 2000, almost six months after the presidential election. Furthermore, the 2000 presidential election occurred a little over two months after Putin took office following Yeltsin's surprise resignation on January 1.

Nonetheless, Putin had held the prime minister's office since August 1999, and he was soon acknowledged as the de facto head of state and state executive during the twilight of the Yeltsin administration. At the same time, he represented a continuation of the Yeltsin regime, in that Yeltsin had hand-picked him as a successor. Therefore, despite the fact that Putin had not held a full term in office before the presidential election, I argue that there is still some value in comparing this "incumbent" to the more conventional gubernatorial incumbent, Iurii Goriachev. As a final word in support for this choice, I would also point out that, working with the data set collected by Timothy Colton and William Zimmerman during the 1995

Table 4.5. Support by Economic Assessment

Variable or Measure	Incumbent Governor	Putin
Absolute sociotropic	0.32***	0.04
Pocketbook	0.10	0.03
Relative sociotropic	0.45***	–0.01
Age	–0.07	0.09
Female	0.07*	0.05
Urbanization	–0.07	0.11*
Level of education	–0.12*	0.05
Employment status		
Unemployed	–0.11**	0.09
Pensioner	0.16	0.02
Student	–0.04	–0.00
Party support		
Communist Party	0.17***	–0.49***
SPS, Yabloko	0.12	–0.31***
Bloc Zhirinovsky	0.07	–0.38***
Model χ^2	244.79***	179.64***
Pseudo R^2	0.22	0.15
N	881.00	881.00

* $p \le .05$, ** $p \le .01$; ***$p \le .001$.
Note: SPS = Union of Right Forces.

presidential and parliamentary elections, I also discovered that voters' evaluations of regional and local performance were significantly more weakly related to incumbent presidential support than evaluations of the national economy.[69]

With all these points in mind, this and the subsequent analyses focused on party-list choice in the December 1999 elections should be taken as a rough approximation of the role that considerations of economic performance may have played in voters' decisions to support a given party or presidential candidate during these earlier federal contests. These findings are not central to the argument regarding voter calculi in gubernatorial elections but are presented primarily as additional suggestive evidence for the contention that jurisdictional considerations are taken into account by regional voters.

Comparing the effects of the predictors across the gubernatorial and presidential support models, the economic assessment measures provide very strong predictors of incumbent governor support while offering almost no leverage in explaining support for the president. The best predictors of presidential support in the model are found among the party variables where, considering the use of the quasi-presidential party Unity as a baseline

Table 4.6. Party Support (Multinomial Logit)[a]

Variable or Measure	Liberal Democratic Party	Unity	Yabloko	SPS	OVR	Likelihood Ratio Test[b]
Absolute sociotropic	−0.03	0.04	0.00	−0.01	0.01	5.28
Pocketbook	−0.03	−0.11	0.01	0.14**	0.07	12.68*
Relative sociotropic	0.02	−0.15*	0.00	−0.01	−0.02	7.53
Age	−0.23***	−0.29***	0.02	−0.09***	−0.00	76.90***
Female	−0.02*	−0.02	−0.01	−0.00	−0.01	6.92
Urbanization	−0.03*	−0.05	−0.02	−0.01	−0.02	14.21*
Level of education	−0.01	0.09**	0.12***	0.02	−0.01	30.94***
Employment status						
Unemployed	0.05*	−0.03	0.01	0.01	0.02	6.31
Pensioner	0.04	−0.02	−0.03	0.01	−0.01	6.59
Student	−0.02	−0.17	0.04	−0.01	0.03	3.43
N = 876						

* $p = .05$, ** $p = .01$; ***$p = .001$.
Note: SPS = Union of Right Forces; OVR = Fatherland–All Russia.
[a] Communist Party voters are the baseline.
[b] H_0: Coefficient = 0.

measure, it is not surprising that supporters of the remaining parties were less likely to cast their votes for Putin.

Similar results are evident when comparing support for the governor with behavior in the 1999 Duma elections. Table 4.6 presents a multinomial logit model of party-list voting decisions during the December 1999 elections. Here again, I emphasize that because this particular survey was administered nine months after the Duma elections, there is a much stronger potential for respondents to mistakenly recall or even fabricate their vote choices. Furthermore, the economic assessments asked the voter to assess change of the past twelve months, putting the reference point only three to four months before the election in question. Nonetheless, as additional suggestive evidence regarding the role that different assessments played in the respondents' vote choices, the analysis provides further support for the jurisdictional voting argument outlined above.

Multinomial logit tables are inherently "messy" affairs because they present sets of coefficients for each independent variable *and* each category of the dependent variable. An examination of the columns under each party category shows that some indicators had stronger effects on the likelihood of certain vote choices than others but provides less of an idea of which indicators provided the most leverage in predicting a party choice among the entire field of available contenders. One means to circumvent this problem is to conduct a likelihood-ratio test, which assesses the null hypothesis that all coefficients for the independent variable in question are simultaneously equal to zero—in other words, that the variable provides no leverage in helping us determine an individual's choice among the field of parties. In this instance, significant outcomes for an independent variable (denoted by asterisks in table 4.6) indicate that this particular measure provides sufficient leverage to help us determine voters' party choice based on the nature, presence, or absence of this factor.

With this in mind, table 4.6 indicates that, once again, the voting decisions in federal elections were largely independent of regional-level economic assessments. An examination of the results of the likelihood tests indicates that, of the variables included in the model, static socioeconomic factors like the respondent's age, level of education, and whether or not he or she lived in an urban or rural setting provided the best predictors of party support, whereas the only economic assessment predictor significantly related to party support was the personal pocketbook measure.[70] Clearly, assessments of regional conditions factored very weakly into voters decisions to vote for or against any particular party.

Conclusions

In terms of holding governors accountable for economic performance outcomes, the above results indicate that voters in Ul'ianovskaia Oblast exhibited elements of the type of jurisdictional voting behavior necessary to hold their incumbent responsible for the results of his policies. First, as indicated above, the economic test indicators returned strong coefficients relative to the other noneconomic controls. This lessens the possibility that the economic assessment measures are simply picking up the effects of other variables like employment status, education, place of residence, and so on.

Second, pocketbook measures performed much worse than sociotropic measures, suggesting that the incumbent was less likely to be punished for the more idiosyncratic turns in respondents' personal fortunes than for the downturn in the regional economy as a whole. Third, relative sociotropic measures played a strong role. Respondents weighed their region's performance against that of other regions, holding their incumbent responsible for those outcomes that fell within his jurisdiction. The importance of this last point cannot be underestimated. Should the relative measure have been much weaker than the other two economic measures or had it been closely correlated to the absolute measure, then one could argue that Goriachev was "punished" for factors external to his policy responsibilities. Fourth and finally, the type of behavior noted in the gubernatorial support model appears to be unique to elections at that particular level. Predictors of behavior in Duma and presidential elections differed substantially from those determining gubernatorial support, with regional economic factors playing a negligible role in federal-level elections.

This study also offers a telling glimpse into the media issues surrounding regional-level opinion formation. The elimination of independent media outlets like NTV and TV-6 has increased awareness about the weak state of Russian media independence at the *federal* level. However, regional media conditions receive far less scrutiny, and comparatively few individuals living outside any given region are either aware of or interested in whether the region's governor cracks down on local newspapers or uses the budget-financed regional television station for campaign agitation. For residents dependent solely on regional media outlets for information about their immediate environment (federal-level newspapers and television stations naturally focus on national issues and events in Moscow), such questions take on a greater importance.

Fortunately, the results suggest that, though a biased media is certainly a matter of concern, one should demur from portraying Russia's regional-level voters as mindless receptors for whichever message a particular media outlet chooses to purvey.[71] The interrelationship between respondents' social standing and their newspaper consumption suggests that readers recognize various papers' biases and are attracted to those sources that best reflect their own views. The press may reinforce and focus political opinions, but there is little evidence that it actually forms them. Ul'ianovskaia Oblast's newspapers very rarely forged a Goriachev opponent from a respondent whose other characteristics predisposed him or her to support the governor (or vice versa).

However, broadcast media offers a clear exception. The resilience of the GTRK Volga indicator shows that an administration-controlled television station *can* act as a means of persuasion. As indicated above, this relationship was likely amplified in the Ul'ianovskaia Oblast case (and that oblast's media structure is typical of many regions of Russia, especially in the so-called red belt) by a lack of alternative regional-level stations and the station's near monopoly as a source for regional information in the oblast's rural areas. In comparison to choosing a newspaper, television viewing is relatively cost free, and the lack of alternatives meant that GTRK Volga's audience spanned many social divides. Nonetheless, while GTRK Volga probably created a number of Goriachev supporters before the 2000 election campaign, the election results demonstrate that even a loyal and preponderant (in relation to other stations) regional television station is insufficient to save an unpopular governor facing a strong and well-supported opponent.

From Behavior to Outcomes

This initial foray into the behavioral aspect of the regional electoral accountability issue yielded surprisingly encouraging results. Ul'ianovskaia Oblast's voters clearly took region-specific performance into account when deciding to support or oppose their incumbent, and the strength of the relationship—especially when compared with behavior in federal elections—suggests that they were even more jurisdictionally oriented than many of their counterparts in other parts of the world. If Ul'ianovskaia Oblast's voters were representative of other regions (and there is little a priori reason to assume that they were not), then the Russian voter was most likely voting "correctly."[72]

But what of the voter's institutional context? What happens when the voter disapproves of an incumbent but sees no viable alternative? Might election rules and various other machinations undertaken in the course of a campaign block the full manifestation of individual jurisdictional voting calculi? These questions and others constitute the next step in our exploration. Chapter 5 takes us from the realm of the individual voter to an examination of the past decade of election trends for all of Russia's eighty-eight federal subjects (minus Chechnya) and explores whether Russia's regional electoral system was a help or a hindrance to the jurisdictionally minded voter.

Notes

1. To a lesser extent, the particular nature of the case also speaks to the criteria of a viable opposition and media (criterion 4) and the ability to replace incumbents with challengers (criterion 2). Aspects of the case relevant to these two issues will be discussed as they arise.

2. N. Morozov and Iu. Semykin, "Kratkii istoricheskii ocherk Ul'ianovskogo Povolzh'ia," in *Kto est' kto v Ul'ianovskoi oblasti Rossiiskoi Federatsii,* ed. Viachislav Kudinov (Ul'ianovsk: Kumir, 1999), 8–24.

3. Ul'ianovskaia Oblast Committee of State Statistics, *Ekonomicheskoe polozhenie Ul'ianvoskoi Oblasti v 1999 godu* (Ul'ianovsk: Ul'ianovskaia Oblast Committee of State Statistics, 2000).

4. Viktor Sidorenko, interview by the author, Ul'ianovsk, Ul'ianovskaia Oblast, November 17, 2000.

5. V. S. Shuvalova and Y. N. Shuvalov, "Sotsial'no-politicheskoe soznanie naseleniya Ul'ianovskoi Oblasti mezhdu vyborami v Rossiiskii Parlament 1990 i 1993 g.g." (Ul'ianovsk: Perspektiv, 1993), 4.

6. Robert McIntyre, "Regional Stabilization under Transitional Period Conditions in Russia: Price Controls, Regional Trade Barriers and Other Local-level Measures," *Europe-Asia Studies* 50, no. 5 (1998): 866.

7. Egor Il'in, "Synok," *Simbirskii Kur'er,* December 22, 2000.

8. Thanks to Andrei Lavrov of the Russian Ministry of Finance for providing budgetary data.

9. Despite the region's "outlier" status in average budget deficits, it fell well below the Russian Federation average in terms of federal transfers as a percentage of adjusted regional expenditures. Between 1992 and 1997, these averaged 15.08 percent, which placed the region under the federal average (29.99 percent) and within the first quarter (Q1 = 19.29) of Russia's regions.

10. Unlike the AvtoVaz plant in neighboring Samarskaia Oblast, which despite all the economic hardships of the post-1991 crisis never once halted its conveyer, UAZ was plagued by periodic stoppages caused by breakdowns in the quasi-Soviet barter system by which it obtained parts and raw materials.

11. See, e.g., John McMillan and Christopher Woodruff, "The Central Role of Entrepreneurs in Transition Economies," *Journal of Economic Perspectives* 16, no. 3 (2002): 153–70; Janos Kornai, "Ten Years after 'The Road to A Free Economy': The Author's Self-Evaluation," paper presented at the Annual World Bank Conference on Development Economics, Washington, April 2000; John McMillan and Christopher Woodruff, "Interfirm Relations and Informal Credit in Vietnam," *Quarterly Journal of Economics* 114, no. 4 (1999): 1285–1320; Yingyi Qian and Chenggang Xu, "Why China's Economic Reforms Differ: The M-Form Hierarchy and Entry/Expansion in the Non-State Sector," *Economics of Transition* 1, no. 2 (1993): 135–70; Andrea Richter and Mark Schaffer, "The Performance of *De Novo* Private Firms in Russian Manufacturing," in *Enterprise Restructuring and Economic Policy in Russia,* ed. Simon Commander et al. (Washington, D.C.: World Bank, 1996); Per Ronnas and Bhargavi Ramamurth, eds., *Entrepreneurship in Vietnam: Transformation and Dynamics* (Copenhagen: Nordic Institute of Asian Studies, 2001); Leila Webster, *The Emergence of Private Sector Manufacturing in Hungary: A Survey of Firms,* World Bank Technical Paper 229 (Washington, D.C.: World Bank, 1993); World Bank, *Ukraine: Restoring Growth with Equity* (Washington, D.C.: World Bank, 1999); Harry Broadman, "Reducing Structural Dominance and Entry Barriers in Russian Industry," *Review of Industrial Organization* 17, no. 2 (2000): 155–75; and Jiahua Che and Yinkyi Qian, "Industrial Environment, Community Government, and Corporate Governance: Understanding China's Township Village Enterprises," *Journal of Law, Economics and Organization* 14, no. 1 (1998): 1–23.

12. Viktor Sidorenko, interview by the author, Ul'ianovsk, Ul'ianovskaia Oblast, November 17, 2000.

13. Iurii Lebedev, interview by the author, Ul'ianovsk, Ul'ianovskaia Oblast, November 15, 2000.

14. S. P. Kashkorova, "Maloe predprinimatel'stvo Ul'ianovskoi oblasti: Kamo gri-adeshi?" *Simbirskii VIP-Bulletin,* January–February 1998.

15. *Selektornoe soveshchanie* was a program broadcast every Saturday morning, during which the governor and members of the administration discussed regional problems, took telephone calls from citizens, made policy pronouncements, and publicly attacked challengers. Toward the end of the administration's rule, this paternalistic show became one of the administration's primary instruments for "ruling" the oblast.

16. Gennadii Iakimchev, "Aleksandr Nabegaev provali, pervoe zadanie," *Simbirskii Kur'er,* April 11, 2000.

17. Igor Egorev refers to a survey of more than 100 small enterprise owners conducted by Ul'ianovsk State Technical University, in which 69 percent of the individuals blamed oblast policies and 71 percent blamed municipal authorities for the poor quality of small business conditions.

18. McIntyre, "Regional Stabilization under Transitional Period Conditions in Russia," 866.

19. Ul'ianovskaia Oblast Committee of State Statistics, *Ekonomicheskoe polozhenie Ul'ianovskoi Oblasti v 1999 godu* (Ul'ianovsk: Ul'ianovskaia Oblast Committee of State Statistics, 2000).

20. Ul'ianovskaia Oblast Committee of State Statistics, *Ekonomicheskoe polozhenie Ul'ianovskoi Oblasti v 1999 godu.*

21. Igor Egorov, interview by the author, Ul'ianovsk, Ul'ianovskaia Oblast, November 23, 2000.

22. In the 1993 Federal Assembly elections, held at the height of the Ul'ianovsk model, Goryachev was elected to one of the oblast's two seats with 90.1 percent of the vote. The other seat was won by the mayor of Ul'ianovsk and ally of Goriachev, E. Yermakov.

23. Rustam Bikmetov contends that the absence of legislative organs in the oblast allowed this commission to play a much stronger role in the political decisions of the oblast—ultimately contributing to the content of the regional charter. Given the fact that this commission was initially answerable only to the Governor, the administration had a strong partner in what was an ostensibly independent institution geared toward the protection of regional election rights. See P. M. Bikmetov, "Izbiratel'nyi protsess, vlast' i oppozitsiia v Ul'ianovskoi Oblasti," *Polis* 3 (1999): 121–22.

24. See Ukaz Presidenta RF, no. 1765, October 27, 1993. According to Decree 368, the Ul'ianovsk Legislative Assembly would consist of two chambers—one derived from single-mandate districts based on existing administrative units, the second derived from single-mandate districts in newly created "territorial okrugs." The combination of these two chambers led to gross disproportions in the representation of various regions and not surprisingly, those regions which were over represented happened to be the same areas that had traditionally supported the governor. As just one example, Zasviyazhskii Okrug 5, a traditionally strong source of opposition to the governor and the location of the State University, contained 173,700 voters, while Bazarnosyzranskii Okrug 48, a rural region that had shown strong support for Goriachev, contained 10,335. In total, the populations of Dimitrovgrad and the city of Ul'ianovsk, despite the fact that they made up 56 percent of the voters, received only 36 percent of the seats in the Legislative Assembly. See Vladimir Kazantsev, "Ul'ianovskie Vybory—'95: Itogi proshlogo i uroki dlia budushchego," photocopy, Ul'ianovsk, 1998.

25. Following publication of the court's decision, Goriachev made a public statement in *Narodnaia Gazeta,* saying that, "a group of individuals, politicians, under the

banner of the 'Bloc of Democratic Forces' had taken advantage of the pre-election situation to undermine the social-political situation in the oblast"; *Narodnaia Gazeta,* March 19, 1992.

26. Arbakhan Magomedov, "Khronika politicheskikh sobytii," in *Regiony Rossii: Khronika i rukovoditeli, tom 7,* ed. Kimitaka Matsuzato (Sapporo: Slavic Research Center, 1999), 186–87.

27. Alexander and Vladimir Kazantsev were kind enough to provide a list of indicators to demonstrate how the legislative assembly was not a "check" in the normal sense of a system of checks and balances. These included the complete absence of any vetoed legislation in the course of the assembly's tenure, the fact that the majority of representatives from rural regions were also heads of regional administrations (appointed by Goriachev before 1996), the legislature's support for decisions that are most key for the administration, and legislative support for economic and financial legislation which benefits firms close to the administration. An illustrative example of the third point was the legislature's 1999 decision to allow Goriachev to run for a third term based on the fact that the existing law was changed to state that a governor could not be *elected* to a third term and Goriachev had been appointed to his first. See P. M. Bikmetov, "Izbiratel'nyi protsess, vlast' I oppozitsiia v Ul'ianovskoi Oblasti," *Polis* 3 (1999): 125.

28. The nature of the data precludes me from undertaking more advanced correlational analysis, but the patterns described are mostly clear from a glance at figure 4.1.

29. Liubov' Balakina, "Pavel Romanenko: 'Oblast'—bankrot,'" *Ul'ianovsk Segodnia,* October 17, 2000.

30. Natal'ia Zhidkikh, "Kirienko ponial shto oblastnaia vlast' durila nam golovy," *Ul'ianovsk Segodnia,* November 17, 2000.

31. Data for the survey were drawn from an oblast-wide 1,630-respondent survey undertaken in September of 2000 by the Ul'ianovsk State Technical University's Perspektiv Sociological Laboratory (Valentina Shuvalova, director). A full description of the survey follows in this chapter.

32. As a more extreme example of the virtual absence of policy discussion in this campaign, a member of the board of directors of Ul'ianovsk State University told of one meeting between Shamanov and the board at which the general talked exclusively of his war experience (this despite the fact that the vice chairman of the board is a Muslim) and any attempts to move onto more relevant topics proved fruitless.

33. Sergei Gogin, "Teplovoi udar," *Simbirskii Kur'er,* November 16, 2000.

34. V. Kuznetsov, "C. Kirienko: 'Vpechatlenie ot oblasti? Khoroshee!'" *Simbirskie Gubernskie Vesti,* November 17, 2000; Aleksandr Dmitriev, "Vizit polpreda v Ul'ianovsk," *Molodezhnaia Gazeta,* November 17, 2000. The report in Molodezhnya Gazeta even went so far as to suggest that Marusin was embezzling payments to energy providers, thus creating the municipal debt.

35. Jubilees mark every decade of an individual's life. E. Sul'dina, "Vizit Polpreda: Posleslovie k krivotolkam," *Narodnaia Gazeta,* November 17, 2000.

36. Sergei Gogin, "Teplovoi udar."

37. *Narodnaia Gazeta,* December 8, 2000.

38. *Narodnaia Gazeta,* December 8, 2000; E. Sul'dina, "Obstanovku v nashei oblasti V. Putin otsenivaet ob'ektivno," *Narodnaia Gazeta,* December 8, 2000; S. Aleksandrov, "President podderzhal gubernatora Iu. Goriacheva," *Simbirski Gubernskie Vesti,* December 8, 2000; "Proshu podderzhat' gubernatora," *Ul'ianovskaia Pravda,* December

9, 2000; "Goriachev—Putin: Razgovor o glavnom," *Molodozhnaia Gazeta,* December 15, 2000. In addition to the articles and news programs dealing with the president's request to "support the governor," sometime around December 15, campaign posters with Goriachev and Putin shaking hands (caption: "President Supports the Governor") appeared around the city. Later, the paper *Ul'ianovsk Segodnia* sent copies of these pamphlets to the presidential administration, demanding an explanation—no response was received. For details of this exchange, see "Putin tokogo ne podderzhit!" *Ul'ianovsk Segodnia,* December 19, 2000.

39. G. Nekhoroshev, "Novaia Kurskaia bitva: Vpervie oblastnoi sud v poslednii moment snimaet s vyborov deistvuiushchego gubernatora, imevshego shansy na pobedy," *Nezavisimaia Gazeta,* October 24, 2000; E. Gamaiun, "Pike Rutskogo," *Moskovskii Komsomolets,* October 21, 2000.

40. The first involved an October 4 discussion of the regional elections and the second, broadcast on October 23, discussed the decision to remove Governor Rutskoi in Kursk Oblast.

41. *Simbirskii Kur'er,* October 26, 2000.

42. In this instance, referendum voting connotes a situation in which voters cast votes to "punish" a subnational incumbent because of his or her perceived ties with an unpopular federal-level executive.

43. In any case, Yeltsin no longer held office at the time of the election. Furthermore, Goriachev's ambivalent relationship with the president exempted him from anti-presidential referendum voting.

44. As the former chairman of the oblast soviet and oblast executive committee, Goriachev's career as a regional decisionmaker extended back well before the early 1990s.

45. However, this is not to say that the elected challenger will necessarily reverse a region's economic fortunes. Under the Shamanov administration, Ul'ianovsk continued to suffer economic stagnation, energy crises, and payment difficulties (although these are in part the legacies of the Goriachev era).

46. For a comment on other locus-related issues and the place of jurisdictional voting in this extant literature, see n. 31, chap. 2.

47. Bernard Manin, Adam Przeworksi, and Susan Stokes, "Introduction," in *Democracy, Accountability and Representation,* ed. Adam Przeworski, Bernard Manin, and Susan Stokes (Cambridge: Cambridge University Press, 1999), 14–15.

48. One manifestation of this issue is the tendency of opposition candidates in many regional elections to provide comparisons between regional performance measures taken in 1991 with those drawn from the election year. Of course, nearly every comparison points to a catastrophic decline. However, because these figures also reflect a nationwide problem generally beyond the control of any one governor, one should also look at the relative performance of the region—an outcome for which the incumbent is arguably more responsible.

49. In certain respects, this is similar to the distinction that Atkeson and Partin draw between "referendum" and "retrospective economic" voting in their study of U.S. gubernatorial elections. Referendum voting punishes or rewards governors for the success or failure of national policies, making no distinction between regional and national performance. Atkeson and Partin's "retrospective economic" voting involves more sophisticated assessments as voters assign responsibility based on the policy jurisdictions of

each level of government. See L. R. Atkeson and R. W. Partin, "Economic and Referendum Voting: A Comparison of Gubernatorial and Senatorial Elections," *American Political Science Review* 89 (1995): 99–107.

50. This factor speaks to the potential role of elections in the so-called market-preserving federalism literature. For a more detailed treatment of the economic conditions driving regional convergence in federations, see Barry Weingast, "The Economic Role of Political Institutions: Market Preserving Federalism and Economic Development," *Journal of Law, Economics and Organization* 11 (1995): 1–31; G. Montinola, Yingyi Qian, and Barry Weingast, "Federalism, Chinese Style: The Political Basis for Economic Success," *World Politics* 48 (1996): 50–81; Darrell Slider, "Russia's Market-Distorting Federalism," *Post-Soviet Geography and Economics* 38 (1997): 445–60; and Olivier Blanchard and Andrei Shleifer, "Federalism with and without Political Centralization: China versus Russia," National Bureau of Economic Research Working Paper, March 2000, http://www.nber.org/papers/w7616.

51. When including a categorical measure in a logistic regression model, a baseline value is specified as a reference point for the remaining values. In this case, the result for the "student" value indicates the degree to which a student is more or less likely than a working respondent to support the incumbent.

52. At this point, it is necessary to describe briefly the relationship between the local Communist Party organs and the communist (with a small "c," as opposed to a member of the region's Communist Party organs) Governor Goriachev. Despite apparent ideological similarities—particularly regarding Goriachev's stance on social and economic policies—the Communist Party was one of the Goriachev administration's most vocal opponents throughout much of the 1990s. In the 1996 gubernatorial elections, the first secretary of the Ul'ianovskaia Oblast Committee of the Communist Party, Aleksandr Kruglikov, ran against Gorachev and actually won in the city of Ul'ianovsk. During the 2000 gubernatorial election, the regional committee of the Communist Party strongly endorsed General Shamanov's campaign. The party organized rallies and meetings for the general, and Kruglikov sat in for Shamanov during televised debates. During the debate broadcast on December 8 by GTRK Volga, both Goriachev and Shamanov were absent, ostensibly as a reaction to the "dirt" being thrown about during the campaign.

53. For one of the more important works on this topic, see: John Zaller, *The Nature and Origins of Mass Opinion* (Cambridge: Cambridge University Press, 1992). For an examination of similar issues within the postsocialist setting, see Raymond Duch, "A Developmental Model of Heterogenous Economic Voting in New Democracies," *American Political Science Review* 95 (2001): 895–910.

54. There are also numerous other publications with smaller press runs and distribution. These include newspapers from universities, *raion* administrations, special-interest papers, and others. In addition, during an election campaign, candidates often publish separate newspapers that exist only for the duration of the campaign. These are exclusively propaganda publications, and given the self-selection process described in the main text, their impact on the course of a campaign is probably minimal.

55. According to Marc Heatherton, this phenomenon is not restricted to Russia's regions. In his analyses of the 1992 U.S. presidential elections, he demonstrates that media coverage promoted negative assessments of the economy that masked an actual recovery going into the election. He argues that these assessments played an important role in Bush's eventual election defeat. See Marc Heatherington, "The Media's Role in

Forming Voters' National Economic Evaluations in 1992," *American Journal of Political Science* 40 (1996): 372–95.

56. Of the newspapers included in the analysis, *Narodnaia Gazeta, Ul'ianovskaia Pravda,* and *Molodezhnaia Gazeta* were unequivocally progubernatorial. Antigubernatorial newspapers published in the region included *Simbirskie Gubernskie Vedomosti, Simbirskii Kur'er, Ul'ianovsk Segodnia,* and *Zhizn' Ekonomika.* "Central" newspapers with regional inserts included *Komsomol'skaia Pravda* and *Argumenty i Fakty.* *Simbirskie Gubernskie Vesti,* another infamous progubernatorial paper (rather more for its scandalous content than a voluminous press run), was not explicitly listed on the survey and thus fell into the "other newspapers" category. This particular publication printed scathing shock articles directed against the governor's enemies while using a format similar to *Simbirskii Gubernskie Vedomosti* in the hope of confusing readers. Nevertheless, its actual influence should not be overestimated. The volume of the paper's press run remained a mystery to most local analysts and copies were generally difficult to come by.

GTRK Volga, as the oblast administration–sponsored television station, was naturally progubernatorial. Mixed loyalties and recent staff changes made other television stations more difficult to classify. TNT had ties to Sergei Riabukhin (speaker of the oblast legislature and a late-running gubernatorial candidate), and some members of the station's staff acted as his campaign representatives. However, due to the speaker's longtime loyalty to Goriachev, both his campaign and TNT's coverage were relatively neutral toward the incumbent. Reporter's director was a recent Goriachev appointee, but the station ran advertisements and reportage that would be difficult to label as overwhelmingly "progubernatorial." The station 2x2 was inclined toward the opposition but also divided its airtime between the candidates. In any case, the signal from the last three stations was so weak that only low-quality reception was available in most areas of the oblast. Overall audience rates for TNT, Reporter, and 2x2 were 9, 15, and 10 percent, respectively. In several rural areas, not a single respondent claimed to receive Reporter or 2x2.

57. During one iteration of the general model, the variables were grouped according to their classifications (progubernatorial, antigubernatorial, and center) and these groups were included in lieu of the individual variables. This resulted in insignificant coefficients for each of the three groups.

58. The Ul'ianovsk survey included a question measuring the extent to which respondents agree with the following statement: "Some people think that law and order is greater in those regions where the governor is a former military officer (general)." Respondents had the option of answering (1) strongly agree, (2) agree, (3) uncertain, (4) disagree, and (5) strongly disagree. The answers were coded in the same order as in the questionnaire, with nonresponses coded as missing.

59. Arkady Ostrovsky, "Putin Sends General to 'Retake' Old Outpost of the Red Economy," *Financial Times,* December 23, 2000; Maura Reynolds, "Russia's 'Cruel' Soldier Comes Home," *Los Angeles Times,* January 19, 2001. In an interview, Arbakhan Magomedov presented a slightly different viewpoint. Magomedov indicated that Ul'ianovskaia Oblast's citizens exhibited a particular preference for "heroes." During the early 1990s, Goriachev was a "hero" battling the deprivations of liberalization. The 2000 elections brought a different hero, General Shamanov, who would battle against the stagnation and corruption of Goriachev's late-1990s regime. Given the continued stagnation in the region following Shamanov's election, one might wonder from where

the next "hero" will come. Arbakhan Magomedov, interview by the author, Ul'ianovsk, Ul'ianovskaia Oblast, March 24, 2001.

60. For information about this technique, see Alfred DeMaris, *Logit Modeling: Practical Applications* (Thousand Oaks, Calif.: Sage Publications, 1992); David Hosmer and Stanley Lemeshow *Applied Logistic Regression* (New York: Wiley, 1989); J. Scott Long, *Regression Models for Categorical and Limited Dependent Variables* (Thousand Oaks, Calif.: Sage Publications, 1997); and J. Scott Long and Jeremy Freese, *Regression Models for Categorical Dependent Variables Using Stata* (College Station, Tex.: Stata Press, 2001).

61. E.g., analysts like Anthony Downs and Samuel Popkin see party identification as an "information shortcut," which voters use to reduce information costs. See Anthony Downs, *An Economic Theory of Democracy* (New York: Harper Brothers, 1957); and Samuel Popkin, *The Reasoning Voter* (Chicago: University of Chicago Press, 1991), 51. Warren Miller and Merrill Shanks take a more nuanced view, indicating that "long-term partisanship exerts an indirect influence on vote choice by shaping voters' attitudes toward many of the short-term forces in a given campaign, as well as by exerting some direct or unmediated influence of its own on the vote decision"; Warren Miller and Merrill Shanks, *The New American Voter* (Cambridge, Mass.: Harvard University Press, 1996), 284. In both of these instances, the authors suggest that party identification is a form of group identity greater than the sum of an individual's particular policy preferences or ideological orientation. This identity in turn has at least some direct causal impact upon a voter's choice of candidates.

62. On the basis of this argument, one might expect the age control to have exhibited a larger coefficient. However, most of the age effect was absorbed by the education and employment status measures. One's position within the oblast social structure was apparently more indicative of support for the Governor than one's age.

63. In this instance, the exponentiated odds ratio of 0.44 is multiplied by the variable's range of four.

64. *Molodezhnaia Gazeta* was an "independent" (from official involvement by regional political organs) newspaper that, in 2000, was under the financial control of "OOO Molodezhnaia Gazeta." From 1989 to 1991, the paper's chief editor, Zakhar Misanets, served as the Regional Committee first secretary in the Leninskii raion Komsomol and was thus closely tied with Goriachev's circle. During the 2000 election campaign, the newspaper presented a selection of anti-Shamanov attack articles mixed with apparently more objective reporting and public interest items.

65. Statements to this effect are relatively common in Russian media reports and analyses and appear quite frequently in Western treatments of regional politics. For examples, see Sergei Ryzhenkov, "Ul'ianovskaia Oblast': Perekhod bez smeny elit," in *Rossiia regionov: Transformatsiia politicheskikh rezhimov,* ed. Vladimir Gelman, Sergei Rizhenkov, and Mikhail Bri (Moscow: Ves' Mir, 2000), 257–93; Darrel Slider, "Pskov under the LDPR: Elections and Dysfunctional Federalism in One Region," *Europe-Asia Studies* 51 (1999): 755–67.

66. The apparent strength of *Molodezhnaia Gazeta's* indicator in the general model probably says very little about the paper's actual influence relative to other outlets. The newspaper was not widely distributed and only 3 percent of the sample claimed to have read it (a paltry forty-one respondents). Furthermore, with a significance level of 0.052, the relationship between this variable and incumbent support is clearly less stable than for those of the other predictors. As for the "other newspapers" measure, the mixed bag of publications represented by this measure provides little grist for anything but the most

speculative conclusions. Therefore, for the purposes of this study, there is little to gain from speculation about these results.

67. In his classic study on the effects of mass communication, Joseph Klapper defines selective exposure as "the tendency of people to expose themselves to mass communications in accord with their existing opinions and interests and to avoid unsympathetic material"; Joseph Klapper, *The Effects of Mass Communication* (Glencoe, Ill.: Free Press, 1960), 19. Indications of selective exposure frequently arose in discussions between the author and local observers and analysts. An interviewee might complain that pro-gubernatorial media shaped people's understanding of the region but then go on to say that opponents of the governor either ignored such media sources or read and viewed them only for amusement. Supporters of the governor usually referred to antigubernatorial newspapers as "yellow" and therefore ignored them.

68. These observations coincide with research conducted by Larry Bartels and others demonstrating that, for many individuals, television viewing has a greater impact on political preferences and performance evaluations. Larry Bartels, "Messages Received: The Political Impact of Media Exposure," *American Political Science Review* 87 (1993): 267–85. For another important work on the effects of media on political support and perceptions, see Shanto Iyenger and Donald Kinder, *News That Matters: Television and American Opinion* (Chicago, University of Chicago Press, 1987).

69. The 1995–96 Russian Election Study, commissioned by Timothy Colton and William Zimmerman and conducted by Paulina Kozerova's Demoscope public opinion organization, was a panel survey consisting of three nationwide surveys of 2,841 respondents. Interviews were conducted face to face with respondents chosen via multistage area probability sampling. The waves were timed to occur before and after the December 1995 parliamentary elections and after the June 1996 presidential contest. Additional information about the survey is included on the Web site of the Inter-University Consortium for Political and Social Research (http://www.icpsr.org) and in Timothy Colton, *Transitional Citizens: Voters and What Influences Them in the New Russia* (Cambridge, Mass.: Harvard University Press, 2000).

70. The likelihood ratio test is a test of the null hypothesis that all coefficients associated with the independent variable in question are equal to 0. Statistically significant results indicate that the independent variable offers some explanatory power for at least one of the outcomes in the nominal dependent variable. See Long and Freese, *Regression Models for Categorical Variables Using STATA*, 182.

71. In his book *Transitional Citizens,* Colton makes a similar point asking, "Are we to infer, then, that Russian's transitional citizens have nothing to say in the matter, that they are docile couch potatoes who absorb every sound bite fed to them in the mass media?" Colton answers in the negative indicating that, "popular awareness of media favoritism is widespread in the Russian Federation." See Colton, *Transitional Citizens,* 61.

72. As in Diana Mutz's U.S. state-level analyses of media effects on economic assessments, a single region study should not pose any major generalizability problems for the particular behaviors examined here. Logically, one would expect voters in other region's to process and apply political and economic information in much the same way. The most significant differences will probably occur with regard to the controls because these most closely reflect the particular relationship between the incumbent and different social groups. See Diana Mutz, "Mass Media and the Depoliticization of Personal Experience," *American Journal of Political Science* 36, no. 2 (1992), n. 15.

Chapter 5

Aggregate Economic Performance
and Election Outcomes

—We've arrived at a political situation that is closer to American standards. There
they have the expression "incumbent." This is how they call the acting governor
who always has a better chance of keeping his seat. And usually 65 to 70 percent
of "incumbents" are reelected.
—In other words, we've caught up to America?
—Passed them! We've got it even better! In fact, this time we've reelected 80 percent of our governors.

—Interview with Dmitrii Oreshkin

Chapter 4 painted a portrait of a sophisticated regional voter who, despite
the challenges of "federal confusion," a heavily biased regional media, and
one of the more stagnant and politically repressed oblasti in Russia, cast his
or her vote according to rough assessments of his or her region's performance relative to those of others. By this standard, the Russian voter appears
more "jurisdictionally oriented" than her American counterpart, who tends
to cast his vote in state elections according to party affiliations and assessments of the U.S. president. Hence, if Russian regional elections have failed
to elicit even a modicum of accountability, the fault does not lay with the
provincial voter.

Unfortunately, "good voters" do not necessarily yield "good outcomes."
A vast number of factors like the quality of challengers, proincumbent election rules, dirty campaigning, ballot fraud, and various nefarious election
tactics might intervene to shield incumbents from a discontented electorate.
As indicated in chapter 3, incumbents maintained an extensive arsenal of
methods to secure their position in the face of marked opposition. Furthermore, the "jurisdictional voter" might decide to support or oppose an incum-

158

bent based on comparative, yet entirely miscalculated, assessments of regional conditions.[1] If jurisdictional voters are making seeming random assessments of their region's relative performance, then their ability to assign responsibility across levels of government is lost for want of reliable perceptions of local conditions.

This chapter builds upon the survey analyses of chapter 4 by examining the nexus between incumbent success and aggregate-level regional economic performance. In doing so, I investigate to what extent various measures of economic performance provide leverage for predicting the odds that the incumbent executive (or incumbent regime) maintained office. When combined with the analyses in chapter 4, this portion of the study allows us to not only determine how closely regional voters' assessments of the regional economy coincided with objective economic measures but to also determine whether the nature of Russia's regional electoral institutions effectively blocked the manifestation of popular discontent in election outcomes. Given the obstacles alluded to throughout this book, the case for economic accountability through elections certainly remains to be proven.

In light of the extant literature and the conventional wisdom surrounding Russian gubernatorial elections, the results of the study are quite surprising. The introduction of the annually standardized measure of regional growth into the models results in a strong and rather robust relationship between economic growth and incumbent success. Such results suggest that, despite the numerous shortcomings of Russian regional elections, incumbent governors were more likely to retain their posts in regions where the economy improved at a faster rate relative to other regions during the election year in question. Though one would be naive to tout these results as proof of Russia's vibrant regional-level democracy, they do challenge the most dire assessments of its provincial elections as they existed during the period from 1996 to 2001.

Data Sources

The analyses draw upon a database that I developed for the 1996–2001 elections. The database contains more than 100 political, economic, and institutional variables for all the oblast, *krai,* "city of federal importance," republic, autonomous *okrug,* and autonomous oblast elections that occurred between June 1996 and April 2001 (the discussion in chapter 1 describes the data limitations influencing the choice of time periods). Economic measures are official data drawn from the Russian State Statistical Agency's (Goskomstat's) annual "Regions of Russia" statistical collection.

A combination of Internet sources and official print publications provided the bulk of election statistics and background information. These included the Central Election Commission's *Vybory glav ispolnitel'noi vlasti sub'ektov Rossiiskoi Federatsii, 1995–1997* and *Vybory v organy gosudarstvennoi vlasti sub'ektov Rossiiskoi Federatsii 1997–2000,* the official Web site of the Central Election Commission, Grigoryi Belonuchkin's "Politika" Web site, and electronic versions of regional newspapers too numerous to list here. Institutional variables like election laws were drawn from official regional government sites, the "Panorama" Web site (which contains regional election laws for each region through 1997), and once again the official publications of the Central Election Commission.[2]

Preview and Summary of Results

As with the survey analyses in chapter 4, the analyses presented in the remainder of this chapter paint a relatively (at least in comparison with the conventional wisdom on the topic) positive picture of Russian regional executive elections, indicating that, despite a vast number of shortcomings, these contests did enforce a degree of accountability for economic performance. Examining the results of the models presented in this chapter, one sees that changes in regional quality-of-life indicators (in this case, changes in adjusted wages) relative to those throughout Russia as a whole provided substantial leverage in determining incumbent success. In other words, incumbents ruling over regions in which wages were increasing at a higher rate relative to the national average were more likely to retain their posts but those in regions that lagged behind national dynamics were more likely to be voted out of office.

One should note that incumbents were not punished or rewarded for the absolute standard of living in their regions. Had this been the case, one might argue that incumbents in regions whose economic structure offered them certain advantages over poorly endowed regions would simply benefit from these fixed advantages and retain office regardless of the policies pursued during their terms. Instead, incumbents were sanctioned and rewarded for *relative changes* in regional performance before the election—a measure that at least partly reflects the success of regional economic policies in creating higher standards of living for local citizens. Finally, given the

Figure 5.1. Incumbent Electoral Success

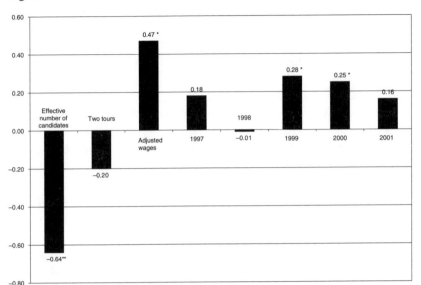

$*p \leq .05, ** p \leq .01; ***p \leq .001.$

fact that the relative standard-of-living measures are drawn from official economic statistics, the results of the aggregate analyses in this chapter suggest that the ballpark relative assessments made by voters in the survey analyses of chapter 4 roughly approximate the objective relative standing of regional economies.

Figure 5.1 provides a graphical summary of the results discussed in further detail throughout the remainder of this chapter. Similar to the histogram presented in the previous chapter, each bar in the figure represents the strength and direction of the relationship between the independent variable in question and the odds of a particular incumbent maintaining his or her post during an election. A comparison of the strength and directions of each relationship provides a sense of which factors were more determinant of incumbent success relative to all the other possible factors included in the model. The results indicate that after including controls for electoral competition (the "effective number of candidates" indicator) and electoral institutions (the "two tours" indicator), a measure of the growth or decline in the regions' adjusted wages relative to the national average change in adjusted wages exhibited a strong relationship to incumbent success. The year dummies, indicating the year that the election took place, also provide a good indicator of the fluctuations in incumbent success relative to those elections held in 1996. With the exception of slightly lower odds of re-election in 1998, regional executive incumbents experienced a marked increase in success rates relative to the 1996 contests, thus bearing out the observations discussed in chapter 3.

Nonetheless, a caveat is in order. The fact that the regional election competition measure provided a strongly significant indicator of incumbent success suggests that the impact of economic measures was partially dependent upon the degree of elite competition in regions. When this variable was removed from the model, the adjusted wage measure predicted little variation in incumbent success. Hence, if incumbents could use their positions at the head of regional political institutions to undercut potential competitors before and during electoral contests, they could deny voters of a choice of candidates and effectively shield themselves from a disgruntled electorate. Elections held incumbents accountable for the relative prosperity of the electorate, but only in those instances where viable alternative candidates were available to the voter.

Test Variables and Controls

Analysts generally measure electoral accountability by testing hypotheses relating various (usually socioeconomic) independent variables to measures of either vote shares or wins and losses.[3] For the sake of brevity, and in the interest of maximizing comparability with the Ukrainian case (after all, we cannot measure "how close" a Ukrainian governor came to being dismissed), this study subscribes to Manin, Przeworski, and Stokes's maxim that "what ultimately matters for accountability is not the popularity or even the share of the vote but survival in office."[4] Even if incumbents are "punished" with low shares of the vote, other factors—both systematic and purely coincidental—may intervene to prevent voters from "throwing the rascals out." In this respect, it is important to determine if "citizens can discern whether governments are acting in their best interest and sanction them appropriately, so that those incumbents who satisfy citizens' demands remain in office and those who do not lose it."[5]

To identify relationships of interest across such a diverse set of cases, one must carefully select controls to filter the effects of other factors influencing vote percentages and perhaps wins and losses. To begin, elections in Russia's regions occurred within subnational political systems characterized by marked variation in levels of political competition. Whereas the incumbent in a place like Tatarstan enjoys a widely acknowledged monopoly on regional political power, the incumbent in Pskovskaia Oblast's 2000 election faced opponents from a variety of regional political and economic interests. These different regional political structures may have a marked impact on incumbent vote shares that, in a cross-sectional study, might mask any relationship between regional performance and incumbent success. Some means must be identified to control for such variation without resorting to a region-by-region—and inevitably subjective—study of local competition.

A control variable representing the effective number of candidates in the first round of each election provides one solution to this problem. As indicated in chapter 3, the "*effective* number of candidates" measure (once again, see the appendix for the formula to calculate this measure) provides some sense of the extent of inter-elite competition by indicating the *quality* of opponents participating in the election. Elections in which the opponent ran against one strong candidate will yield a higher number of *effective* candidates than one in which a strong incumbent ran against several weak challengers.[6] Not only does this provide some indicator of the strength of opposition in the region, but it also controls for those cases in which the ballots were marked by excessive numbers of weak—and perhaps "fake"—candidates.

I also control for elections whose outcome is resolved in a second tour and for any impact of the number of candidates not accounted for in the *effective* number of candidates measure by including a variable indicating the *raw* number of candidates in the final election round.[7] In two respects, elections settled in the second round suggest higher levels of intraregional competition. First, the candidate clearly could not muster sufficient support in the region to obviate the second round. Second, regions in which the regional executive held sway over the greatest political and economic resources tend to have legislatures that support the regional executive. In many cases, these same legislatures passed election laws allowing the governor to win with a simple plurality. Thus, in combination with the effective number of candidates measure, these two controls should deal with much of the variation across elections resulting from differences in the strength and numbers of elites vying for power in the region.

The final set of controls consists of year dummy variables indicating whether or not the election in question occurred during a particular year. By including these dummy variables, I control for the year and cycle-specific conditions that might have had a universal impact on incumbent success during the period under examination. As discussed in chapter 2, in any given year of an election cycle, a number of general factors (e.g., the state of the national economy and the predominance of Yeltsin appointees during the 1996–97 cycle) may have increased or decreased the chances that *all* incumbents in a given year might successfully retain their office.

With regard to the economic indicators, what type of aggregate-level economic indicators might have an impact on support for incumbents in the Russian subnational setting? Regional economic growth, as measured by gross regional product (GRP), presents an obvious option, but it also raises a number of problems. Most important, as economic trends from 1999 to 2001 indicated, growth in such an indicator as GRP does not automatically translate into improved living standards for the population. In fact, during the year spanning December 1998 to December 1999, measures of real wages and pensions as a percentage of regional subsistence income continued to decline despite a broad upturn in many aggregate measures of productivity. Logically, voters within a setting in which macroeconomic growth indicators improve but standard of living continues to deteriorate might give precedence to those issues closest to their own well-being, such as real wages and pensions, unemployment rates, wage arrears, and regional poverty levels. Given these considerations, the analysis must include a full range of economic indicators.

Aside from asking which *type* of indicators might affect incumbents' election fortunes, another important issue concerns whether this effect is linked to static measures (e.g., GRP in 1999) or dynamic measures of change for the given indicators (e.g., change in GRP from 1998–99). A situation in which incumbents of regions characterized by high static measures of any given indicator are more likely to win elections than their counterparts in regions exhibiting lower static measures does not necessarily suggest accountability for regional performance. To take the Tiumenskaia Oblast example, the region's abundance of oil and other natural resources gives it an inherent economic advantage relative to other regions. However, the fact that the region had the highest real wage levels of any of the 1999–2001 election case regions provides little indication of the incumbent's effectiveness as an administrator. In fact, though the region exhibited the highest *static* real wage values, as a percentage of the regional cost of living, these wages were decreasing at a sharper rate than in any of the other case regions. Such a sharp decrease suggests changes in the regional economy that one might logically attribute to fluctuations in regional performance under the existing administration.

Conversely, one could also conceive of a poorly endowed region with relatively low static performance measures experiencing marked improvement in these measures under an able administrator. In either case, if election success is contingent upon static measures, there is little incentive for incumbents in naturally well-endowed regions to pursue policies that benefit their constituents, and incumbents in poorly endowed regions are doomed to be punished by an electorate discontented with factors that lie beyond the administration's control. Hence, accountability for economic performance is best promoted if the incumbent's election success is related to those measures that most logically represent the fruits of the incumbent's policies— change in economic indicators at some point before the election.

Another issue concerns the particular *form* in which variables should be included in the analysis. In choosing whether (and how) to transform the variables included in their models, analysts of Russian regional executive elections have essentially applied the logic of national-level elections to the subnational level.[8] In most cases, this entailed including measures of change or absolute levels of various economic indicators in the models and assessing how these measures were related (or not) to incumbent turnover. However, the often tepid results of these studies, which generally indicated little or no relationship between economic performance and incumbent success, and my own struggles with weak and sometimes fleeting associations, suggested some fault either with the measures employed or the viability of the economic voting thesis itself.[9] The latter contention certainly has its supporters among Russian and Western observers; however, my observations of numerous regional election campaigns in 1999–2001 consistently revealed a great deal of economic content in candidates' statements, campaign coverage, and media commentaries. Campaigns were so charged with talk of economic performance that it seems difficult to believe that, in the aggregate, some economic link to incumbent success does not exist. Furthermore, Russian's strong identification with their regions and the tendency to refer to governors as *khoziain* (literally, a manager or lord) suggests that regional voters would tend to attribute local conditions to governors' policymaking activities.

This hunch spurred a lengthy reexamination of the types of measures being employed in these studies and how they are related to both the psychology of the Russian regional voter and the means by which campaigns are carried out. The core issue concerns how voters measure the performance of a regional economy embedded within a larger national economic space. Do they see regional performance in absolute terms, so that *any* increase or decrease is taken as an indication of good governance over an improving economy? What if the average wages in a voter's region improved by 200 rubles while the rest of the country experienced increases of 500 or more? Would voters be thankful for the increase, or "punish" their incumbents for weak growth during an economic boom?

Drawing upon the logic of regional-level electoral accountability and research experience in Russia's provinces, I propose that regional voters most likely respond to their best assessments of their region's performance relative to the perceived concurrent performance of the rest of Russia during a certain period before elections. This apparently straightforward formulation carries two important methodological and empirical implications, which have generally been ignored in the extant literature.

First, a "best assessment" does not suggest that voters enter the polling station carrying the latest copy of Goskomstat's *Regiony Rossii* and make their voting decisions on the basis of complex comparisons of exact figures. However, the findings in chapter 4 and countless discussions with "provincials" from various walks of life strongly suggest a tendency to rank one's region among others on the basis of information gleaned from the media, personal interactions, visits to other regions, and the regional conventional wisdom that, though very apparent, defies any attempt to pinpoint its source. Of course these are mere sketches of the actual underlying realities, but if referenced in citizens' voting decisions, they may result in trends that roughly parallel variation of major indicators like GRP.

The second implication relates to the methods employed to measure performance. As indicated in chapter 2, many studies of subnational elections (and all known studies of subnational elections in Russia) tend to address the economic voting issue through the inclusion of raw performance indicators (either static measures or various measures of change) in their models. Unfortunately, in this particular case, this approach actually measures regional performance relative only to a limited subset of regions. In instances when all subnational units undergo elections during a relatively brief period, this poses no problems for the behavioral assumptions indicated above—the measure for the given region during that year is included in the regression model with measures from all other possible regions. However, in cases like Russia, where historical circumstances result in regional elections occurring in fits and starts across long cyclical periods, the inclusion of raw indicators for only the subset of elections under observation creates a situation in which the analyst is only measuring regional performance relative to those regions having elections during the same period. In essence, this approach implies that, in a year in which five regions underwent elections, voters in each of the five regions would assess their region's performance relative only to those of the four others—a clearly dubious proposition in a country with eighty-nine regions spanning eleven time zones.

If, as indicated in chapter 4, voters hold an impressionistic sense of their regions' standing relative to the rest of the country, measures must be employed that actually reflect regions' performances relative to the concurrent performance of the *entire* country.[10] Therefore, I break with the existing literature on Russian regional elections by employing annually standardized measures of change for each of the economic indicators in question. Using a concrete example of the annually standardized GRP measure, the formula is:

$$\text{Per capita GRP} = \frac{(Y_{rt} - Y_{rt-1}) - (\bar{Y}_t - \bar{Y}_{t-1})}{s_Y}$$

In this case, Y indicates the raw per capita GRP value, r the region, and t the year of the election. In essence, such a measure indicates the change on the indicator relative to all other regions during the election year by assessing the case region's distance above or below the national mean growth rate for that year.

Model and Final Results

In light of the binary nature of the dependent variable, this analysis employs logit techniques to help determine whether fluctuations in economic performance contributed to the odds of an incumbent maintaining office. Going into the initial tests, I expected positive relationships between incumbent victories and such factors as real and adjusted wages and pensions, budget revenues, and GRP, and a negative relationship with unemployment. More detailed descriptions of each of the independent variables are presented in the appendix. I ran numerous iterations of the model including the various economic indicators both singly and in clusters. However, because of the high correlations between the economic indicators, the clusters essentially "washed out" the effect of any single indicator.[11]

Furthermore, after estimating models including, individually, the variables

Table 5.1. Russian Incumbent Regional Executive Probability of Winning, Total Effects

Measure	Model 1	Model 2	Model 3
Effective number of candidates[log]	−0.63**	−0.64**	−0.64**
Two tours	−0.19	−0.17	−0.20
Δ Adjusted wages		0.38[a]	0.47*
1997	0.12	0.13	0.18
1998	−0.20	−0.12	−0.01
1999	0.27*	0.28*	0.28*
2000	0.25*	0.26*	0.25*
2001	0.16	0.13	0.16
Pseudo R^2	0.20	0.22	0.26
Model χ^2	35.64***	38.96***	44.50***
N	133.00	133.00	129.00

* $p \leq .05$, ** $p \leq .01$, *** $p \leq .001$.
[a]$p = 0.096$.

for wages, pensions, adjusted wages, adjusted pensions, unemployment, percentages of unprofitable firms, adjusted budget revenues, and GRP, I find that the adjusted wage measure yielded the most leverage in explaining incumbent election outcomes. Therefore, for the sake of parsimony, table 5.1 presents only the outcomes for the model including the annually standardized change in adjusted wages indicator.

Once again, the results are presented as *total effects,* indicating in this case the change in the likelihood that an incumbent governor wins an election as one moves from the independent variables minimum to its maximum value and while all other independent variables in the model are held at their means. Therefore, a value of −0.63 for the effective number of candidates variable indicates that, with all other variables held at their means, an incumbent governor's probability of winning in a region with the maximum effective number of candidates decreases by a factor of 0.63 when compared with an incumbent contesting an election in a region with the minimum effective number of candidates.

The column in table 5.1 headed "Model 1" indicates the results from a model estimated using only the candidate, tours, and year dummy controls. As expected, a higher number of effective competitors and a second election round significantly lower the probability of incumbent success by factors of 0.63 and 0.19, respectively. With the addition of the standardized change in adjusted waged measure, Model 2 indicates a respectable improvement over the previous model. The results for the adjusted wage measure indicate that an increase from the minimum to maximum standardized wage value increases the probability of an incumbent maintaining his or her position by a factor of 0.38. Furthermore, the increase in the model's χ^2 and pseudo R^2 provides further evidence for the relevance of the economic performance measure to incumbent success.

Of course, the relatively small number of cases raises the risk that even a single influential case might inordinately influence the size and direction of the coefficient and return results that might represent the impact of a small number of outliers rather than a general trend across all the cases.[12] Therefore, some diagnostic method should be employed to verify the presence or absence of such influential cases. The Cook's distance is a measure of influence that identifies the individual impact of each observation on a linear regression model with an eye toward determining whether a specific case or small number of cases had an inordinate impact on the results.[13] It does this by indicating the effect on the model of removing each observation from the sample and then assigning a distance coefficient to that case. Because the Cook's distance is used with linear regression models, the table plotted here actually represents an equivalent to the Cook's distance derived for use with nonlinear regression models like logit.

A perusal of figure 5.2 readily indicates that four cases (Tiumenskaia Oblast's 2001 election, Evenkiiskii Autonomous Okrug's 1997 election, Tul'skaia Oblast's 2001 election, and Lipetskaia Oblast's 1998 contest) stand out with Cook's distances greater than 0.3. Pending further investigation of these cases, they were removed before estimating Model 3. The results indicate that the removal of these cases actually strengthens the impact of the standardized adjusted wage measure, increasing the expected probability to 0.47 and improving the general fit of the model.

Overall, these results demonstrate the utility of the standardized economic change measures and suggest some provocative conclusions. As pointed out above, previous studies of economic voting in Russian gubernatorial elections indicated that, if economic voting was a factor at all, it was only relevant to a select number of cases during specific time periods.[14] However, the results for the standardized economic performance measure uncover a trend suggesting that the voting calculi exhibited by our voter in chapter 4 manifested itself in aggregate outcomes as well.[15] Furthermore, the fact that indicators of relative economic *change* during the past year featured strongly in the incumbent success model suggests that it was precisely policy outcomes rather than fixed regional economic advantages that determined voters'

Figure 5.2.   Scattergram Showing Cook's Distances, Incumbent Win/Loss Model

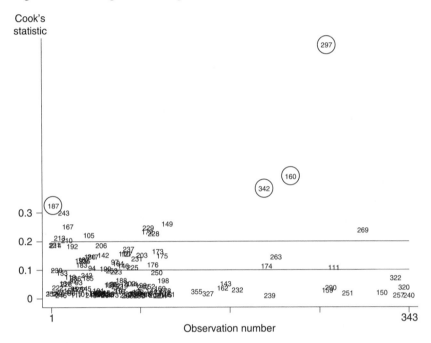

Note: Circled observation numbers represent influential cases dropped from Model 3 in table 5.1.

decisions to cast their votes for the incumbent. The model presented above explicitly focuses on relative change regardless of the particular fixed advantages or disadvantages that a region enjoys.

However, the model still points to the potential impact of incumbents' efforts to shield themselves from electoral competition through the use of various election tricks and the abuse of state office ("administrative resources"). The electoral competition variable, operationalized with the number of effective candidates in each election, also exhibited a strong relationship to incumbent success. As operationalized in this model, electoral competition might be affected through the use of clones, phony candidates, and efforts between elections to undercut potential candidates within the region. Earlier iterations of this model that excluded the electoral competition variable resulted in negligible relationships between various economic performance indicators and incumbent success.

Because the models presented above indicate that *with all other conditions held equal,* regional performance and the electorates' economic welfare has an impact on incumbent success, one can thus conclude that elections in which incumbents faced weakened opponents were less likely to return accountability-promoting outcomes. The extent of an executive's control over the regional political process and his or her ability to manipulate election outcomes with clones, phony candidates, and other dirty tactics could thus have a substantial impact on the accountability question. Though the results diverge significantly from conventional wisdom, which held that these elections were fully controlled by entrenched incumbents, the significance of the electoral competition indicator suggests that the system left much room for improvement. This issue will be taken up in further detail in chapter 7.

Elected versus Appointed Executives

This chapter has presented a number of surprising and encouraging results regarding the link between elections and regional economic performance in Russia. Despite the claims that elections legitimize—or even promote—the pilfering of regions by predatory political elites, the outcomes of this analysis indicate a robust link between growth in regional wages and incumbent electoral fortunes. In the aggregate, successful regions appeared to promote successful incumbents.

Nonetheless, merely demonstrating a positive relationship between regional performance and incumbent electoral success tells us too little about the relative effectiveness of a centralized system of appointees versus a system of regionally elected officials in the post-Soviet setting. Furthermore, the work of public finance specialists in other "transition" cases like China has suggested that systems of appointed officials better promote subnational economic growth. Though anecdotal accounts and a quick perusal of performance measures suggest that regions in the unitary states of the former Soviet Union are no better off than Russia, an explicit exploration of the appointment process in these states promises to provide both a better indication of the relative effectiveness of the two systems and a means to draw out some of the implications involved in the establishment of either type of state structure. Chapter 6 presents such a comparison through an exploration of regional executive turnover in Russia's western neighbor—Ukraine.

Notes

1. Witness the elderly woman overheard on a bus in Samarskaia Oblast complaining about local conditions and explaining how life is much better in "Lenin's homeland"—stagnant Ul'ianovskaia Oblast, where even the region's famed social safety net had failed. Another example comes from the director of Permskaia Oblast's Goskomstat office, who sneeringly asked the author why he was working from a backward agricultural region like Samarskaia Oblast instead of a resource rich industrial giant like Permskaia Oblast. In fact, both regions share similar performance measures and Samarskaia Oblast is certainly known more for its energy, transportation, and industrial resources (including the giant AvtoVAZ) than its farms.

2. The appendix contains descriptive statistics for each of the measures.

3. More often than not, the focus is on the incumbent party or governing official. For an exception, see Joshua Tucker, "Reconsidering Economic Voting: Party Type vs. Incumbency in Transition Countries," paper presented at the Annual Meeting of the American Political Science Association, Atlanta, September 1999.

4. Bernard Manin, Adam Przeworksi, and Susan Stokes, "Introduction," in *Democracy, Accountability and Representation,* ed. Adam Przeworski, Bernard Manin, and Susan Stokes (Cambridge: Cambridge University Press, 1999), 18.

5. Jose Antonio Cheibub and Adam Przeworski, "Accountability for Economic Outcomes," in *Democracy, Accountability, and Representation,* 225. Nonetheless, an examination of the connection between regional conditions and incumbent vote shares is a potentially interesting way to assess the effects of various tactics employed by unpopular Russian governors to maintain office with a minimum of popular support.

6. The actual analysis uses a *logged* effective number of candidates. A histogram of a variable indicating the raw number of candidates in each election indicated that the distribution was skewed quite strongly to the right. The log transformation results in a distribution more closely approximating normal distribution.

7. For the raw number of candidates variable, the "final round" may be a first- or second-round election. First-round elections will include those where plurality rule-based regional election laws made provisions only for a single round or where one of the candidates took more than 50 percent of the vote in a majority-rule-based system. Second-round elections include those held in regions characterized by majority-rule-based elections and where two candidates entered a second election round after no candidate succeeded in gathering more than 50 percent of the vote in a first election round.

8. Steven Solnick, "Gubernatorial Elections in Russia, 1996–1997," *Post-Soviet Affairs,* 14 (1998): 48–80; G. V. Golosov, "Povedenie izbiratelei v Rossii: Teoreticheskie perspektivy i rezultaty regionalnikh vyborov," *Polis* 4 (1997): 44–56; Andrew Konitzer-Smirnov, "Incumbent Election Fortunes and Regional Economic Performance during Russia's 2000–2001 Regional Executive Election Cycle," *Post-Soviet Affairs* 19 (2003): 46–79; Christopher Marsh, "Social Capital and Grassroots Democracy in Russia's Regions: Evidence from the 1999–2001 Gubernatorial Elections," *Demokratizatsiya: The Journal of Post-Soviet Democratization* 10 (2002): 19–36; Bryon Moraski and William M. Reisinger, "Explaining Electoral Competition across Russia's Regions," *Slavic Review* 62 (2003): 278–301.

9. E.g., in an earlier study, I identified a relationship between economic performance and incumbent success during the 2000–1 elections but not during the 1995–96

contests. See Konitzer-Smirnov, "Incumbent Election Fortunes and Regional Economic Performance."

10. Another interesting path of inquiry is to measure regional performance relative to other regions within a specific federal district (*okrug*).

11. By itself, the correlations between the converted economic performance measures lend additional credibility to this method of adjusting performance measures to the federal mean. Indicators like raw adjusted wages, industrial output, and unemployment figures are poorly correlated with raw GRP figures. However, when adjusted to the federal mean, the resulting correlations demonstrate that the variables in question follow the same upward and downward trends, indicating that this adjustment represents the general relative performance of the regional economy. Exceptions to this rule were found in the cases of unemployment and the relative change in the percentage of unprofitable firms—both measures that are particularly subject to misreporting.

12. Analysts should especially be cautioned when including Moscow, Saint Petersburg, and other particularly resource rich regions like Khanty-Mansiiskii Autonomous Okrug in their quantitative analyses.

13. See J. Scott Long and Jeremy Freese, *Regression Models for Categorical Dependent Variables Using Stata* (College Station, Tex.: Stata Press, 2001); and D. Pregibon, "Logistic Regression Diagnostics," *Annals of Statistics* 9 (1981): 705–24.

14. Konitzer-Smirnov, "Incumbent Election Fortunes and Regional Economic Performance."

15. Readers familiar with my previous work in this area might note that these results differ somewhat from those presented in earlier analyses, where relative change in GRP stood as a strong indicator of incumbent success. This is mostly attributable to the different time spans under examination. The key issue is whether incumbent success is tied to a major indicator of economic success—something that the conventional wisdom on the topic denies. Hence, for the purpose of this study, it is less important whether the best indicator is wages or GRP; and in any case, these two indicators correlate rather strongly with one another (with a correlation coefficient of 0.69).

Chapter 6

Russia's Regional Executive Elections in Comparative Perspective

Tam khorosho, gde nas net. (Life is good, wherever we don't live.)
—Russian Proverb

The results of the analyses in chapters 4 and 5 suggest that, despite a host of seemingly insurmountable challenges and a popular consensus that discredited their worth as accountability mechanisms, regional elections in Russia appeared to have served some accountability function. Voters focused their attention on regional executives and weighed their performance on the basis of assessments of the region's well-being relative to that of other regions. Aggregate-level analyses also demonstrated some link between incumbent success and economic growth, as measured with the annually standardized gross regional product (GRP). Though individual cases still indicated that "bad" governors managed to maintain their hold on power, overall trends suggested that voters could use the ballot box to enforce some measure of responsibility for regional performance.

But merely demonstrating a degree of regional-level accountability within a single federal system featuring elected subnational officials proves insufficient to challenge the arguments of those who contend that a centralized system of subnational appointees might perform *even better.* During the middle to late 1990s, a particular strand of institutional economics going by the name of "market-preserving federalism" focused its attention first on China's system of subnational governance and then on that of Russia, arguing that one of the explanations for China's apparent economic success, and Russia's continuing decline, lay with specific features of each country's state and political structures.

Although the bases for this conclusion rested on a number of factors other than the method of choosing and removing leaders, work by other analysts suggested that subnational elections were partially responsible for the malaise Russia faced in the late 1990s. According to these analysts, elected officials in office during a highly decentralized economic transition like the one under way in Russia simply maintained too much control over regional political systems to be held responsible for economic outcomes. Furthermore, the temptation to undertake populist policies, or simply forgo the austerity measures necessary to push the country through the difficult transition, was much greater for elected officials than for their appointed counterparts.

Looking at the results of the previous chapters, one may find some bases to reject such conclusions. However, without an explicit comparison with a system of appointed subnational figures, one might still contend that, though Russia's elections appear to have squeezed some measure of accountability from regional-level political institutions, a system of appointed governors might have yielded even better outcomes. This is essentially a question of efficiency—the electorate may be capable of punishing or rewarding its governor, but all the populism, vote fraud, and election manipulation inherent in Russian regional elections makes this a much less efficient process than a system of appointees operating under a conscientious, objective, and development-oriented central government.[1] Through a focused comparison of unitary and federalized former Soviet states, this chapter provides a better means to assess the relative advantages of each system in the post-Soviet context.

Theoretical Expectations . . . and Disappointments

Proponents of democratic decentralization tend to present a common set of benefits that theoretically accrues to a decentralizing political system.[2] These benefits typically include greater accountability for policy outcomes, higher levels of responsiveness to citizens' needs, greater civic engagement among citizens, the promotion of plurality (both political and ethnic/cultural), and the provision of a counterweight to authoritarianism. Though each benefit is a key component of the decentralization argument, given the focus of this study, I forgo discussion of the last three benefits and concentrate instead on issues of accountability and responsiveness.

Theoretically, decentralization promotes accountability and responsiveness because the proximity of local governments both focuses the attention of local policymakers on the needs of their constituents and improves the ability of citizens to monitor and assign responsibility for policy outcomes. As Diamond indicates, it is difficult for national governments to recognize, or even care about, the specific needs of individual localities. A lack of incentives and the sheer difficulty of monitoring and prescribing policies for myriad jurisdictions prevent national actors from producing tailor-made policies to meet local needs. Furthermore, disgruntled citizens of one locality face nearly insurmountable obstacles when attempting to "punish" a national lawmaker. In this instance, by devolving government responsibilities to a lower level and allowing citizens to choose their local administrators, it becomes easier to monitor and impose electoral sanctions on lawmakers.[3] As Joseph Shumpeter puts it, decentralization promotes citizen participation by narrowing one's political space to "the little field which the individual citizen's mind encompasses with a full sense of its reality."[4]

The case for the link between decentralization and accountability is also echoed among economists and specialists in public finance. Regional and local governments theoretically provide more efficient outcomes by allowing localities to set tax rates, policy priorities, and other economic and financial goods according to the specific needs of the region in question. When combined with free factor flows and clearly defined policy jurisdictions, decentralized policymaking can promote a sort of interregional competition that spurs local governments to persistently seek out the most efficient policy packages for their jurisdictions. In this instance, governments are punished or rewarded for policy outcomes by citizens who either "vote with their feet"—or with their ballots.[5]

Unfortunately, as indicated in chapter 3, the empirical record provided by subnational election studies across the globe suggests only a tenuous link between decentralization and accountability/responsiveness. Though seldom cited in discussions of decentralization, democratization, and development, an extensive body of work focused on the United States, Canada, Western Europe, and Latin American countries indicates rather murky connections between the success of elected subnational governments and measures of subnational economic performance.[6] In the case of countries with stronger party systems, this often reflects the tendency of citizens to cast votes for regional officials on the basis of whether or not they share party affiliations with more prominent central government actors—what Niemi, Stanley, and Vogel refer to as a presidential referendum effect. In these cases, elected regional officials are often punished or rewarded for factors and outcomes that lie entirely beyond their official responsibilities.[7]

Systems of elected regional officials in postcommunist states—specifically Russia—raise additional challenges. The number of potential obstacles to electoral accountability in Russia has been alluded to throughout the text and will be treated in more detail in chapter 7. However, for the purposes of this chapter, I briefly recapitulate the four obstacles that I feel are most relevant to the study at hand.

First, though weak party systems substantially reduce the likelihood of the referendum effect evidenced in countries like the United States, the individualistic nature of political competition raised its own obstacles to accountability by complicating voters' support calculi and lessening the incentives for elected officials to follow any particular set of policies during their term in office. Second, poorly established norms of competition (as best exemplified by the prevalence of bomb threats, beatings, and contract killings during regional election campaigns); poor supervision and enforcement of election laws; and, again, weak party structures reduced electoral competition to an all-or-nothing contest between regional power elites who can (and have) resorted to almost any means to win. Voters were subjected to a cacophony of often baseless claims in regional media, "phony" candidates, vote fraud, legal battles, and unpredictable election processes that may or may not reach their resolution according to established election laws. Third, poorly defined policy jurisdictions, budgetary structures that remove the incentive to pursue performance-oriented policies, and a lack of budgetary transparency undermined the ability of even economists to assess the actions of incumbents. Fourth and finally, legacies of the Soviet past combined with the universal tendency of voters to focus on short-term, quality-of-life issues (if not their pocketbook per se) resulted in a certain voter myopia that could reward incumbents for short-lived increases in living standards or punish them for perhaps more prudent long-term policies. In terms of issues facing a typical Russian region, a rising gross national product might not have yielded election dividends when accompanied by slow wage growth and price liberalization in the housing and energy sectors.[8]

These factors, along with certain implications of the so-called market-preserving federalism (MPF) literature, led some policy advisers and analysts working within the sphere of economics and public finance to suggest that a system of appointed regional officials might provide certain economic growth advantages over the regional electoral institutions currently operating in Russia. In particular, Montinola, Qian, and Weingast's somewhat loose application of MPF to the case of China spawned a series of comparisons between the relative success of China's system of subnational administration and that currently practiced in Russia.[9] Though most of the comparisons undertaken in the wake of this study focused on the issue of budget constraints, central government restraint, and clearly defined policy jurisdictions, Blanchard and Shleifer suggested that China's combination of market reforms without democratization provided the degree of central control necessary to pursue and enforce reforms in the regions—in other words, much of the blame for Russia's current troubles lay with the system of elected regional executives.[10]

But like the broader literature on decentralization and local democracy, Blanchard and Shleifer's tentative conclusions—and the MPF theory in general—remain hampered by a lack of empirical support. Examining one of the theory's flagship cases, Landry demonstrated that, whereas China may exhibit some of the fiscal prescriptions of MPF, there is little evidence supporting the implication that Chinese subnational officials are removed or promoted according to the success of the economy within their jurisdictions.[11] Hence, MPF theorists created an elegant institutionalist model without demonstrating whether central governments actually focus on subnational performance and impose the necessary sanctions (e.g., dismissal) to ensure that subnational policymakers concentrate their efforts upon the success of their jurisdictions. Just as advocates of democratic decentralization too readily assumed that regional elections provide a smooth mechanism of subnational accountability, proponents of centralized reform seem too quick to make rather demanding assumptions regarding the prescience and interests of central authorities.

One might, however, also level the criticism that, despite the loosely analogous economic reforms being undertaken in China and Russia, these states share little in terms of history, culture, and systems of government. Therefore, as the premise for this study, perhaps a better test of the relative accountability of appointed as opposed to elected officials within states undergoing market transformations might be found in a comparison between the two former Soviet states of Russia and Ukraine.[12] Having a common history dating back to the state of Kyiv Rus and having been constituent parts of the same state (be it the Russian Empire or Soviet Union) since the Periaslav Treaty of 1654, modern-day Ukraine and Russia share a large number of historical, cultural, political, and economic characteristics that allow us to "control out" many of the potentially influential factors that might hinder comparisons of cases like Russia and China. Hence, the juxtaposition of the recent political and economic histories of Ukraine and Russia promises to offer further insights into the relative advantages of different state structures within the former Soviet Union.

On the face of things, these two cases raise a set of challenges to the thesis that centralized authorities are more successful in promoting regional growth. In the most general terms, despite the differences in their state structures, Ukraine and the Russian Federation have experienced roughly parallel economic fortunes, with Ukraine actually suffering a substantially deeper contraction from its preindependence gross national product.[13] Furthermore, both suffered harsh economic downturns throughout the 1990s, which reversed themselves only after economic crises in 1998 and a turn to steady growth in 2000. Certainly these similarities, and Ukraine's relatively poorer economic performance, could be traced to any number of other factors, such as differences in natural resources, geopolitics, and sheer geographic size and potential. However, a closer examination of the actual workings of Ukraine's unitary state structure provides further evidence against the applicability of MPF-based arguments promoting the appointment of subnational policymakers.

Looking more closely at the specific mechanisms prescribed by analysts like Blanchard and Shleifer, both journalistic accounts and the work of Kimitaka Matsuzato suggest that, ever since the brief flirtation with regional executive elections in 1994–95, Ukrainian regional executive turnover has been determined more by the political expedience of actors in Kyiv than by considerations of the executives' performances as managers of their regional economies. Among the most common accusations is that President Leonid Kuchma dismissed governors who failed to mobilize a sufficiently large number of voters in support of propresidential parties. Aside from elections, Igor' Guzhva suggests that Ukraine's unitary state structure also helped the president stamp out occasional political fires by controlling information in the relatively more isolated provinces. Taking a recent example, Guzhva attributes the relative calm in Ukraine's regions following the 2000 "cassette scandal" to the spin control of the president's loyal regional executives.[14] These factors alone challenge the contention that centrally appointed officials might yield anything other than a regional governing elite beholden to the political interests of its president.

The above discussion perhaps raises more questions than answers, but it also demonstrates how the juxtaposition of regional governance structures in Russia and Ukraine might provide an opportunity to examine the relative benefits of appointed and executive regional officials in post-Soviet states.

What types of outcomes are promoted through these different state structures? Which structures better promote regional living standards? Are certain structures more likely to reflect narrow elite interests? In the remainder of this chapter, I examine these and other questions through a comparison of the quantitative relationships between regional conditions and executive turnover in Russia and Ukraine.

Ukraine

For the first half of the 1990s, Ukrainian center–region relations appeared to hang in the balance between a unitary state and varying degrees of decentralization. Ukraine's Law on Local Self Government (February 1992) established the legal basis for post-Soviet subnational governance and placed substantial policymaking powers in the hands of regional councils.[15] Nevertheless, the center's attack on regional prerogatives began almost immediately. In March 1992, a presidential decree established presidential representatives in each of Ukraine's regions who would effectively act as the executives of regional governments and report directly to the president.[16] However, Leonid Kravchuk's effort to reign over the regions proved short-lived. Ukraine's deepening economic crisis resulted in greater pressure for regional autonomy in the eastern regions, and strikes and unrest eventually led to Kravchuk's late 1993 decree granting greater autonomy to regional administrations, in particular eastern oblasti, for a period of two years. With presidential elections approaching, parliament took advantage of Kravchuk's vulnerability to pass the Law on the Formation of Local Government Bodies. This law stipulated the elimination of all presidential representatives as of June 26, 1994, and established elected oblast council heads as effective regional executives. In effect, these changes freed regional governments from direct subordination to the presidential representatives and made them "adjuncts" of the Verkhovna Rada (the national parliament).

Despite eleventh-hour efforts to recast himself as a supporter of regional autonomy, Kravchuk lost to the challenger Kuchma during the July 1994 presidential elections. Nonetheless, the balance of power once again shifted against the regions—for despite having run on a platform promoting greater decentralization, Kuchma immediately embarked on a long struggle with the parliament to once again centralize the nation under presidential control. Heading off an attempt by the parliament to hand even more powers to regional legislative bodies, Kuchma issued an August 1994 decree subordinating the heads of oblast councils to the president. The Law on Power (June 1995) granted Kuchma the power to appoint all chairmen of local councils as heads of regional and local administrations. These were followed by later decrees in January 1996 that subordinated village, settlement, and city council chairs to the president and gave them extended executive powers within their regions.

This process of centralization was extended and crystallized in the 1996 Constitution. Following the long struggle with the parliament, the Constitution went beyond the Law on Power to firmly establish Ukraine as a unitary state. Regional executives no longer concomitantly held positions as heads of regional councils and instead became part of a strong vertical executive power running from the president down to the village level.[17] As indicated in figure 6.1, Kuchma made sufficiently frequent use of his power of appointment—particularly following the 1998 parliamentary elections.

However, the legal changes of 1995–96 once again failed to fully institutionalize Ukraine's unitary state structure, and soon after, the diffusion of political power to the regions began anew. Before the presidential election of 1999, Kuchma faced a problem similar to his predecessor's before the 1996 elections. Lacking strong party structures in the regions, the president was forced to rely on his appointees in the regions to organize campaigns and mobilize voters. To expand the power of these executives and tie them to the president's campaign, Kuchma gave unprecedented powers over key assets in their regions. Restructuring in the gas and energy sectors furthered the process of regionalization by transferring valuable energy assets from Kyiv oligarchs to regional business elites.[18]

These developments—combined with growing challenges to the political order established under Kuchma (beginning with the cassette scandal in 2000 and continuing through the current struggle over constitutional reform) and political maneuvering before and after the 2004 presidential elections —once again raised the issue of expanded regional powers, including the institution of elected regional executives. Calls for such a reform arose from a number of different quarters, including Kyiv mayor Alexander Omelchenko, Nasha Ukraina faction leader Viktor Yushchenko, and even Premier Minister Anatoly Kinakh.[19]

As one might expect, the response within the presidential administration was decidedly cooler and exhibited elements of Kuchma's ongoing attempts to maintain the delicate balance between sufficiently powerful but subordinate regional officials. Characteristic of this gambit were Kuchma's statement that "in order to have elected governors, we need constructive (political)

Figure 6.1. Quarterly Ukrainian Regional Executive Turnover, June 1995–December 2000 (number of persons is shown on top of bar; below bar, "1995–3" = third quarter of 1995, etc.)

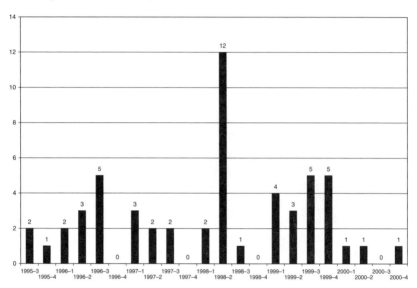

Note: Turnover figures for a given year may differ slightly from those in Matsuzato's work discussed in the main text. This reflects a different approach to coding "promotions" of regional executives. In most instances, turnover was treated as a dismissal unless there was strong evidence that this was in fact a promotion to a higher position.
Source: Slavic Research Center, Hokkaido University, "Politichna elita ukrains'kikh regioniv," at http://src-h.slav.hokudai.ac.jp/ukrregions/index.html.

counterbalances" and a quote from vice head of administration Oleg Demin stating, "*In time* [author's emphasis], I think we will come to a system of elected governors."[20]

The events surrounding the 2004 presidential elections completely altered Ukraine's political landscape, and at the time of writing the future of center-periphery relations under the Yushchenko administration remains uncertain. However, given Ukraine's history with appointed regional executives and the challenges presented by Kuchma's appointees in the regions, one should expect a continuation of "business as usual"—appointed executives ruling at the bidding of the president—in the near term. Looking further into the future, the question remains as to whether Yushchenko will implement the regional elections that he himself supported during his time as an opponent of the Kuchma regime.

Preview and Summary of Results

The analyses presented in this section challenge the arguments offered by proponents of appointed regional executives and indicate that regional executive dismissals in Ukraine were driven largely by the president's narrow political interests rather than by concerns over regional conditions. The success of the incumbent president and his affiliated parties during national elections provided much stronger indicators of regional executive security than did regional economic performance.

These results indicate that regional executive appointees were held more responsible for the strength and success of their regional electoral machines than for nurturing regional economic development. In the broader context of this study, for all the Russian regional executive electoral system's flaws, these contests still yielded better accountability for regional executive election outcomes than the system of appointees operating in neighboring Ukraine.

Looking ahead, the results also bear negative implications for the future of a Russia without regional executive elections. Contemporary Russia and Ukraine share a number of political, economic, and social characteristics, and we might expect a Russian system of regional appointees to work much in the same manner as its counterpart in Ukraine. Hence, the citizens in Russia's regions stand to lose a great deal from the elimination of regional executive elections.

Figure 6.2 provides a graphical summary of the results discussed in further detail throughout the remainder of this chapter. As in the summary figures in previous chapters, each bar in the figure represents the strength and direction of the relationship between the independent variable in question and the odds of a particular appointed regional executive maintaining his or her post during a given three-month period. A comparison of the strength and direction of each relationship provides a sense of which factors were more determinant of the odds of retaining office relative to all the other possible factors included in the model.

A perusal of the results clearly indicates that regional executives were sanctioned and rewarded largely for their ability to get out the vote for the

Figure 6.2. Ukrainian Regional Executive Turnover (percent)

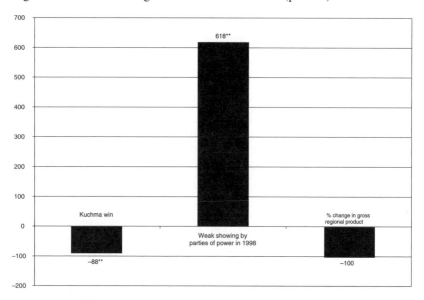

* $p \le .05$, ** $p \le .01$; *** $p \le .001$.
Source: Graphic representation of the author's logit results presented in this chapter.

incumbent president and affiliated political parties. Economic variables were weakly related to an increase in the odds of dismissal, but this relationship proved less stable than that between the odds of dismissal and the incumbent president's electoral success in the region in question. Furthermore, when compared with the economic change indicator, the variable measuring the success of the propresidential parties during the 1998 Verkhovna Rada election provided vastly greater leverage in determining the odds of incumbent governor dismissal.

A Closer Look at Ukraine's Appointee System

Aside from the occasional media report speculating about the causes of a recent dismissal, regional executive turnover in Ukraine remains a relatively underexamined issue. In one of the few exceptions, Kimitaka Matsuzato presents an exploration of potential economic and political factors contributing to Ukrainian president Kuchma's decisions to remove regional executives during the period from 1996 to 2000.[21] Matsuzato argues that regional outcomes in federal election campaigns were the best determinant of executive turnover with regions where the "parties of power" gained the most votes demonstrating the lowest rates of turnover.

Unfortunately, though Matsuzato's study is remarkable as being one of the few to deal directly with this topic, the author's reliance on simple bivariate correlations, questionable choices of variables, and sometimes generous interpretations of the data leave some doubt about the validity of the results. Nonetheless, Matsuzato's work suggests a number of potential indicators and provides a useful point of departure for this study. First and foremost, the analysis emphasizes the potential importance of political factors such as election outcomes in determining the odds of incumbent turnover. As Matsuzato suggests, regional executive performance may be more determined by the ability to "get out the vote" for the incumbent president and "parties of power" than any measure of the executive's performance as a regional manager.

To address this issue, two election variables are included in the model. The first consists of a simple dichotomous measure indicating a value of 1 for each quarter if President Kuchma attracted the most votes in the region during the final round of the most recent presidential election. This indicates the extent to which each region's executive was able to maintain popular support for Kuchma and transform this support into votes during elections. However, as the remarkable increase in the number of executive dismissals following the 1998 Verkhovna Rada elections suggest, parliamentary elections may also have an important impact on regional executive turnover.

Drawing upon the arguments of Matsuzato and other observers, I include another dichotomous measure indicating the electoral fortunes of a bloc of parties of power during the 1998 Verkhovna Rada election.[22] The indicator takes a value of 1 during the first two quarters of 1998 if, within the region in question, the sum of the vote percentages for eight political parties tied to the Kuchma administration falls below the median (calculated across all Ukraine's regions) summed percentages of these parties.

To assess the potential impact of the clearest alternative to an explanation based on voter mobilization, I also consider performance measures—particularly the success of the regional economy during the term of an appointed executive's tenure. As in the Russian case, certain considerations about the nature of subnational accountability and conditions unique to systems characterized by appointed regional executives demanded a careful selection of indicators.

Appointees and elected officials theoretically "serve different masters." Appointees are ultimately responsible to the appointing authority, whereas elected officials—once again, at least in theory—must serve the needs of their electorate. With regard to choices of economic indicators, this suggests that different types of measures will be more or less important for different types of executives. One would expect the economic performance of an elected official to be weighed more in terms of those issues that affect the electorate the most—employment, wages, cost of living, and so on. Appointees, conversely, are beholden to central authorities who, among other things, are most interested in tax revenues from the region in question. Hence, though still testing the effects of more direct standard-of-living measures like wages and employment, I expect measures of tax revenues or aggregate performance measures like GRP (which are more likely to directly effect the tax base) to play a more important role.

Furthermore, the choice between static measures as opposed to measures of growth and decline also arises in the Ukrainian case. As in the Russian model, I stand by the assertion that changes in economic measures during the year before the turnover event are more likely culprits for an executive's dismissal than a static measure. To echo arguments from the Russian case, if static measures "matter," then the regional executive of Zakarpattia (one of Ukraine's more poorly endowed regions) is in perpetual danger of removal, regardless of economic trends within his oblast.[23]

With all these considerations in mind, the Ukrainian turnover models included measures of the percentage change in regional per capita GRP, employment, average household wages, investment in fixed capital, small enterprises, and regional tax revenues along with the electoral indicators described above.[24] In terms of the dependent variable, for each of the region-quarters, a simple binary dismissal variable indicates whether an executive was dismissed during that quarter in question.[25]

I employ a fixed-effects, cross-sectional, time-series logit model with year dummies to estimate the impact of the above-listed independent variables on the likelihood of a regional executive dismissal. To remind the reader of the technique briefly described in the appendix, the cross-sectional, time-series approach examines the relationship between a dependent and set of independent variables for a particular cross-section of cases (here, Ukrainian regions) during a period of time. In this specific instance, I examine the relationship between a set of political and economic indicators and the odds of a particular executive's dismissal during any given three-month period from 1996 to 2000 for each of Ukraine's twenty-seven major subnational units.

Because this model employs a binomial (dismissal/nondismissal) dependent variable, I then analyze the cross-sectional, time-series data with the same logit technique employed in the previous two chapters. The main difference in this case is that, because I examine the same set of regional cases across a period of twenty quarters, I cannot use standard logit techniques because fixed features specific to each region will violate specific assumptions of the technique and yield biased results. One way to resolve this problem is to parse out those fixed features of each region and examine only the relationship between variables that actually "vary" and the dependent variable. The fixed-effects estimator accomplishes this by eliminating a host of unobserved effects characteristic of each of the regions in question while the year dummies control for conditions specific to each of the years covered in the analysis.[26]

The combination of these two approaches allows the analyst to focus primarily on the relationship between his or her variables of interest by clearing up much of the "noise" resulting from fixed characteristics of different regions and idiosyncratic features of a given year, which affected all regions similarly. Having controlled for these factors, the resulting coefficients are then interpreted in much the same way as with a standard logit model. Like the cross-sectional models in previous chapters, each value indicates the impact of a particular independent variable on the odds or probability of a specific outcome (in this case, retention of office) of the dependent variable when all other variables in the model are held at their means. However, in interpreting the results, I remind the reader that table 6.1 presents odds ratios rather than predicted probabilities. A brief explanation indicating how to interpret these odds ratios is presented in the appendix. The results for the model are presented in table 6.1

Five different models were estimated, starting with a model containing the full set of political, economic, and year dummy variables. As anticipated, the predictors indicating whether Kuchma won during the most recent election and whether the combined vote of the parties of power fell below the national median during the 1998 elections provide the most leverage in determining the odds of dismissal. The explanatory power of these indicators is further demonstrated by their apparent impact on the other nonpolitical variables in the model. As shown in table 6.1, a comparison of Models 1 and 2 clearly reveals major changes in the economic measures' odds ratios (most particularly, the employment and wage measures) after the removal of the political indicators in Model 1. Such results are attributable to the large amount of variance accounted for by the political variables, which

Table 6.1. Ukrainian Regional Executive Turnover, Odds Ratios

Measure	Model 1	Model 2	Model 3	Model 4	Model 5
Kuchma win	0.10**	—	0.12**	—	0.13**
Parties of power in 1998	9.03**	—	7.18**	—	7.14**
% Δ gross regional product	0.00	0.00[a]	0.00[b]	0.00*	—
% Δ employment	24.99	4.76	—	—	—
% Δ budget revenues	1.21	1.15	—	—	—
% Δ average income	68.60	1.07	—	—	—
% Δ investment	0.50	0.69	—	—	—
% Δ small enterprises	0.19	0.35	—	—	—
1997	0.17	0.10*	1.32	0.36	10.46*
1998	0.11	0.13	0.98	0.53	11.42*
1999	—	—	14.16	4.49	19.39***
2000	0.03*	0.18	—	—	—
Model χ^2	44.26***	22.95**	39.80***	21.04***	35.35***
N	368.00	368.00	368.00	368.00	368.00

* $p \le .05$, ** $p \le .01$, *** $p \le .001$.
[a] $p = 0.062$.
[b] $p = 0.051$.

essentially consume much of the noise in the model (nonetheless, the correlations between the economic and political variables are minimal, and the economic variables remain statistically insignificant).

In contrast to the other economic indicators, the per capita GRP measure also provided a relatively strong and significant predictor, which increased in relevance when the political variables were removed from the equation in Model 2.[27] Model 3 eliminated all the economic measures except per capita GRP and combined this with the year dummies and electoral measures. This produced a model relatively strong in predictive power and efficiency, but the borderline ($p = 0.051$) significance exhibited by the GRP measure suggests that even this economic factor was less stable than the political measures. The remaining two columns of table 6.1 (Models 4 and 5) further demonstrate the strength of models using only the electoral or the GRP measure with the year dummies. A comparison of the two models again suggests that the political measures still account for the most variance in Model 1, which includes both the political variables and the GRP measure.

Overall, the results for the Ukrainian model bear out many of the notions presented by previous commentators. National election results appear strongly linked to the odds of dismissal and easily outweigh the effects of various performance measures and region-specific factors. This suggests that the primary measure of one's success as a Ukrainian executive under the Kuchma administration was to mobilize voters for the president and his parties of power. In this respect, speculations by analysts like Blanchard and Shleifer that appointed officials may provide more efficient means to promote reforms and economic growth appear to fail in the Ukrainian case. For Ukraine, unitary government simply brought Kyiv's political struggles to the regions.

Nonetheless, as with the standardized adjusted-wage measure in the Russian case, the analysis of Ukrainian turnover yielded one surprise. To remind the reader, Matsuzato argues that economic factors played no role in the decision to remove governors and that the current system therefore provided little or no linkage between regional economic performance and political outcomes. However, the persistence of the measure indicating the percentage change in per capita GRP suggests that, even after controlling for the electoral interests of the Kuchma administration, economic performance played at least some small role in decisions to remove regional executives.[28] Given the predominance of the electoral factor in the model, this observation perhaps provides little consolation for Ukraine's future economic development. Nonetheless, it challenges some of the most negative assessments of Ukraine's existing system of center–region relations and once again points to the importance of moving beyond simple bivariate correlations when assessing regional political developments (or nearly any political phenomenon, for that matter).[29]

Conclusions

The current debates about the relative effectiveness of elected versus appointed subnational governments in so-called transition states has recently produced a growing number of arguments in favor of the latter. However, results from this comparison of Russia and Ukraine challenge the suggestion that appointed subnational governments increase accountability for economic outcomes. The Ukrainian case demonstrates exactly the types of dynamics that many proponents of federalism most fear: a central government making decisions about the nature and quality of subnational government on the basis of its own narrow political interests. As imperfect as it was in promoting accountability for regional conditions, Russia's system of elected officials apparently provided a better alternative to the type of centralized system concurrently operating in Ukraine.

For now, this comparison of regional-level economic accountability in

Ukraine and in Russia provides valuable insights for the issues currently being debated among political elites and analysts in both countries. The populations of Russia's regions will likely gain very little in a shift from elected to appointed officials, and promises of budgetary savings and centrally imposed accountability must be assessed against the evidence from the Ukrainian case. For Ukraine, the results provide less clear-cut prescriptions. Though a newly empowered regional electorate might gain the means to "throw their rascals out," the fact that calls for elected regional executives arise precisely among those political actors who garner their support from outside Kyiv suggests that a Ukraine with elected regional executives could face the same rampant regionalization that Russia experienced during the second half of the 1990s. Whether the potential gains in accountability outweigh the economic, political, and emotional costs of Russian-style regional executive elections remains a question.[30]

Notes

1. The reader may smirk at this "philosopher king" approach, but both the democratic decentralization literature and the proappointment public finance theorists oftentimes speak in the language of ideal types.

2. Andrew Selee and Joseph Tulchin, "Decentralization and Democratic Governance: Lessons and Challenges," in *Decentralization, Democratic Governance, and Civil Society in Comparative Perspective,* ed. Joseph Tulchin and Andrew Selee (Baltimore: Johns Hopkins University Press, 2004).

3. Larry Diamond, *Developing Democracy: Towards Consolidation* (Baltimore: Johns Hopkins University Press, 1999), 117–60. Nonetheless, decentralization also carries certain liabilities, and its advantages are often more evident in theory than in practice. Under certain conditions, decentralization may actually raise barriers to accountability. As Diamond indicates, stronger, more autonomous local and regional governments can sometimes promote authoritarian enclaves, intolerance for local minorities, greater geographical inequality, and waste. As will be discussed in further detail below, a growing number of analysts examining cases in Latin America and the former Soviet Union provide empirical evidence of the dark side of certain forms of decentralization and weak federalism.

4. Joseph Shumpeter, *Capitalism, Socialism and Democracy* (New York: Harper Brothers, 1950), 258.

5. Wallace Oates, *Fiscal Federalism* (New York: Harcourt Brace Jovanovich, 1972); C. Tiebout, "A Pure Theory of Local Expenditures," *Journal of Political Economy* 65 (1956): 416–24; Shadid Burki, Guillermo Perry, and William Dillinger, *Beyond the Center: Decentralizing the State* (Washington, D.C.: World Bank, 1999); Elinor Ostrom, L. Schroeder, and S. Wynne, *Institutional Incentives and Sustainable Development* (Boulder, Colo.: Westview Press, 1993); Ronald McKinnon and Thomas Nechyba, "Competition in Federal Systems," in *The New Federalism: Can the States Be Trusted?* ed. Barry Weingast and John A. Ferejohn (Stanford, Calif.: Hoover Institution Press,

1997); Barry Weingast, "The Economic Role of Political Institutions: Market Preserving Federalism and Economic Development," *Journal of Law, Economics and Organization* 11 (1995): 1–31; G. Montinola, Yingyi Qian, and Barry Weingast, "Federalism, Chinese Style: The Political Basis for Economic Success," *World Politics* 48 (1996): 50–81.

6. Stephen Turret, "The Vulnerability of American Governors, 1900–1969," *Midwest Journal of Political Science* 15 (1971): 108–32; John Chubb, "Institutions, the Economy, and the Dynamics of State Elections," *American Political Science Review* 82 (1988): 133–54; Malcolm Jewell and David Olson, *Political Parties and Elections in American States* (Chicago: Dorsey, 1988); Michael Lewis-Beck and Tom Rice, *Forecasting Elections* (Washington, D.C.: CQ Press, 1992). For evidence of the absence of a subnational economic voting effect in Latin America see Karen Remmer and François Gélineau, "Subnational Electoral Choice: Economic and Referendum Voting in Argentina, 1983–1999," *Comparative Political Studies* 36 (2003): 801–21.

7. Richard Niemi, Harold Stanley, and Ronald Vogel, "State Economies and State Taxes: Do Voters Hold Governors Accountable?" *American Journal of Political Science* 39 (1995): 936–57.

8. The disconnect between aggregate economic performance measures and standard of living was most recently demonstrated in the results for the Social Innovation Foundation's study, "Quality of Life of the Population in Russia's Regions." According to a series of reports published in *Rosbalt,* despite three consecutive years of growth in gross national product, roughly 30 percent of the population indicated that its income placed it below the subsistence wage, and the proportion of respondents characterizing their lives as "unsatisfactory" ran from 30.6 percent in Vologodskaia Oblast to 42.2 percent in Kaliningrad. Nearly half the respondents indicated that Vladimir Putin had done a poor job in supporting "dignified lives for the citizens of Russia." See Ekaterina Ivanova, "Reiting narodnogo nedovol'stva," *Rosbalt,* July 24, 2003, http://www.rosbalt .ru/2003/07/29/110997.html; "Vladimir Putin plokho obespechivaet dostoinuiu zhisn' grazhdan, schitaiut 50 protsent rossiian," *Rosbalt,* July 23, 2003, http://www.rosbalt.ru/2003/07/23/110637.html.

9. Montinola, Qian, and Weingast, "Federalism, Chinese Style."

10. Weingast, "Economic Role of Political Institutions"; Darrell Slider, "Russia's Market-Distorting Federalism," *Post-Soviet Geography and Economics* 38 (1997): 445–60; Olivier Blanchard and Andrei Shleifer, "Federalism with and without Political Centralization: China versus Russia," National Bureau of Economic Research Working Paper, March 2000, http://www.nber.org/papers/w7616.

11. Pierre Landry, "Performance, Markets and the Political Fate of Chinese Mayors," paper presented at the Annual Meeting of the American Political Science Association, Boston, August 2002.

12. Furthermore, in normative terms, the nature of Ukraine's centralized state (particularly with regard to the central government's use of force), makes this particular form of centralization more acceptable than current government practices in China. Hence, any indication of the merits of centralization in Ukraine will prove a bit more palatable than similar statements related to the often-inhumane authoritarian government of China.

13. European Bank for Reconstruction and Development data, as cited in Gzhegozh Kolodko, *Ot shoka k terapii: Politicheskaia ekonomiia postsotsialisticheskikh preobrazovanii* (Moscow: Zhurnal Ekspert, 2000), 83.

14. Igor' Guzhva, "Ukrainskaia vertikal," *Ekspert,* March 4, 2002. In fact, among

the many hours of conversations contained in the Melnychenko audiotapes are rather bold statements by Kuchma regarding the need for regional and local governments to maximize votes (in one fashion or another) for pro-Kuchma parties during the 1999 parliamentary elections. The author thanks Yoshiko Herrera for bringing these statements to his attention.

15. Budgetary power was a different story. The law contradicted the 1999 Law on Budget Systems, which allowed upper-level governments to determine jurisdictional responsibilities. See Paul D'Aieri, Robert Kravchuk, and Taras Kuzio, *Politics and Society in Ukraine* (Boulder, Colo.: Westview Press, 1999), 125–26.

16. Later, parliament inaugurated this institution into law with the Law on Presidential Representatives in Ukraine.

17. Taras Kuzio, Robert Kravchuk, and Paul D'Anieri, *State and Institution Building in Ukraine* (New York: St. Martin's Press, 1999), 162–69; D'Aieri, Kravchuk, and Kuzio, *Politics and Society in Ukraine,* 125–32).

18. R. F. Turovskii, "Sravnitel'nyi analiz tendentsii regional'nogo razvitiia Rossii i Ukrainy," *Polis* 6 (1999): 49–61; Guzhva, "Ukrainskaia vertikal."

19. Kinakh was dismissed six months later. "Kinakh vystupaet za vybornost' gubernatorov," *Ukraina.Ru,* May 27, 2002; Natal'ia Talalai, "Mikhail Pogrebinskii: Snachala nado povysit' uroven' mestnoi demokratii, a potom perekhodit' k vybornosti gubernatorov," *Ukraina.Ru,* May 29, 2002; "Omelchenko predlegaet izbirat', a ne naznachat' gubernatorov," *Ukraina.Ru,* May 24, 2002.

20. "Kuchma: Dlia vybornosti gubernatorov nuzhny konstruktivnye protivovesy," *Ukraina.Ru,* June 18, 2002; Natal'ia Talalai, "Dumaiu, shto k vybornosti gubernatorov v Ukraine my vse zhe pridem," *Ukraina.Ru,* May 14, 2002.

21. Kimitaka Matsuzato, "All Kuchma's Men: The Reshuffling of Ukrainian Governors and the Presidential Election of 1999," *Post-Soviet Geography and Economics* 42 (2001): 416–39.

22. The parties include Narodno-demokratichna partiia, "Trudova Ukraina," Partiia regionov, "Blok Demokratichnik partii–NEP," Partiia natsional'no-ekonomichnogo rozvitku Ukraini," Partiia pratsi ta liberal'na partiia–RAZOM," Agrarna partiia Ukraini, and "SLOn–Sotsial'no-Liberal'ne Ob'ednannia." A two-quarter (six-month) "lag" was chosen to compensate for the fact that an overview of media sources appeared to indicate that Kuchma removed "problem governors" roughly three to six months after the 1998 parliamentary elections. Thanks to Lucan Way for his assistance in selecting these parties.

23. Natalia Zilgalova, "Zakarpats'ka oblast," in *Regional'nii portret Ukraini,* ed. Iulia Timoshenko (Kyiv: Ukrain'ski nezalezhnii tsentr politichnikh doslidzhen', 2003), 111–20. This book consists of a collection of chapters focused on the political, social and economic conditions in each of Ukraine's major subnational units (with the exception of the city of Sevastopol) and is an excellent resource for regional information.

24. Because economic measures for all regions were included in each quarterly "slice" of the cross-sectional time-series analysis, there was no need to standardize the variables in the same way as in the Russian case. Thanks to Lucan Way for providing regional-level budgetary and tax revenue data.

25. The conditions surrounding a turnover "event" were checked to ensure that turnover did not result from the death of the current executive or a promotion to a more prestigious position (usually in the central government). Turnover data through 1999 was drawn from Hokkaido University's Slavic Research Center Web site, "Politichna

elita Ukrains'kikh regioniv," at http://src-h.slav.hokudai.ac.jp/ukrregions/index.html. Iurri Marchenko of the Kyiv Information Service provided turnover data after 1999.

26. Observers of Ukrainian politics may have already noted the absence of certain "staple" indicators germane to nearly all studies of Ukrainian political developments, like the "east/west divide," the special status of Crimea, and other factors specific to certain regions of the country. These are purposely excluded because fixed-effects models isolate time-constant factors (thereby accounting for consistent factors such as cultural differences between eastern and western provinces), and the inclusion of indicators that do not vary across time can actually result in a misestimated model. For more information about fixed-effects models, see Jeffrey Wooldridge, *Econometric Analysis of Cross Section and Panel Data* (Cambridge, Mass.: MIT Press, 2001); and Jeffrey Wooldridge, *Introductory Econometrics: A Modern Approach* (Cincinnati: South-Western College Publishing, 2002).

27. Acknowledging the potential impact of correlations between the economic variables, the author also estimated models including each variable by itself and in subsets. The GRP measure provided the best indicator.

28. This effect may also suggest that regions suffering from a strong economic downturn are perhaps more likely to feature strong support for antipresidential parties and challengers. With only municipal and central government officials available for "punishment," voters may be more likely to lash out at the central government. Therefore, though the Ukrainian presidential administration's strongest incentive is to sanction and reward regional executives for "getting the vote out," it is also not in the president's interest to have regions pushed to the edge of economic collapse. Even the strongest regional election machine might not overcome the impact of abject poverty.

29. The nature of the economic indicators that provided leverage in both the Russian and the Ukrainian models also follows a certain logic. As mentioned in chapter 5, GRP does not translate automatically into outcomes that more closely affect the lives of voters—i.e., wages and cost of living. Hence, we might expect that, in a system of elected officials, incumbent success would be tied to wages rather than such macro indicators as GRP, expansion of industrial production, etc. In a system of appointed officials, the central government's main concern would be tax revenues and national election outcomes. The former is much more closely related to GRP than to wages and other such indicators. As suggested in the text, Ukrainian and Russian governors really do "serve different masters"—at least during the first post-Soviet decade.

30. At any rate, as with the debates under way in Russia, the fact that an increasing number of Ukrainian political actors are speaking out for regional level electoral institutions does not guarantee the establishment of such institutions in the near term. The pattern established during the past decade suggests that the decentralization issue has become a popular campaign tool for presidential challengers and that this tool is easily discarded following the establishment of the new regime in Kyiv. A successful opposition candidate, upon establishing his or her ruling circle in Kyiv, could do an about-face on the decentralization issue similar to that of Kuchma following his win over Kravchuk.

Chapter 7

Making the Worst of a Bad Situation?

Luchshee—vrag khoroshego. (The best is the enemy of the good.)
—Russian proverb

Thus far, this analysis of regional executive accountability during Russia's first post-Soviet decade has yielded rather surprising results. Respondents in the regional election survey exhibited jurisdictional economic support calculi suggesting that voters take into account economic conditions in their particular regions when deciding to support or oppose incumbents. Contrary to the popular discourse surrounding regional-level democratic processes in Russia, a link has been established between regional economic performance and incumbent success. Furthermore, the specific nature of this link suggested that *policies* mattered by indicating that changes in regional performance were more important than static measures resulting from features inherent to the given region. In broader terms, these results belie the popular 1990s image of unaccountable regional executives driving their regions into economic ruin for their own political gain by instead suggesting that incumbents had to tend to regional living standards or pay some price at the polls.

Nonetheless, just as the analyses raised interesting challenges to existing perceptions of regional executive elections, they also highlighted the numerous flaws existing within the system up through the first years of Vladimir Putin's administration. Poorly defined policy jurisdictions; a biased, unethical media; few established political organizations; incumbents' use of "administrative resources"; and generally weak norms of competition placed tremendous informational and even emotional costs on the voter. In large

194

part, the linkage between voting and economic performance existed *in spite of* this clearly hostile election environment.

The years between the consolidation of Putin's power in 2000 and 2001 and the elimination of popularly elected regional executives at the end of 2004 proved to be an interim period between the freewheeling decentralization of the Yeltsin era and a decisive shift to a more centralized system featuring appointed executives. Reforms implemented in the course of the Putin administration's first term suggested that the central authorities hoped to dispel much of the chaos in the regions and perhaps put in place the changes necessary to enhance regional democratic processes and promote accountability through democratic elections. Apparently, resolute actions were taken to better define jurisdictional responsibilities, lessen governors' control over administrative resources, recast regional media environments, and promote the growth of lasting regional political organizations and parties. On paper, many of these changes held out the hope of a more rational and consistent set of relations between the federal center and the regions, and as Gordon Hahn suggested, such developments promised to yield positive outcomes for regional-level democratic processes.[1]

But as with many Putin-era policies, a tension was evident between the stated goals of implementing an impartial "dictatorship of the law" and both the settlement of political scores and the continued reliance on regional executives in a system lacking federation-wide party structures. Though the administration apparently identified most of the critical weaknesses of Yeltsin-era federalism, its actions were characterized by half measures, arbitrary implementation, and attempts to force changes through legislation of issues that could only be resolved through an evolutionary process of economic, social, and political cultural development. Furthermore, as Putin's first term wore on, it became ever more apparent that the federal government valued a more centralized system as a goal in and of itself, and such other issues as accountability and stronger regional and local democratic institutions often barely figured in the administration's reforms.

During this period of attempted reforms before the elimination of elections in December 2004, the Putin administration's medicine for the regions' electoral woes proved more harmful than the disease. In an ostensible effort to remove the obstacles to regional electoral accountability, the central government began to strip the elections of their substantive meaning and risked alienating regional and local populations from subnational elections. In the end, the damage rendered to the system of regional executive elections during this interim period of reform was stopped, not by a return to the Yeltsin-era status quo but by the elimination of elections in their entirety.

This final chapter further describes the obstacles to electoral accountability in the Yeltsin and early-Putin eras, goes on to examine the Putin administration's efforts to mitigate these obstacles, and provides a set of preliminary observations on the possible implications of Moscow's centralization efforts for the accountability question. In the wake of the positive findings of the analyses in previous chapters, I identify a set of troubling trends that appeared during Putin's first term. The president's pre–December 2004 reforms resulted in a transmuted system of regional elections where the contests were increasingly determined by the interests of the center and where regional voters had less ability to control outcomes and "punish and reward" their executives. Had this system remained in place, one could expect that the accountability gains realized during the chaotic 1990s would have been largely erased by the encroachment of Putin's "managed pluralism" into regional politics.[2]

Hence, when the question is asked whether Russian democracy suffered a setback with the elimination of regional executive elections, one could still answer in the affirmative, but the elections that occurred in the last half of Putin's first term were a far cry from the contests that played out from 1995 to 2001. Had elections continued under the system that slowly evolved during this interim period, it is very likely that the outcome of contests would reflect the will of Kremlin tacticians rather than the needs of regional populations.

Having discussed the period spanning the last half of Putin's first term and the first year of his second term, I conclude with some possible implications of a Russia without regional executive elections. Given the results of the Ukrainian analysis, the prognosis is not optimistic. The new laws will allow the president to select officials who are subject only to the approval of United Russia–dominated regional legislatures and will thereby create a system of effective appointment. Under these circumstances, one can expect regional executives to be assessed less on their ability to advance the development and interests of their regions and more on their ability to mobilize popular support for the president's initiatives and "get out the vote" during presidential and Duma elections. Given its sheer size, Russia continues to face its age-old dilemma of choosing between good governance and centralized control. This latest round of reforms finds the central government decisively opting for the latter option, and today Moscow once again confronts all the challenges of ruling far-flung regions from a remote metropolis.

Five Post-Yeltsin Challenges . . . and Putin's Solutions

Although the past six chapters revealed an extensive and varied set of short-comings in Russian federal relations, the structure of regional government, and the conduct of campaigns, one can categorize these challenges into five general obstacles to accountability: (1) administrative resources and dirty campaigning, (2) poorly defined policy jurisdictions, (3) regional mass media conditions, (4) the underdevelopment of political parties, and (5) arbitrary intervention from the federal center. Despite efforts during the Putin administration's first term to implement changes in the first four of these areas, these obstacles continued until the very end of Russia's regional executive election experiment to exacerbate the normal "federal confusion" that any voter faces within a federated system. Furthermore, despite the regime's expressed interest in perfecting regional and local structures of governance, the administration's efforts to overcome these obstacles—and in the case of intervention, an increased tendency for the federal government to arbitrarily interfere in regional politics—actually worsened the conditions for electoral accountability.

Chernaia Tekhnologiia and Administrativnye Resursi

Although the models in chapters 4 and 5 suggest that regional elections were performing their accountability function to a certain (and significant) degree, the very nature of electoral competition suggests that Russia's regional elections fell short of any ideal of electoral accountability. Throughout the 1990s, a number of high-profile examples of election manipulation made a tangible mark on the outcomes of certain regional executive elections. Nearly every election yielded its own examples of "dirty tricks" (*chernaia tekhnologiia*), ranging from little more than "negative campaigning" to physical violence and bomb threats. However, certain tactics are worth noting, both for the amount of attention they attracted in the press and for the fact that they were later adopted and imitated in other regions. Looking at various forms of election manipulation in regional executive elections occurring between 1999 and 2001, Joel Moses speaks of certain "alternatives," which

became terms of the Russian political lexicon in the media known by the name of the region in which they first occurred. . . . The four most conspicuously labeled in the Russian media were the "Belgorod alternative," the "Kursk alternative," the "Briansk alternative," and the "Orel alternative."[3]

The first tactic, the "Belgorod alternative," involved collusion between the regional executive and legislature whereby the latter makes changes in election rules that move the scheduled election date forward and reduce the margin necessary to win the election. During this alternative's seminal election in Belgorodskaia Oblast, the regional legislature moved the election date forward by eight months and changed the election laws to allow for victory with a simple plurality in a single election round. The unexpected change in election dates undercut opponents' plans, leaving candidates scrambling to gather signatures and mount an effective campaign in the sharply abbreviated period before the election.

During the 1999–2001 election cycle, the Belgorod alternative once again appeared before the Kirovskaia Oblast election. There, Governor Vladimir Sergeenkov and the legislature moved the election from its scheduled autumn 2000 date to March and again changed the rules governing election victories from majority to simple plurality criteria. As indicated in chapter 3, "partial-Belgorod alternatives," in which legislatures changed elections to simple plurality rules but left election dates as scheduled, were also evident in Altaiskii Krai and in Murmanskaia, Pskovaia, Brianskaia, Kirovskaia, and Volgogradskaia, Oblasti.

The farcical "Briansk alternative" featured candidates registering "clones" (*dublery*) bearing names similar to those of major opponents. With like-named candidates competing in the election, the sponsor hoped that voters would misinterpret campaign tactics and perhaps accidentally cast their votes for the clone instead of their main rival. By itself, Brianskaia Oblast demonstrated the extremes to which such tactics were taken. At one point in the oblast's election campaign, of the fourteen candidates registered with the regional election commission, there were three "Denins," two "Lodkins" (including the incumbent), and two "Demochkins."[4] To make matters worse, the "cloning" in Brianskaia oblast was not limited to candidates. During the campaign, a political bloc called "For Putin" arose around a local engineer by the name of Vladimir Borisovich Putin. This "movement" allegedly attempted to capitalize on the popularity of the president and stir up support for the "real Denin," Nikolai Vasil'evich.[5]

During Orlovskaia Oblast's 1997 election, oblast governor Yegor Stroev established the "Orel alternative" by forcing opposing candidates from the race through a combination of coercion and legal action and replacing them with a single inexperienced "challenger." With the regional press questioning the background, intentions, and loyalties (particularly with regard to his "rival"—the governor) of this largely unknown opponent, few voters supported the late-runner. During the 1999–2001 election cycle, the "Orel alternative" was successfully imitated in Rostovskaia Oblast, resulting in a similarly overwhelming victory for the incumbent.[6]

Another variant employed during Samarskaia Oblast's 2000 and Kemerovskaia Oblast's 2001 elections featured the incumbent governor forcing an early election by resigning his post before the scheduled end of his term. In both cases, the early resignation significantly shortened the time remaining for would-be opponents to prepare their campaigns and allowed the candidates to avoid any charges of using their "administrative resources" to gain an unfair advantage over their opponents. Interestingly, both incumbents who resorted to the "Kemerovo/Samara alternative" in 2000 were opponents of Putin in the 2000 presidential election. This suggests that both Titov and Tuleev feared either that a federal government-backed candidate might mount a particularly strong campaign before the originally scheduled election date or that they would be subject to Kremlin intervention similar to that which occurred in Kurskaia Oblast in October 2000.[7]

This set of campaign tactics provides only some indication of the tools available to candidates and other interested parties seeking to manipulate election outcomes, and each election cycle was fraught with instances of incumbents and opponents alike violating the spirit and letter of regional and federal election laws. However, as with many other concepts popularized in the regional and national media, one should assess the impact of these tactics with a certain degree of skepticism. The apparent use of any of these tactics does not automatically imply the counterfactual—that outcomes would have been different in their absence. As Olga Shevel' indicated (see note 6), the Rostovkaia Oblast governor's use of the "Orel alternative" was entirely unnecessary. Titov's victory in the Samarskaia Oblast elections was perhaps less a result of his early resignation than of recent policies that gained him the support of the region's pensioners.[8] Conceivably, the decision to move the election forward in Kirovskaia Oblast helped the incumbent win the election, but changing the victory requirements to a simple plurality proved unnecessary—the incumbent won with 58 percent of the vote.

Nonetheless, other cases suggest that such tactics had an important impact. As indicated several times throughout this text, results from the Pskovskaia and Brianskaia Oblast elections signify what a combination of *dublery,* stand-ins, and low victory thresholds can do for even an unpopular incumbent's election chances.[9] The Volgogradskaia Oblast election demonstrated one of the more blatant, yet successful, attempts to implement the "Belgorod alternative." In this instance, a change in the regional election law allowing the governor to win the election by a simple plurality was tabled in early August and rapidly pushed through the regional legislature before the end of September.[10] During Volgogradskaia Oblast's December 24 election, the victorious incumbent gathered only 37 percent of the votes cast, while the next three strongest candidates accounted for 49.17 percent. In this instance, a two-round majority-rule election might have elicited a substantially different outcome.

As three of the more egregious instances of incumbent regimes' "electioneering," the Pskovskaia, Brianskaia, and Volgogradskaia Oblasti cases shared certain noteworthy characteristics. Incumbents in poorly performing regions won elections with very low portions of the overall number of eligible voters, thanks in part to election laws pushed through loyal (and communist- or Liberal Democratic Party–dominated) legislatures. "Democratic" and "Liberal" incumbents certainly demonstrated their aptitude for *chernaia tekhnologia* and the abuse of administrative resources, but it was in regions like Pskovskaia, Brianskaia, Volgogradskaia, and Tulskaia Oblasti where the 1999–2001 elections' most blatant violations occurred. In each case, traditional, "red" or "brown" governors garnered strong support among a larger (as compared with the federal average) conservative electorate, and through various legal and quasi-legal measures excluded or simply neutralized (through plurality voting rules) the remaining voters.

From the standpoint of enhancing regional democracy, Moscow's attempts to eliminate dirty election tactics stand as one of the successes of Putin's first term in office. In the wake of the 2000–2001 election cycle, changes to the Basic Guarantees came into effect stipulating that regional executives were exempted from running in elections brought about by their own resignation (thus eliminating the "leave so you can return" tactic practiced in Samarskaia and Kemerovskaia Oblasti) and requiring that all regional executive elections must be decided by majoritarian election rules. This latter move lowered the incentive to enter clones and *dublery* in regional elections because, though these phony candidates could siphon off a certain percentage of a challenger's vote and strengthen the odds of an incumbent winning in a single-round, plurality-rule-based election, a majority-rule-based election would most likely eliminate all clones and *dublery* in the first election, leaving the incumbent to face off against his or her strongest challenger in the final round.

Nonetheless, some candidates still saw an incentive to resort to cloning. During Brianskaia Oblast's 2004 election, candidates once again opted for the tactic that the region had made famous in 2000. During the 2004 contest, the incumbent Iurii Lodkin's main opponent, Nikolai Denin, found himself facing off against one Mikhail Denin. As in the 2000 race, both candidates shared not only their last names but also very similar occupations—both the "real" and "phony" Denin were directors of enterprises named Snezhka. Furthermore, Mikhail Denin was not the first clone to appear before the Brianskaia Oblast's 2004 election. In September, a transient with a history of frequent name changes received a passport bearing the name Iurii Lodkin—the same moniker as the region's incumbent governor. The "new" Lodkin, claiming to be the director of the enterprise Denin Finance Limited, later attempted to register as a candidate. For Nikolai Denin (the "real" Denin), this was a clear attempt to discredit his upcoming campaign by implicating him in the use of cloning tactics, and the candidate immediately took the matter up with the general prosecutor.

Brianskaia Oblast's incumbent went on to discover that cloning and other election tactics were no longer tolerated—especially when employed by a "red" governor against a United Russia–backed opponent. Iurii Lodkin "the clone" was never allowed to register as a candidate, and the "real" Iurii Lodkin was disqualified from the race for "numerous infringements of the law" (curiously, the two cloning attempts were not listed among the claims).[11] By itself, Governor Lodkin's downfall in 2004 provides additional evidence of the change in political conditions since 2000. During the 2000 election, Lodkin successfully subjected Nikolai Denin to many of the same tactics as those that resulted in his disqualification in 2004. Two important factors differentiated the 2004 race from the 2000 contest: Moscow was much stronger vis-à-vis the regions, and Nikolai Denin was now a member of United Russia. Denin went on to win the race.[12]

Another challenge to the conduct of fair elections at the regional level was of course the issue of administrative resources. As indicated throughout the text, during the period under examination, regional executives made extensive use of the resources proffered by their office to mobilize support during election contests, undermine other candidates, and prevent a solid opposition from developing between campaigns. Until the gradual consolidation of the Putin administration's power vis-à-vis the regions that occurred during the interim period before December 2004, these resources could serve *any* executive regardless of his or her relations with the Kremlin. In large part, this once again reflected the fragmentation of political and economic space within the Russian Federation during the first post-Soviet decade. One was as likely to see complaints from federal-level officials and media outlets about the abuse of administrative resources as from opposition candidates and media within a region.

With the election and subsequent consolidation of power under Putin, the nature of "administrative resources" gradually changed. As will be further described in the section below on political parties, the expansion and consolidation of the United Russia party structures in the regions soon posed a simple choice for regional executives accustomed to employing their full range of administrative resources in electoral competitions. If they aligned with United Russia, they maintained relatively full and unfettered access to the resources proffered by their office, gained the support of their region's United Russia structures, and could rely on additional backing through federal structures and media outlets.

However, those who refused to align with the federal center and the party of power faced full enforcement of a new array of legal restrictions on the use of state property, personnel, and other benefits of their office.[13] Essentially, the establishment of stronger vertical executive power from 2001 to 2004 eliminated the unfettered abuse of administrative resources, instead making the use of these resources the primary domain of the party of power and its allies. In exchange for their support of the federal center and its party (particularly during key elections), regional executives gained a powerful machine to back their own election bids and a certain immunity from laws regulating the electoral behavior of incumbents and other candidates.

Poorly Defined Policy Jurisdictions

To return the reader to our working definition of accountability, Cheibub and Przeworski state that a situation of accountability holds when "citizens can discern whether governments are acting in their best interest and sanction them appropriately, so that those incumbents who satisfy citizens' demands remain in office and those who do not lose it."[14] As was indicated above, the first half of this definition requires that voters enjoy access to reasonably objective information about conditions within a given policy jurisdiction and a practical grasp of the distribution of responsibility for these outcomes across all jurisdictions. Lacking this, the voter either misperceives conditions in the region or lays responsibility for outcomes upon incumbents who lack any means to actually influence them.

Yeltsin-era federalism presented the voter with a tangle of overlapping and poorly defined policy jurisdictions, "unfunded mandates" for which incumbents were responsible but lacked the financial means to implement, and a generally inadequate level of budgetary supervision that permitted the diversion of billions of rubles into uses other than those specified in annual budgets. Aside from lowering the incentives for individual policymakers to serve the needs and interests of their constituencies, these factors permitted a great deal of "ruble" passing before election campaigns, and incumbents often found it in their interest to maintain this jurisdictional murkiness and deliberately confuse their electorate. One can imagine that, when even economists found the tangle of economic and fiscal relations difficult to assess, the less specialized voter certainly lacked the time, information, and understanding to make informed and rational decisions.

Mostly in recognition of the fact that the Yeltsin-era status quo cost Russia billions in unrealized development potential, waste, and corruption, but also with a nod to the ideal of promoting subnational accountability, the Putin administration quickly took steps to reform Russia's budgetary policies and federal fiscal structures. In the summer of 2001, the administration established a commission under the vice chairman of the presidential administration, Dmitrii Kozak, to develop proposals for major federal reforms. The Kozak Commission set to their task with a highly publicized effort to include a wide range of social organizations, government agencies, and representatives of the general public in the process. As described by Leonid Smirniagin, events included "large conferences in the cities of Togliatti and Nizhnyi Novgorod, roundtables and meetings of various municipal organizations specifically created to discuss the project, an international conference in Saint Petersburg, countless articles in the central and local press and boisterous television talk shows."[15]

However, as Tomila Lankina relates, the actual development of the projects relied on a much narrower set of interests that largely excluded representatives from the local level of government—the very level toward which many of the reforms were ostensibly directed. According to Lankina, of the twenty-two members of the Commission, only two (the Novgorod mayor, Aleksander Korsunov; and the president of the Congress of Municipal Authorities, Oleg Sysuev) represented local interests. Another fourteen members represented the federal government and various executive agencies. Of three representatives of regional interests, two ruled ethnic republics (Tatarstan's Shaimiev and Kabardino-Balkarskaia Republic's Kokov) with a dismal history of local self-government. In Lankina's view, these factors together indicated that the reformers were far less interested in strengthening local self-administration than in further institutionalizing the vertical executive, while at the same time compensating regional leaders for attacks on their prerogatives during the early years of the Putin administration.[16]

In 2003, two laws—Of Amendments and Additions to the Federal Law of General Principles for the Organization of Legislative and Executive Organs in the Subjects of the Russian Federation (June 25); and Of General Principles for the Organization of Local Government in the Russian Federation (September 16)—emerged from the Kozak Commission's proposals. Together, these laws were heralded as major substantive changes to Russian federalism and the structures of regional and local government. A perusal of the laws indicates important changes in three areas. First, the laws firmly established the principle of vertical responsibility, with each level of government held responsible before the next highest level. Second, the laws set out guidelines for the clearer definition of jurisdictional responsibilities— detailed lists of policy areas indicated the distribution of responsibilities across each level of government. Third, financial guarantees were tied to each policy area. This addressed the continuing problem of "unfunded mandates"—the transfer of responsibilities from one level of government to the other without a concomitant transfer of budgetary funds.

Nonetheless, the Kozak reforms left a number of issues unresolved. Most important, regional governments retained the responsibility for distributing budgetary funds among the municipalities within their jurisdictions. Hence, despite the stronger provisions indicating that budgetary funds must be attached to the redistributed policy jurisdictions, the opportunity remained for governors to sanction municipalities that, for whatever reason, acted against the regional administration's interests. Such conditions leave the door open for the buck passing and mutual recriminations between regional and municipal administrations witnessed throughout the 1990s. Once again, if voters are unable to place the blame for conditions within their regions and municipalities, accountability suffers.

At the time of writing, the effects of the Kozak Commission's reforms remain uncertain. The laws were not scheduled to enter fully into effect until 2006, and much could change (particularly considering the 2003 Duma and 2004 presidential elections) before their implementation. Perhaps more important, the electoral reforms ratified in December 2004 will also have implications for local governance. Though the president gained substantial powers over the naming of regional executives, these executives may also acquire the privilege of naming executives to municipalities within their jurisdictions through a process very similar to the one by which the regional executives themselves are selected.[17] Obviously, this move would have a substantial impact on the working of local self-government in Russia, creating a vertical sequence of appointments from the president to municipalities.

With these points in mind, if anything can be said about the deliberations surrounding the Kozak Commission and resulting laws, it is that the nature and shortcomings of this recent attempt at reforming federal budgetary relations illustrates the obstacles that continue to hinder the establishment of clear policymaking jurisdictions. The Kozak reforms, even if implemented in full, are unlikely to establish the clear jurisdictional lines envisioned in the decentralization literature, and the political pulling and hauling over the three years between the laws' signing and their actual implementation may result in an outcome that falls far short of even the imperfect laws of 2003.

The Regional Media

Western studies of public opinion and voting behavior have demonstrated the important role that the media plays in shaping popular support, influencing voters' choice of candidates, and affecting how individuals view conditions within their societies.[18] Depending upon the study in question, exposure to the media may partially determine the types of issues voters consider, how they formulate these issues, and which candidates voters believe stand the greatest chance in the coming election. Media coverage shapes candidates' images and plays a major role in helping voters to associate various issues with specific candidates. In terms of the economy, media exposure can influence the weight that voters place on personal economic fortunes (according to Mutz, voters with more exposure to media are less likely to vote egotistically) and constitutes a major contributing factor in shaping voters' perceptions of broader economic dynamics.[19] With regard to the latter, Hetherington indicates that the media is capable of portraying economic performance as being much worse than it actually is—with sometimes dire consequences for incumbents.[20]

The above-mentioned studies draw primarily upon data from the United States, where a substantially larger advertising market and history of an independent media means that media structures differ substantially from those in Russia's regions. As indicated in chapter 4, taking into account the local business environment, the orientation of the regional government, and a number of other factors, the major players in a "typical" Russian regional media environment generally consist of the oblast-controlled television-radio station (GTRK),[21] a handful of independent stations with varying political loyalties, one or more oblast and/or major municipality-controlled newspapers, a small number of "business" dailies or weeklies, and the regional Communist Party's newspaper. Each of these outlets usually exhibits a rather apparent agenda in their reportage on regional conditions and their support for or opposition to various political actors. Regional administration publications and broadcast media naturally put the best face on the administration's activities and cast the blame for the most obvious regional problems either on other levels of government or upon some other internal or external actors or conditions.[22] Business publications are generally relatively well financed, boast more professional journalists, and display at least an air of objectivity. Nonetheless, such publications carry their own agendas depending upon the incumbent's relationship not only with the regional business sector as a whole but also with various cliques among the business elite.[23] The local communist publication usually varies its stance depending upon both the ideological orientation of the incumbent in question and also that incumbent's relationship with the local party organs (the latter not necessarily determined by the former).

As indicated in the discussion about Ul'ianovskaia Oblast, one does not require sophisticated or extensive content analyses to uncover the general orientation of most regional media outlets. Regional media outlets are characterized by hard-hitting and frequently crude reporting, and editorial staffs and journalists pull no punches in the interest of damaging the political reputation of their opponents. Given the importance of mediated information in formulating perceptions about people and events with which the public has little direct contact, one must consider the potential effects of such an environment.

How might voters react to such conditions? What do these biases imply for voters' assessments of candidates and preelection regional economic performance? Though one might imagine an infinite number of possible effects, three stand out as potential "modal responses" from media consumers. First, voters might unreflectively digest all the information presented in whatever media source they happen to consume and allow these ideas to directly affect their vote choices (a *persuasive* effect). Second, voters with preexisting preferences for specific candidates or groups might identify sources supporting these candidates and groups and trust the information published or broadcast by that media outlet (a *motivational* or *reinforcing* effect). Third, voters may be well aware of the media sources' bias and either reject most of the information presented by the media or attempt to piece together some objective picture based upon a collection of biased sources, personal experience, and other sources of information (personal discussions, etc.).

Although I currently lack the data to rigorously test these three propositions, extensive field experience and work by other researchers provides sufficient grounds to offer a number of speculative arguments.[24] With regard to the persuasive effect, much of the evidence indicates that Russian voters are more sophisticated than the images of mindless, media-consuming golems rendered by arguments promoting the media's role as an opinion maker. Looking at data from the 1995 Duma and 1996 presidential elections, Timothy Colton indicates that "popular awareness of media favoritism is widespread in the Russian Federation" and that "almost 40 percent of citizens espied distortions in media coverage of the 1995 Duma campaign; the next summer more than 50 percent sensed it in the race for the presidency, almost all of them seeing the media product as warped in Yeltsin's favor."[25] However, more recent research, conducted in the wake of the Putin administration's assertion of control over major media outlets, has raised some challenges to Colton's assessments. Among other sources, a paper presented by Stephen White, Sarah Oates, and Ian McAllister at the 2002 American Political Science Association Meeting in Boston suggests that trust in state media increased substantially during the most recent presidential and parliamentary elections.

Nonetheless, during an April 14, 2003, presentation at the Kennan Institute for Advanced Russian Studies in Washington, Ellen Mickiewicz cautioned against making too much of White, Oates and Mcallister's findings. According to Mickiewicz's focus group research, though respondents might respond affirmatively when asked whether they "trust" the state-controlled media, further probing of their attitudes reveals that they continue to either ignore or sift through much of the information presented in media reports. Mickiewicz went so far to suggest that the Russian media consumer, conditioned by years of exposure to politicized media outlets (either under Communism or under the Yeltsin and Putin regimes), demonstrates a higher sophistication in the processing and selection of information than his or her American counterparts. Transferred to the regional level, such awareness suggests that citizens resist and dismantle biased media reports and that a regional administration's monopoly on information sources provides no guarantee of essentially dictating knowledge to the masses.

Discussions, interviews, and other observations in Samarskaia, Permskaia, and Ul'ianovskaia Oblasti also suggest some support for the mobilizational effect—media consumers identify media biases and draw upon those sources that best reflect their particular predispositions. Individuals with stated preferences for one candidate tended to dismiss media sources supporting other candidates as examples of "yellow (*zheltyi*) journalism," while drawing most of their arguments and supporting information from sources favoring their preferred candidates (even when these sources were clearly as biased as any other). Readership also divided along established social cleavages. Pensioners seldom read business dailies, and business people were rarely observed reading the local communist paper. As the "official source" of information in the oblast, regional administration-sponsored media might draw consumers from a broad spectrum of society; but trust in the information seemed to vary depending upon the social requisites of regime support. The results from the Ul'ianovskaia Oblast survey analysis provide some support for this outcome as well. Aside from the broadcast media measures, the effect of the remaining media variables was "washed out" with the inclusion of fixed socioeconomic indicators. This suggests a relationship between one's place in life and the types of information that one consumes and trusts.

The third modal response—that the public distrusts media and must piece together its understanding of events from many different sources—concurs with Colton's and Mickiewicz' arguments regarding the effect of media bias during federal elections upon a society predisposed to mistrusting its mediated information sources. In comparative terms, trust in the Russian media lags significantly behind that found in advanced industrial democracies, where the bulk of media studies are currently centered. For instance, in the period from June 1985 to May 1998, an average of 73.5 percent of respondents to Pew Research Center surveys indicated that they trusted four major American network news programs.[26] In Russia, by contrast, a series of polls taken between 1998 and 2001 indicated that distrust in the objectivity and veracity of the media varied between 60 and 50 percent with no clear trend in either direction.[27] When asked if regional television presented objective information about the region, or painted regional conditions in too positive or negative a light, only 37 percent of the respondents indicated that the broadcast media provided objective information (26 percent indicated that it painted conditions in too positive a light, while a mere 7 percent indicated that the media painted an overly pessimistic picture).[28]

Clearly, trust in the media among Russian voters lagged significantly behind similar measures in the United States. With potential voters skeptical about media information, one might expect them to assemble a patchwork of information from a variety of media sources, interpersonal communication, personal experience, and other sources. In addition to each of these sources' independent effect on opinion formation, combinations of factors—say, a personal experience of unemployment and media reports on high unemployment in the region—might interact to produce particular outcomes independent of any single factor. In this respect, Colton also speaks of the importance of interpersonal communication through "informal peer circles" as an alternative information source.[29] None of the outcomes for the media variables included in the Ul'ianovskaia Oblast analysis would refute such claims. However, to parse out and fully appreciate the means by which the Russian media consumer processes and creates information demands more detailed studies, like Mickiewicz's focus groups.

Nonetheless, the regional voter's ability to piece together information from a variety of sources remains contingent upon the number and quality of sources available. This in turn varies not simply from region to region but also within regions. An examination of the Ul'ianovskaia Oblast case indicates that the highest numbers of viewers of the regional administration-backed television and radio station, GTRK Volga, resided in rural *raion* centers, towns, and villages.[30] Such figures suggest that much of GTRK Volga's broadcast area included a "captive audience" with little or no access to opposing viewpoints. Even allowing for interpersonal communication, it is likely that rural voters had little access to alternative information—most of their interactions would be with similarly situated rural residents. Table 4.2 above graphically demonstrates the potential effects of a regional television station's monopoly on regional broadcast news.

The importance of Russian regional television stations was certainly not lost on the Putin administration or the Central Election Commission. In September 2000, a presidential order, Of State Electronic Mass Media in the Russian Federation, stripped regional executives of their responsibility to appoint directors of regional television stations and transferred the power of appointment to *okrug* presidential representatives. In theory, this move would assist with the development of a "single informational space" throughout Russia and weaken the administrative resources of incumbents. However, weakening regional executives' control over regional television stations, while perhaps eliminating a major source of proincumbent propaganda, would have only a marginal effect on the total volume of slanted campaign coverage in any given region. The fact remained that privately owned stations could throw in their lot with incumbents and other political and economic elites, providing just as effective propaganda as state media. Also, the new presidential order made no provisions to alter the rules of the game for print media. Therefore, the central government pressed for further measures to "save" regional voters from an abusive media.

The Kremlin made its most decisive steps in this direction through a set of amendments to the Basic Guarantees of Citizens Electoral Rights and Rights to Participate in Referendums and other laws pertaining to mass media and advertising. Passed over the first half of 2003, the amendments placed a number of potentially far-reaching restrictions on broadly defined instances of campaign agitation. In addition to these restrictions, the laws also laid out procedures for identifying and punishing offenders—opening the way for federal organs to actually close down errant media organizations. Writing in *Nezavisimaia Gazeta,* Maksim Glinkin identified at least nine potential guidelines which, if violated, could result in the temporary or permanent closing of a media outlet. These included:

- When reporting on preelection events, journalists do not have the right to provide commentary.
- Mass media do not have the right to report on the activities of one candidate of political organization without devoting the same volume or broadcast time to the activities and actions of other candidates.
- Mass media are prohibited to present any, even completely verifiable information, about a candidate if it might damage his or her honor and professional reputation and if the media is not prepared to provide free airtime or print space for his or her response.
- Mass media are prohibited to publish results of surveys without providing details regarding how they were carried out. This information must contain nine points, including margins of error and the name of the individual or organizations that ordered the survey.
- Mass media are prohibited to publish polls predicting election outcomes during the last week of the election campaign.
- Mass media are prohibited to adjust the cost of print space or airtime for different candidates.
- Mass media are prohibited to publish an article on an election theme without reporting who ordered or paid for it.
- Print media, reporting on elections are prohibited from varying the frequency or volume of printruns.

- Mass media are prohibited to publish ads for firms and organizations established or led by candidates or their agents.[31]

Not surprisingly, the broad prohibitions drew protests from liberals, press advocates, and political parties like Union of Right Forces and Yabloko. Most critics argued that the new laws would effectively silence the media during election campaigns —nearly any form of campaign coverage could fall within one of the prohibitions and result in punitive action. On October 30, these efforts bore fruit after 104 Deputies representing every major political party *except* United Russia brought the matter to the Constitutional Court. The Court, recognizing that the portions of the current law that restricted journalists from agitating for a particular candidate could be interpreted as prohibiting any campaign reportage at all, ruled those portions unconstitutional. Furthermore, the Court provided criteria to distinguish agitation from the simple provision of campaign information, specifying that a statement is only "agitation" if it could be demonstrated in court that the statement was made with the journalist's direct intent to support one or the other candidate.[32]

The Constitutional Court's decision to overturn the draconian mass media laws was considered a victory for liberals and other supporters of the free press. However, the course of the few campaigns that occurred under the stricken law provided a troubling indication of the federal government's attitudes toward media campaign coverage and its intentions for using the law as leverage during regional election campaigns. The first electoral contests that occurred under the new amendments suggested that the prohibitions would not apply equally for all regions and that presidential support, or at least disinterest, would yield a certain amount of protection from the broadest interpretations of the media restrictions. For instance, the October 2003 elections in Leningradskaia, Sverdlovskaia, and Omskaia Oblasti exhibited the same unabashed proincumbent campaigning in the regions' media organs as previous elections. In none of these cases did incumbents face candidates supported by the federal government; and in all cases, the incumbent enjoyed support from the regional United Russia party organs.[33] Nonetheless, by themselves, these campaigns might suggest that the new laws were merely ineffective, and that, as was the case throughout the 1990s, weak central state capacity had resulted in another instance of poor enforcement. Unfortunately, events in Saint Petersburg provided clearer evidence of a less benevolent trend.

The October 2003 gubernatorial elections in Saint Petersburg came about after the Putin administration appointed the sitting governor, Vladimir Iakovlev, to the post of vice premier in charge of construction and communal services reform. Media observers and other analysts had long spoken of the Putin administration's desire to remove the governor of Russia's "second capital," and Valentina Matvienko's (then vice premier for social programs) aborted campaign to unseat Iakovlev in March 2000 was widely seen as an initial bid by the Putin administration to achieve this goal.[34]

The year 2003 brought renewed efforts by the Kremlin to remove the governor. First, the Putin administration positioned Matvienko to not only oversee affairs in Saint Petersburg but to also acquire a potential launch pad for another gubernatorial bid in the city by appointing her as the presidential envoy to the Northwest Federal District. Shortly thereafter, an inquiry began regarding the possible diversion of federal funds transferred to support the city's upcoming 300th anniversary.[35] In the event, despite rumors of an imminent plan to replace Yakovlev with Matvienko, the inquiry came to nothing and Yakovlev remained in office until after the jubilee celebrations.

In June 2003, the administration finally succeeded in removing Yakovlev and gave him the undesirable responsibility of overseeing communal services reforms.[36] With Yakovlev removed from the scene and effectively neutralized, elections were announced for October. To no one's surprise, Matvienko announced her candidacy soon after. Both the presidential administration and Matvienko herself made no secret of her relations with the Kremlin, yet the new media laws in place might have prevented the use of state media outlets to agitate for the Kremlin's candidate. In the event, a very selective application of the new laws worked decisively in Matvienko's favor, and events in early September clearly demonstrated that not all candidates were equal before the law.

During every one of their September 8 newscasts, the federal television stations RTR and First Channel broadcast a piece involving a working meeting between President Putin and Matvienko. Even putting aside the issue of the broadcast itself, the very rationale for the meeting smacked of campaign agitation. First, Matvienko met with the president in her capacity as presidential envoy of the Northwest Federal Okrug—a position from which, in accordance with new election laws, she was temporarily furloughed. Second, the working meeting focused on Saint Petersburg's budget for 2004—an issue that lay entirely beyond Matvienko's policy jurisdiction. During the course of the meeting, the president made generous offers of federal support for major construction and renovation projects in the city—a clear suggestion that these projects were dependent upon Matvienko's victory in the upcoming election. Putting all innuendo aside, the president then went so far as to say that "Matvienko could resolve Saint Petersburg's problems 'even better than those who are now responsible for the city.'"[37]

The events of September 8 were particularly troubling because the election was unfolding under the new laws governing media activity during election campaigns. Again, if interpreted in the broadest manner, these laws could have restricted nearly any form of campaign materials in local and federal media outlets. Local outlets, which might have thrown more support behind candidates like Anna Markova (vice governor of Saint Petersburg and Matvienko's main opponent, who ultimately went on to challenge her during the second round of the election), faced the possibility of closure under the fullest application of the law.[38]

Such considerations forced candidates to put more efforts into public meetings, posters, and other nonmediated forms of agitation. Unfortunately, given the already strong name recognition of former presidential envoy Matvienko, such a campaign worked decisively against her opponent. Along with clear support from the presidential administration in the form of billboards featuring the president and Matvienko emblazoned with the phrase "Together we may accomplish everything" and the working meeting mentioned above, the fear of retribution essentially guaranteed the victory of the Kremlin's candidate.

In a final blow to Markova's campaign, the one and only debate before the second round of elections was hosted by TRK-Peterburg, a station whose management was replaced with pro-Kremlin (and hence, pro-Matvienko) personnel just before the election campaign. Immediately following Markova's inevitably poor showing during the debate, the station went on to broadcast an hour-long program describing the lifetime achievements of Valentina Matvienko. Once again, the federally backed candidate appeared to be above the law, making full use of the administrative resources made available in her capacity as the Kremlin's favorite.[39]

By the end of the Saint Petersburg campaign, it was clear that the central government's efforts to "clean up" the regional media were both misdirected and prone to subjective application conditioned upon the political leanings and loyalty of the candidates in question. Incumbents and particularly well-known candidates (like Matvienko) generally benefited from the dampening effect that such laws had upon campaign coverage. As Dmitrii Volgin states, as long as local and regional governments are free to make full use of their administrative resources, and regional and local judicial organs remain subject to pressures by local and regional authorities, such laws could work only against opposition candidates.[40] Fortunately, as indicated above, the media restrictions imposed over the summer of 2003 were struck from the books, leaving regional journalists to go about their reporting in much the same manner as before. Clearly, the return to the status quo left the Russian voter with the same cacophony of biased information as before, but at least federal and regional authorities lacked the legal levers made available through these draconian laws.

In the final analysis, the past decade of Russia's regional media development once again drives home the point that a rich, free, and independent media environment is not something that a government may simply legislate into place. Speaking of the media in developing countries "as a 'development good' capable of contributing to improved accountability, more efficient markets, and more information rich societies," Tim Carrington and Mark Nelson argue that

> one must recognize that all these beneficial outcomes derive from the media's financial independence. That independence, in turn, is a function both of the local economy and of a particular media company's ability to turn a given economic environment to its advantage.[41]

These points are as relevant for today's Russian regional media as they are for other developing states. In the absence of independent and diverse sources of funding and a strong advertising market, media outlets face the choice of selling themselves to the highest bidder or mindlessly following the government line in the hope of receiving subsidies. During Russia's regional executive elections, either option failed to serve the interests of the voter. Until regional economies themselves diversify, we can expect either to observe a continuation of the type of impartiality currently witnessed in most regions or future clumsy and stifling interventions by federal authorities. The rise of more diversified ownership and financial support for media outlets would ideally render moot the speculative discussion on the effects of an impartial media and allow us to examine the role of political awareness per se as it is studied in other settings.[42] Citizens could treat their media as a source of sufficiently objective information rather than a tangle of interests demanding deconstruction and interpretation. As it existed up until the elimination of regional executive elections in December 2004, Russian regional media presented more of a hindrance than an aid to accountability.[43]

Political Parties

The third factor impeding the role of elections in promoting accountability was related to the role that party structures played—or perhaps more appropriately, did not play—in regional executive elections.[44] Even the minimalist accountability model applied throughout this study places significant information burdens upon survey respondents and voters. Aside from gathering the information necessary to make a reasonable assessment of regional-level economic performance, individuals must also determine what the incumbent and his challengers intend to do about the current situation. In assessing challengers' goals and intended policies, voters are faced with an even greater quandary. Though they may assess the incumbent on the basis of the previous term, challengers are relatively unknown figures that must present their programs in a very brief period before the election.

Furthermore, because many challengers have little or no experience in regional political office (the exception being those instances when mayors or regional deputies compete), voters have very few bases to assess whether the challenger has the means or intent to implement his or her campaign promises. With such a dearth of information among voters, incumbents of all types gain a margin of support from the voters' natural fear of the unknown.[45]

A stable, institutionalized, polity-wide party system in which parties advance their own candidates could mitigate these problems. With regard to the information issue, parties provide a useful "information shortcut" for individuals facing uncertain electoral choices. Political parties simplify the election decision by presenting voters with a choice of broad policies embedded within a single party ideology. Drawing upon the original work of Anthony Downs, Samuel Popkin notes:

> Parties use ideologies to highlight critical differences between themselves, and to remind voters of their past successes. They do this because voters do not perceive all the differences, cannot remember all the past performances, and cannot relate all future policies to their own benefits.[46]

In single-mandate-district elections, or elections for executives at any level of government, party identification saves the voter from the task of uncovering information about a candidate who may only recently have emerged from the masses to vie for citizens' votes. Rather than expending the time and effort to familiarize themselves with each candidate's platform, record, and reputation, voters can ease the process by relying upon their particular party identification.

An additional potential advantage behind the emergence of a stable polity-wide party system is the element of accountability and restraint it might lend to regional election processes. In a system characterized by weak parties endorsing candidates who entered the race mostly on their own initiative, candidates have little incentive to forgo even the most base election tactics. This is particularly true for candidates whose primary source of well-being and power lies outside the political arena per se (e.g., business people). If a "dirty tactic" succeeds in undermining the opponent, then the candidate increases his or her chances of taking office. However, even if the tactic fails and the candidate is exposed for resorting to such deplorable methods, he or she can simply exit electoral politics after the race and return to his or her previous occupation.[47] By contrast, in a system where stable parties advance competing candidates for election, the election game becomes iterative whether the candidate wins or not. This factor both raises additional sanctions on terminal incumbents (those in their last term of office), and places the costs for "dirty campaigning" upon parties represented by the offending candidates. Stable political parties are tied to electoral processes and compete in each election with the understanding that their performance will affect their success in future races. If candidates are bound to such institutions, the (mis)behavior of those candidates may have profound consequences for the future of the party. Hence, a stable party system creates an iterative game that places restrictions upon terminal incumbents and "transient" candidates. Both types of candidates might disappear after the elections—political parties hope to survive to participate in future contests.[48]

Unfortunately, throughout the 1990s, Russia's regional-level political parties were characterized by internal divisions, minimal levels of inter-election activity, and little consistency between official party platforms and candidate endorsements. In his study of regional political parties, Grigorii Golosov indicates that "Russia's party systems can be characterized as extremely volatile, while the influence of national political parties over the presidency and federal government seems negligible."[49] Parties divided across levels of government, with municipal, regional, and federal-level party structures endorsing different candidates during the same elections. Regional parties broke into factions as individual political leaders fought for political and economic advantage. Between elections, parties either disappeared entirely or entered a dormant state, rousing themselves (sometimes in an altered form) and reminding regional voters of their existence only months before an election. Finally, if parties indeed act as information shortcuts for partisan voters, Russian regional parties often forfeited such a role by endorsing candidates whose views opposed those of the "official" party platform.

Golosov attributes the underdevelopment of regional-level parties and party systems to a number of specific factors, including Russian presidentialism, a lack of party-structured "founding" elections, certain characteristics of the electorate, and the 1991 ban on the Communist Party.[50] However, approaching the issue of party development as a question of elites' demand for specific political goods that parties might supply, Golosov finds the locus of the party development problem in the fact that, between 1991 and 2003, political actors at the regional and national levels enjoyed access to alternative institutional power bases that could supply the same political goods as parties.[51] The weakness of regional party structures was not a question of an undersupply of party labels—elections featured a flood of party options, which if anything only confused the electorate. Instead, the crux of the matter lay in the fact that political actors could obtain the same political goods from institutions that were readily at hand. Furthermore, because these were often "their" institutions, political actors avoided the difficulty of working and bargaining with political equals within a party organization.

Within the post-Soviet settings parties could prove useful to candidates by nominating them, facilitating their registration (collecting signatures or, later, deposits for candidates), and organizing campaign activities. However, throughout the Russian Federation's first decade, nomination requirements varied from region to region and were often sufficiently lax to allow for nominations by "groups of voters," which could include coworkers, the candidate's relatives, or even the candidate herself. Under such conditions, a party nomination proved to be a significantly more difficult option. Signature gathering could also as easily be undertaken by subordinates in regional administrative structures as by members of a potentially more independent party rank and file. The first decade of elections was replete with stories of hospitals where head doctors would gather signatures from patients, workplaces where employees were encouraged to back a candidate, and universities where students were asked to support nominations. Once again, these preexisting institutions were often more efficient and loyal than the party alternative.

The seeming omnipresence of the term *administrativnye resursi* (administrative resources) in the Russian press speaks to the extent to which incumbents and other candidates could rely on their institutional ties and other resources to effectively campaign for political office. Aside from using state- and candidate-controlled private resources for campaigns (public spaces, media, transportation, etc.), money could also buy a better campaign than regional party organizations could provide. Local and Moscow-based advertising and public relations agencies both drew up strategies and helped executive campaigns. Because many candidates had access to larger monetary resources than political parties, such an option was often more attractive than reliance on political party structures.[52]

The resulting reluctance on the part of political actors to consistently and openly identify with regional parties further exacerbated these problems, creating a sort of vicious circle of party underdevelopment. Through 2003, Russian politics remained a very individualistic pursuit in which political figures relied for victory on their personal popularity and clout rather than their association with larger and more stable political organizations. Candidates sought out party endorsements primarily as part of a broader campaign strategy to appeal to a "critical mass" of demographic groups sufficient to gain office. This approach often resulted in a puzzling together of different parties (and factions of parties). Depending on the change in political tides between elections, the same political figure's patchwork of endorsements (the haphazard nature of this process does not warrant the use of the term "coalition") might change dramatically from campaign to campaign. With candidates essentially choosing their own parties and with these choices based predominantly on vote maximization rather than considerations of ideological consistency, the parties' role as an information shortcut naturally decreases.[53]

The year 2003 witnessed a radical transformation in the fabric of Russia's political party system, without necessarily strengthening or broadening the system beyond Russia's new "party of power." Following the success of Unity during the 1999 parliamentary elections, this new party of power sought to consolidate its position throughout Russia. Two factors contributed to this effort. The first was the overwhelming popularity of Putin who, while not an official member of the party, provided the single focal point for the entire organization. United Russia essentially lacked any unifying political platform other than support for Putin's policies. However, with the president's popularity continuing to hover at above 60 percent, this association was sufficient to make the party a major force in national politics.

The second factor contributing to United Russia's consolidation was the party and election reforms undertaken during Putin's first term in office. These laws placed more stringent requirements on political party participation in the Duma, required that regional election commissions include members nominated by political parties, and stipulated that a portion of regional legislatures be elected through party lists. The last change, established in point 16, article 35, of the June 12, 2002, version of the Basic Guarantees of Citizens Electoral Rights and Rights to Participate in Referendums, stipulated that no more than one half of the regional legislature must be elected through a system of proportional representation. In an article written for the Central Election Commission's publication *Dzhurnal o vyborakh,* M. Lugovskaia indicated that two of the goals for this legislature were to "stimulate the activity of all-Russian political parties in the regions along with their activity in regional elections"; and "limit the participation in regional elections of "leadership" parties, oriented not on the expression of general public interests, but on support for the acting regional leadership."[54]

Between February and September 2003, eighty-eight federal subjects had either passed or had taken under consideration legislation bringing regional election rules into line with the new laws (at the time, Kemerovskaia Oblast stood as the one exception). December 2003 saw the first handful of regional elections to occur under the new system, with other regions scheduled to undergo their first proportional elections as late as December 2007. To date, every region that underwent elections under the new laws returned large United Russia blocs, further augmented by United Russia–affiliated candidates from single-mandate districts.[55]

Given the nature of "partification" in Russia's regions, political leaders were thus faced with two options—take on a national party label or face marginalization and opposition from within their region. With the increasing popularity and administrative strength of both Putin and United Russia, the choice was usually clear. By the end of 2003, more than twenty-seven regional and local executives were included on the United Russia party list, and many more were taking efforts to ensure that the party would not challenge them in the upcoming round of gubernatorial elections.

The political vacillations of Samarskaia Oblast's Konstantin Titov provided a telling indication of the incentives facing regional executives at the end of Putin's first term.[56] Following his puzzling race against Putin in the 2000 elections and his later decision to take a leading position in the Russian Social Democratic Party, Titov found himself in an ambivalent and increasingly difficult position in relation to the federal center. Starting in 2001, criminal investigations of individuals within the oblast administration and loyal heads of regional municipalities suggested an attempt by federal authorities to find some bases for the governor's criminal prosecution.[57] Around the same time, elements within the previously loyal regional media launched frequent attacks on the governor, his family, and political associates.[58] Finally, the 2003 oblast duma elections witnessed, for the first time in the oblast's history, the establishment of an antigubernatorial bloc consisting of United Russia deputies and members of an independent group associated with the oblast center's mayor. Together, this bloc impeded important gubernatorial initiatives and threatened to deny the governor the opportunity to run for a third term. At the end of 2003, the political balance of power in the oblast differed greatly from that which existed at the end of 1999.

However, the 2003 Duma elections provided an opportunity for Titov to solve a number of political problems that had arisen in the wake of his presidential bid. On the eve of the December elections, the Social Democratic Party of Russia, led by Titov and Mikhail Gorbachev, made a strategic alliance with United Russia whereby the Social Democrats agreed to support the "party of power" during the Duma elections. This move extracted Titov from the delicate position of being one of the few regional executives to not support United Russia campaigns in their regions. Furthermore, after the election and at the start of a major administrative reform that would establish a regional government complete with an oblast prime minister, Titov accepted the resignation of his former vice governor, Viktor Kazakov, and named Sergei Sychev as his new vice governor, and future prime minister.

Sychev's appointment marked a major political turnaround for Titov, who was simultaneously able to solve several additional political challenges with a single act. First, the new appointee was a Saint Petersburg (then Leningrad) State University graduate who was rumored to have had some contact with Putin during his time in Leningrad. Second, and most important, Sychev played a major role in the regional United Russia party structure and acted as the head of United Russia's campaign staff during the 2003 Duma elections. In appointing Sychev, Titov selected a representative of the party of power to head an apparently powerful, but still poorly defined, post within his new administrative structure. This promised to resolve the problems with the United Russia block in the regional legislature and, it was hoped, ensure the governor his third term in office. Furthermore, Sychev was likely to head the Samara Oblast campaign activities for Putin's reelection bid in 2004. United Russia's performance in Samara during the 2003 Duma elections left something to be desired, and the party's regional election returns fell below that of the federal average. If the governor was forced to take responsibility for campaign activities in the oblast, he might be "punished" for a poor showing in favor of Putin. Instead, Sychev's appointment provided clear evidence of the governor's intention to support the president during the 2004 elections while providing a scapegoat in the event that the president's showing was weaker than desired.

At the time of writing, the outcomes of this gambit were unknown—and Titov is now facing an appointment decision rather than an election bid. However, the events leading up to the decision and the discussion of the strategies behind Sychev's appointment provide a vibrant illustration of the pressures facing Russia's regional executives during this period of partification and the means taken by some regional executives to retain their grip on power.[59]

The events in Samarskaia Oblast and other examples from throughout Russia lend additional credence to the arguments of such analysts as Henry Hale that Russia is finally witnessing the growth of a political party system.[60] However, from the standpoint of accountability, where political parties must provide information shortcuts and reiterated political contests, and where elections must maintain some element of competition, the particular nature of this partification left little reason for optimism.

As suggested above, United Russia continues to lack any particular platform aside from support for Putin. Essentially, it remains a party of bureaucrats and policymakers who have joined the party to maintain their political standing in the face of increasing presidential power. The rush to join or align with United Russia was too recent and the number of elections too few to make any decisive conclusions about the impact of the party label on member's policy stances, but the diverse range of ideologies, policy histories, and biographies of the various region executives donning the United Russia label suggests that, at least in the near term, voters would have gained little knowledge about a candidate's characteristics through his or her party alignment.

Events in Pskovskaia and Novgorodskaia Oblasti illustrated the questionable extent to which United Russia presents a clear party platform "shortcut" to voters and also demonstrated the risks of regional-level "privatization" of party structures—a common practice during the Yeltsin era, but something that starkly contrasts with the popular perception of Putin's centralization drive. In both regions, the party bosses of the regional United Russia organizations were removed because of their opposition to the sitting governor and replaced with members of the governors' circle.[61]

Turning first to the Novgorodskaia Oblast case, Governor Mikhail Prusak and leader of the Novgorod United Russia organization Evgenii Zelenov were both summoned to a meeting in Moscow where they were expected to work out their differences. During the course of the meeting, Prusak laid out his conditions: If Zelenov leaves, the governor would support United Russia during the upcoming 2003 Duma elections. As a result, Zelenov was offered a new post on the nascent, and still poorly defined, Northwest Regional Coordination Council of United Russia. In Pskovskaia Oblast, a conflict between Governor Evgenii Mikhailov and the regional United Russia party leader, Victor Semenov, had divided the regional party structures into pro- and antigovernor camps. At around the same time as events were unfolding in Novgorodskaia Oblast, Semenov was also removed from his position at the top of the party organs and, like his colleague in Novgorodskaia Oblast, offered a spot on the Northwest Regional Coordination Council of United Russia.

Andrei Riskin's assessment of the situation surrounding the reshufflings in Pskovskaia and Novgorodskaia Oblasti was indicative of the continued strength of gubernatorial "administrative resources," and the dependence of United Russia organizations on particularly strong governors during this interim period before the late-2004 reforms. Support for United Russia in these regions was considered to be quite weak, and without the backing of the governors and their power structures, many expected the party to perform very poorly during the 2003 Duma elections. Riskin makes a rather alarming comment regarding Zelenov's attempts to wield some leverage during his meeting in Moscow. Commenting about the party boss's stated intention to run in the upcoming Duma elections, Riskin asserted that "in any case, the deputy did not take into account that, today, for the 'party of power,' gubernatorial support is more important than dozens of devoted party members."[62]

Hence, the continued reliance on the administrative resources of powerful incumbents allowed these governors to at least partially "privatize" provincial United Russia party structures, incorporating their own ideologies and interests into regional party organs.[63] In the process, from the standpoint of Popkin's work, the party once again fell short of its ascribed role as an information shortcut—the platforms and general policy orientation of United Russia took on the colors of the powerful executives that could "get out the vote" during national elections.

Looking at the regional "partification" process from a different perspective —the remarkable success rate of United Russia–supported regional executives, and reports from elections indicating that the United Russia label gained executives access to a full range of regional and federal-level resources while freeing their hands to employ a range of dirty election tactics—suggested that membership or affiliation with the party of power might have provided executives with the "entrenchment" that they sought, but failed to achieve, throughout the 1990s.

The election results for 2003 (table 7.1) provide some telling indications of the impact that a United Russia endorsement has on incumbents' and challengers' chances of preserving or taking office. Of the twenty-one regional executive elections that occurred between January 26 and December 7, United Russia–backed candidates won in nineteen races. Furthermore, of the two races in which United Russia–backed candidates did not win, only one race, in Magadanskaia Oblast, featured an actual loss by the party of power's preferred candidate. The Karachaevo–Cherkessia race was unique in that the recently established United Russia regional party structures failed to endorse any candidate. Though most of the winners were incumbents, the results of the Tverskaia Oblast election suggested that the party of power could also support winning challengers. Finally, in three of four instances in which the incumbent failed for whatever reason to run for office, United Russia backed the candidate who won the empty seat.

Previous analyses of elections from 1996 to 2001 indicated that an endorsement by any of Russia's political parties bore little relation to the change in odds of regional executive incumbent success, and an endorsement by the party of power (in whichever form it took) offered little or no leverage to sitting executives.[64] The remarkable fortune of United Russia–backed candidates in 2003 suggests very strongly that a United Russia endorsement grew to provide, if not a guarantee, then at least a strong assurance of success in regional executive elections.

Nonetheless, one should be wary of writing the voter entirely out of the equation during the era of United Russia's consolidation. Races in 2004 exhibited less auspicious outcomes for United Russia–backed candidates, and by the end of the year, one could understand why the party of power's leadership might welcome the elimination of popular contests.[65] Of twenty-two races in 2004, United Russia–backed candidates won in sixteen. The party of power's candidates suffered defeats in Arkhangelskaia, Riazanskaia, Pskovskaia, Kamchatskaia, and Volgogradskaia Oblasti; and in Altaiskii Krai, a United Russia–backed incumbent lost to a popular comedian.[66]

In many of these instances, United Russia either backed highly unpopular incumbents or regional party organizations split, supporting two and even three (Volgogradskaia Oblast) candidates.[67] During the last contests of Russia's epoch of regional executive elections, United Russia candidates and party organizations seemed to increasingly resort to eliminating strong

Table 7.1. Regional Executive Election Results for 2003 by Party Support

Date of Final Tour, All in 2003	Election (Incumbent)	Victor (Tour)	Supported by United Russia?
Jan. 26	Governor Taimirskii Autonomous Okrug (incumbent did not participate)	Oleg Budargin (1st)	Yes
Feb. 16	Head of Administration Republic of Mordovia (Nikolai Merkushkin)	Nikolai Merkushkin (1st)	Yes
Feb. 16	Governor Magadanskaia Oblast (Incumbent did not participate)	Nikolai Dudov (2nd)	No
May 25	Governor Belgorodskaia Oblast (Evgenii Savchenko)	Evgenii Savchenko (1st)	Yes
Aug. 31	President Karachaevo-Cherkessia Republic (Vladimir Semenov)	Mustafa Batdyev (2nd)	No[a]
Sept. 7	Governor Novgorodskaia Oblast (Mikhail Prusak)	Mikhail Prusak (1st)	Yes
Sept. 7	Governor Omskaia Oblast (Leonid Polezhaev)	Leonid Polezhaev (1st)	Yes
Sept. 21	Governor Sverdlovskaia Oblast (Eduard Rossel')	Eduard Rossel' (2nd)	Yes
Sept. 21	Governor Leningradskaia Oblast (Valerii Serdiukov)	Valerii Serdiukov (1st)	Yes
Sept. 21	Governor Tomskaia Oblast (Viktor Kress)	Viktor Kress (1st)	Yes
Oct. 5	Governor of Saint Petersburg (acting governor did not participate)	Valentina Matvienko (2nd)	Yes
Dec. 7	Mayor of Moscow (Iurii Luzhkov)	Iurii Luzhkov (1st)	Yes
Dec. 7	Governor Iaroslavskaia Oblast (Anatolii Lisitsun)	Anatolii Lisitsun (1st)	Yes
Dec. 7	Governor Vologodskaia Oblast (Viachislav Pozgalev)	Viachislav Pozgalev (1st)	Yes
Dec. 7	Governor Moscow Oblast (Boris Gromov)	Boris Gromov (1st)	Yes
Dec. 7	Governor Novosibirskaia Oblast (Viktor Tolokonskii)	Vivtor Tolokonskii (1st)	Yes
Dec. 7	Governor Orenburgskaia Oblast (Aleksei Chernyshev)	Andrei Chernyshev (1st)	Yes
Dec. 21	President of Bashkortostan (Murtaza Rakhimov)	Murtaza Rakhimov (2nd)	Yes
Dec. 21	Governor Kirovskaia Oblast (Vladimir Sergeenkov: not running, third time in office)	Nikolai Shaklein (2nd)	Yes[b]
Dec. 21	Governor Tverskaia Oblast (Vladimir Platov)	Dmitrii Zelenin (2nd)	Yes
Dec. 21	Goveror Sakhalinskaia Oblast (incumbent governor deceased; acting governor, Igor Malakhov)	Igor Malakhov (2nd)	Yes

[a] At the time of the election, Karachaevo-Cherkessia held the unique distinction of being the only region in Russia without a registered United Russia Party Structure. See "Karachaevo-Cherkesia nadeetsia na mirnye vybory," *OLO.ru,* August 16, 2003, http://www.olo.ru/news/politic/13307.html.
[b] United Russia supported Shaklain only in the second tour.
Sources: "Predvaritel'nye itogi vyborov glav subektov federatsii, sostoiavshikhsia 7 Dekabria 2003 goda," *Nezavisimaia Gazeta,* December 9, 2003; Andrei Borodianskii, "Vtoroi tur v pol'zu 'Edinoi Rossii,'" *Nezavisimaia Gazeta,* December 23, 2003.

opponents from races through legal mechanisms. In both Brianskaia and Ul'ianovskaia Oblasti, rival candidates were eliminated in the first (Brian-skaia Oblast) or second (Ul'ianovskaia Oblast) election round, paving the way for a United Russia victory.

However, media commentators, analysts, and other observers were often too quick to greet any United Russia defeat as evidence of the party's weakness and the myth of Kremlin supremacy. When looking at the 2004 elections from the perspective of Russia's broader regional election history, one is still struck by the remarkable change in the party of power's success in electing and reelecting governors in 2003 and 2004. Of the forty-three elections held between January 1, 2003, and January 1, 2005, United Russia–backed candidates won thirty-five, for a total success rate of 81 percent. At no other time in Russia's post-Soviet history could another party of power claim similar rates of success, and many commentators' intensive focus on a handful of instances of defeat perhaps only emphasized the extent of United Russian dominance during this last stage of the country's regional executive elections.

The defeats of 2004 do help us explain why the presidential administration might opt to eliminate regional executive elections and why United Russia so keenly backed the president's proposals. As indicated above, during this interim period, United Russia party structures were quite consistent in delivering election outcomes favorable to Kremlin officials. However, the less auspicious 2004 record demonstrated the shortcomings of the existing scheme, and party and central government officials expended vast amounts of resources (financial, political, and other) in efforts to depose some of the strongest anti-Kremlin candidates. With United Russia party blocs established in regional legislatures throughout Russia, "election by recommendation of the president" promised to provide a better guarantee of success while saving party of power resources and avoiding the humili-ation of defeat at the hand of well-entrenched problem governors.

In light of all of these points, what were the implications of the 2003–4 party consolidation for the accountability question? The party construction that occurred in Russia's regions in 2003 and 2004 transformed the nature of "administrative resources," providing incumbents with the much-sought-after security that often eluded them during the 1990s. Throughout Russia's first post-Soviet decade and into the first Putin-era regional executive election cycle, regional executives made extensive use of the resources proffered by their office to mobilize support during election contents, undermine other candidates, and prevent a solid opposition from developing between campaigns. Until the gradual consolidation of the Putin administration's power vis-à-vis the regions, these resources could serve *any* executive regardless of his or her relations with the Kremlin. In large part, this once again reflected the political and economic fragmentation within Russia during the first post-Soviet decade. One was as likely to see complaints from federal officials and media outlets about the abuse of administrative resources by regional executives as from opposition candidates and media within a region.

As stated above, with the election and subsequent consolidation of power under Putin, the nature of "administrative resources" changed. First, control over these resources was effectively "confiscated" by the federal center as it took the power to appoint directors of regional broadcast media away from executives; implemented the institutions of federal districts with presidential envoys to watch for election infractions; and forced regional laws, some of which augmented incumbent regime's grip on the reigns of power, into line with federal standards. Following upon these efforts, the expansion and consolidation of United Russia party structures in the regions posed a simple choice for regional executives accustomed to employing their administrative resources in campaign competition. If they aligned with United Russia, they regained the full use of their administrative resources, enjoyed the support of their region's United Russia party structures, and could rely on additional backing through federal structures and media outlets. However, those who refused to align with the federal center and the party of power faced the full enforcement of a new array of legal restrictions on the use of state property, personnel, and other benefits of their office.[68] Essentially, the establishment of stronger vertical executive power did not eliminate the abuse of administrative resources but instead made the use of these resources the principal domain of the party of power and its allies. In exchange for their support of the federal center and its party (particularly during key elections), regional executives gained a powerful machine to back their own election bids and a certain immunity from laws regulating the electoral behavior of incumbents and other candidates.

Events in Sverdlovskaia, Irkutskaia, and Kirovskaia Oblasti provided instructive illustrations of the exchange of party support and administrative resources during the United Russia era. In Sverdlovskaia Oblast, the regional legislature's United Russia faction agreed to reschedule the region's 2003 gubernatorial election from September, the month when Rossel's four-year term actually expired, to December 7, 2003—the same day as the elections to the Russian Duma. The official reasoning behind this legislative effort, which actually involved extending the governor's officially sanctioned four-year term until the election of a new governor, were budgetary savings to the tune of 180 million rubles. However, while officials close to the administration denied that the change was made to further ensure an electoral victory for Rossel (throughout the period under examination, regional executives tended to enjoy greater support, and guaranteed turnout levels, when they held elections concomitantly with federal contests), recent expressions of support from Putin and United Russian party organs only further suggested that Rossel enjoyed the fruits of his close relationship with the party of power.[69]

Changes in Irkutskaia Oblast's electoral legislation provided another illustration. In November 2003, the United Russia faction in the oblast legislative assembly successfully pushed through two initiatives, one to replace the existing vice speaker of the assembly and the other to allow gubernatorial incumbent Boris Govorin to run for a "third" term. In comments made to *Kommersant Daily,* the previous speaker, Sergei Shishkin, indicated that he was certain that his removal resulted directly from his opposition to extending Govorin's stay in office. Curiously, in the course of the legislative debate, the United Russia faction based its support for the bill on the basis of bringing the regional legislation into line with federal laws—an argument that has been most frequently employed to *limit* the number of terms for governors.[70]

Events in Kirovskaia Oblast offer an example of the turn in fortunes of regional executives who failed to carefully nurture ties with local United Russia fractions. In October 2003, the incumbent governor, Vladimir Sergeenkov, approached the regional assembly with a proposal to change the existing oblast charter to allow the same individual to hold the governor's office for more than two times in a row. Kremlin opposition to the move was well known, and according to an unnamed source in the Putin administration, resulted in large part from the fact that "the governor had come forth in open confrontation with the federal government and could not guarantee the effective development of the oblast."[71] After some deliberation, the initiative was voted down and Sergeenkov was forced to leave office at the end of his term. In the subsequent election, the United Russia–backed candidate, Nikolai Shaklein, took the governor's seat in the second election round with 62.77 percent of the vote.[72]

The full implications of these developments for regional-level electoral accountability are, and will probably forever remain, unknown. Only a relatively small subset of elections occurred during this interim period, and the economic data are not yet available to run models similar to those presented in this book. Furthermore, the elimination of regional executive elections at the end of 2004 means that no further elections will occur under the conditions described above. But certain aspects of the interim status quo paralleled some of the conditions outlined within the Ukrainian case. With regional executives gaining full control over enhanced administrative resources (those resources inherent within their office itself, plus federal resources and the resources of United Russia party structures) in exchange for loyalty to the center, future electoral success would have been determined more by alignment with Moscow than by the executive's success or failure as the region's *khoziain.*

Taking this logic a step further, the conditions may also have been established for a form of center–region clientelism, whereby regional executives mobilize support for the party of power and presidential incumbent in exchange for the full backing by these same organs during the executive's subsequent election. Under these circumstances, regional-level electoral success would then be determined more by the strength of the executive's electoral machine during key federal elections and relations with regional United Russian party structures between election periods than by conditions within his or her region.[73] In both cases, the resulting situation, while retaining the institutional trappings of regional elections, might have approximated the state of affairs in unitary Ukraine, where executives are removed or retained based on their success in getting out the vote for Kyiv.

Returning again to the accountability criteria referenced throughout this study, voters must be able to sanction or reward candidates at the ballot box. This means that voters must possess the necessary information to assess incumbents, and that the electorate must be capable of voting unpopular incumbents out of office. The past decade of party development in Russia's provinces witnessed an evolution from a fragmented and weak party system that executives simply ignored to a situation where executives of various stripes are flocking to a party of bureaucrats with no defined platform aside from support for a strong, pragmatic president. At no stage in the process have party affiliations provided the information short cuts, or perhaps even the intraparty accountability necessary to enhance elections as accountability criteria.

Moving to the second accountability criterion, if membership or alignment with United Russia during the 2003 and 2004 elections slanted the playing field in favor of a particular candidate (as it most demonstrably did during the 2003 Saint Petersburg election), then the voter's ability to sanction poorly performing incumbents was severely curtailed, thus violating the second principle. Hence, with regard to both criteria, United Russia's rise perhaps presented more of an obstacle than an aid to electoral accountability.

Arbitrary Federal Intervention

To once again resurrect the image of Russia as patient, the Putin administration's efforts to rein in the regions introduced an attempt to cure the "regionalized autocracies" problem, which in the end proved more harmful than the illness. Either directly (Kurskaia Oblast and Saint Petersburg, among others), or through various mediaries (Sergei Kirienko's somewhat clumsy intervention during the Republic of Mari-El's 2000 presidential campaign), Moscow interfered with election campaigns on several occasions with the apparent goal of removing various "problem governors." Though the governors' "black list" may have—either intentionally or otherwise—served to place all regional executives on notice, the selective nature of the Kremlin's interventions undermined its credibility as an impartial champion of the "dictatorship of law."[74] During the second half of Putin's first term in office, the effort to remove problem governors took a different turn as the general prosecutor undertook various types of criminal proceedings against executives in regions like Kamchatskaia, Saratovskaia, and Tverskaia Oblasti and the Koriaskii and Nenetskii Autonomous Okrugi.

Commenting upon this new strategy, Igor' Bunin of the Center for Political Technology indicated that the general prosecutor's efforts resolved three separate tasks. First, the criminal proceedings discredited the incumbents in the eyes of voters (many of these efforts took place before the beginning of electoral campaigns). Second, when those regional executives under investigation began their campaign seasons, they would be far more limited in their choices of electoral technology. And finally, such attacks would send voters a clear sign that, in an era in which such ties apparently proved of increasing importance, their incumbent had lost the support of the Kremlin authorities.[75]

Many commentators have criticized the Putin administration's seemingly personalized attacks on oligarchs and political opponents—and unfortunately, its approach to regional governance bore similar markings. Though, as in the case with oligarchs like Berezovskii, Gusinskii, and Khodorkovskii, there were most likely serious grounds for investigation in each of the cases against regional executives, the attacks nonetheless exhibited an arbitrary character in that they fell primarily upon actors who

Table 7.2. Saint Petersburg's 2000 and 2003 Elections (percent)

Election	Turnout	Against All
Saint Petersburg, 2000	47.74	3.72
Saint Petersburg, 2003 (final)	28.25	11.75
Federal average, 1995–2000	54.14	5.99

Source: Central Election Commission of the Russian Federation, http://www.cikrf.ru.

maintained hostile, or at least tepid, relations with the Putin administration. The implications for the promotion of regional economic performance were disturbing and threatened to destroy the delicate relationship between the vote and accountability outlined in previous chapters.

Later elections during this interim period suggested the potential effects of Kremlin intervention—both real and imagined—in regional and local elections. The turnout for Saint Petersburg's September 2003 elections was dismally low (see table 7.2), and analysts painted a portrait of an electorate that was disgusted with Moscow's heavy-handed intervention and fatigued from the relentless dirty campaigning for a contest that many felt had already been decided.[76] In broader terms, the race in Saint Petersburg suggested dangerous signs of a citizenry that discounted the importance of local elections in an era when local and regional power appeared to weaken and federal authorities could clearly intervene to remove and then elect executives.[77]

To a large extent, subnational electoral accountability may be as much a matter of society's *perceptions* of the importance of local and regional government as it is a matter of the actual distribution of decisionmaking power and financial resources. With regard to the latter, for months after the reforms' implementation, many analysts remained unconvinced that Moscow's efforts to tinker with Russia's center–periphery relations had actually engendered a substantive and lasting shift in power from the regions to the center.[78] However, if potential voters perceived such a shift in the statements of political figures, the media, and other sources, they might follow their counterparts in other centrist federations and focus their energy on federal-level elections. The increasing frequency of federal government interventions in regional contests during this interim period might have seriously undermined the potential accountability gains (as demonstrated in chapters 5 and 6) garnered from a system of elected regional and local officials—

federal authorities would continue to intervene when desired, and the electorate could do little or nothing to resist these interventions.

Toward a System of Appointed Regional Executives

December 12, 2004, marked the end of the interim period during which the Putin administration attempted to tinker with Russia's center–periphery relations and regional political institutions. In an alleged response to a series of terrorist attacks that culminated in the tragic hostage crisis in Beslan, Russia's voters lost their right to directly influence the selection of regional executives and Moscow acquired the means to dominate the most influential political organ in Russia's eighty-nine regions.

The process of selecting regional executives stipulated in the new revisions to Russia's election laws retains some of the trappings of democracy while providing the president and his circle with an overwhelming degree of control over the office. Though candidates are nominated for approval by regional legislatures, these bodies are increasingly dominated by United Russia blocs, which consistently toe the line of the president. Under such circumstances, it is difficult to imagine a situation in which the president's chosen candidate will not receive the necessary support. In the event that a legislature rejects the candidate after three considerations, the president can then disband the regional legislature and call new elections. Given the strength of United Russia party organizations in the regions, and the evident tendency for legal restrictions on campaigning to be applied most forcefully to United Russia opponents, such an action is likely to result in the elimination of opposition legislatures and the establishment or strengthening of United Russia blocs. In other words, the new election laws may allow the Putin administration to kill two birds with one stone: Moscow gains both more control over regional executives and the means to change the alignment of regional legislative bodies.

As indicated in previous chapters, the move toward a system of quasi-appointments will likely have a major, and negative, impact on the question of accountability for regional living standards and economic performance. By effectively reversing the decentralization tendencies evident during the 1990s, and by removing the regional voter from direct participation in the executive selection process, the system of quasi-appointments will be selecting, evaluating, and removing executives on the basis of the political and economic interests of federal authorities rather than the needs and interests of citizens within their policymaking jurisdictions.

The Ukrainian case placed the potential dangers of such an arrangement into very sharp relief. Ukraine's president acquired the authority to appoint regional executives in 1996 and apparently made use of these powers to punish regional executives for failing to "get out the vote" during presidential and national legislature elections. Regional conditions appeared to play some small role in the decision to remove or retain governors, but this consideration was largely trumped by the narrow political interests of the national government and its associated political parties. Furthermore, the president also used regional executives to control regional information sources and restrict public demonstrations over issues close to his interests.

Part of the difficulty in promoting accountability within a system of appointed regional executives is informational—central authorities often simply lack the information and resources to monitor local conditions and make fine-tuned decisions from faraway capitals. If this problem is evident in Ukraine with its twenty-seven subnational units, one can expect even greater difficulties within Russia with its eighty-nine subjects (the inefficiencies of the last attempt at centralized control, the Soviet Union, also gives reason for pause). But aside from the information issue, self-interest also plays a strong role in undermining the accountability dynamic. If faced with the decision to maintain a good *khoziain* who may otherwise fail to support Moscow's political and economic interests in a region, rational political actors in the Kremlin are likely to pursue their immediate self-interests and replace such an executive with a more reliable subject. In the worse scenario, regional governance could be dominated by politically loyal actors interested in the needs and interests of their local populations only to the degree that constituents would not respond to poor conditions by voting against the party of power during national contests.

At the time of writing, the last remaining regional executive elections are playing out across Russia (the last election is scheduled in Nenetskii Autonomous Okrug on January 23, 2005), and a substantial amount of time will be necessary to trace out the actual impact of the December 12 reforms on Russian subnational accountability and governance. Nonetheless, the evidence presented throughout this work speaks against the claims of the most ardent supporters of Putin's decision to eliminate regional executive elections. The years before the interim period described in this chapter demonstrated that, for all their failings, Russia's regional elections were an institution that was worth saving. If there is some truth to the argument that

Russia has lost very little from the elimination of this institution, it is only with respect to the system as it existed from 2001 to 2004.

Furthermore, while supporters of the reforms claim that the changes will improve upon a system of subnational governance in which rampant decentralization and local fiefdoms have rendered government wholly unaccountable, the evidence presented in this and previous chapters suggests instead that the December 12 reforms did not present a decisive move away from regional level accountability because the interim-period reforms had already introduced a state of strong central control over the regional election process. In the aggregate, a system of appointees may produce the same body of loyal regional executives that would otherwise be produced by the somewhat less reliable system of centralized control created from 2001 to 2004.

Conclusion

In the wake of Moscow's decision to eliminate directly elected regional executives, what has Russia lost? While the 1990s witnessed the threat of "uncontrolled" decentralization, subnational fiefdoms, and regional autocracy, the evidence from the analyses above indicates that the Russian voter managed to eke out some modicum of electoral accountability for economic performance. During this period, the public was all too aware of the disproportionate strength of regional executives, but in some respects, this forced voters to focus on the regional level and express their discontent through subnational elections. The governor was *khoziain,* and though this title sometimes implied the ability to protect incumbents from a disgruntled electorate, it also meant that the public could justifiably hold him responsible for the success or failure of his fiefdom.

In a perverted sense, "wild" decentralization functioned to promote accountability at the subnational level. Still, rampant disregard for the spirit and letter of election laws, uncertain policy jurisdictions, a dearth of reliable mediated information, and weak political parties continued to impair elections as accountability mechanisms. Patterns of accountability were evident at both the individual and aggregate levels, but these other factors indicated ample room for improvement.

During his first term, the selective nature of Putin's "dictatorship of the law" ate away at the modest gains of the Yeltsin era. While the imperfect nature of existing institutions certainly played a key role in the confused election campaigns of the 1990s, factors beyond the competency of legislation played an equal role in blocking the process of electoral accountability. The administration attempted to force change in all areas, apparently under-appreciating or ignoring the fact that problems like the development of po-litical parties and a free and relatively objective media are as much a result of Russia's current stage of socioeconomic and political development as of any shortcoming in existing laws. To exacerbate matters, the administration applied new restrictions arbitrarily, targeted some violators while ignoring others, and took additional steps to convince the public that the federal cen-ter could intervene at will in regional politics.

Reforms begun during the 2001–4 period had already undermined many accountability gains realized during the 1990s, and had this system contin-ued, it is very likely that the future outcomes of Russia's regional executive elections would have reflected the desires of Kremlin tacticians rather than the needs of local populations. Nonetheless, the Putin administration's de-termined effort to concentrate power in the executive branch, along with public dissatisfaction with existing electoral institutions, opened the way for an even stronger attack on regional democratic institutions and moved the Russian voter further away from the levers of regional power. The reforms of December 12, 2004, stand as a major turning point in Russia's experience with federalism and subnational democracy and represent an important vic-tory for centralists. Given the sophistication and resolve demonstrated by the regional voter before 2001, the elimination of popular elections consti-tutes a setback for Russia's effort to democratize. The coming decade will reveal the socioeconomic and political implications of this reversal.

Notes

1. Gordon Hahn, "The Impact of Putin's Federative Reforms on Democratization in Russia, *Post-Soviet Affairs* 2 (April–June 2003): 114–53.
2. For a description of Russia's "managed pluralism," see Harvey Balzer, "Man-aged Pluralism: Putin's Emerging Regime," *Post-Soviet Affairs* 19 (2003): 189–227.
3. Joel Moses, "Political-Economic Elites and Russian Regional Elections, 1999–2000: Democratic Tendencies in Kaliningrad, Perm, and Volgograd," *Europe-Asia Studies* 54 (2002): 907. Because the "Kursk alternative" involved external intervention by the Kremlin and this section focuses on tactics employed by incumbents, this alter-native is excluded from the subsequent discussion.
4. The official Central Election Commission report indicates that only nine candi-dates participated in the election. These included one "Demochkin," two "Denins," and two "Lodkins." This suggests that two of the clones left the race before the election. See the Central Election Commission Web site, http://www.fci.ru/elections/default_gl.htm.
5. Boris Zemtsov, "Piarom po reitingu," *Nevavisimaia Gazeta,* December 14, 2000; Vladimir Petrov, "dvoiniki i dublery," *Vesti.ru,* December 9, 2000.

6. Dar'ia Guseva, "V Rostove oprobovali 'upravliaemuiu demokratiiu,'" *Vremia novostei,* September 25, 2001; Ol'ga Shevel', "Vybory bez vybora," *Vremia novostei,* September 25, 2001. In the latter article, Shevel' makes the interesting observation that the oblast administration was nearly guaranteed a victory without any attempts to manipulate the election but that the incumbent's staff "could not resist using the notorious administrative resources."

7. Aleksandr Sadchikov, "Uiti, shtoby vernut'sia: Prezident presek khitrosti gubernatorov," *Izvestiia,* February 27, 2001.

8. Yevgenii Molevich, interview by the author, Samara, Samarskaia Oblast, October 15, 2000. See also Zoia Andreeva, "Yevgenii Molevich: Titov sam sozdal sebe oppozitsiiu," *Reporter,* July 21, 2000.

9. This factor must be taken into account in studies that uncritically apply the effective number of candidate estimate as a means to measure political competition and therefore *democracy.* For instance, Moraski and Reisinger cite Pskovskaia Oblast's 2000 election as very competitive due to its effective number of candidate's score of 6.48. However, as this author's interview with a local newspaper editor indicates and as further demonstrated by Andrei Morozov, some of the candidates participating in the election were in fact backed by the regional administration and its circle in an effort to divide the opposition vote and gain another term for Evgenii Mikhailov. This approach tends to yield a high effective number of candidates scores (the split often leaves three or more candidates with 10 to 25 percent of the vote), but whether we can truly treat such instances of electioneering as examples of "competition" and particularly "a facet of democracy" is questionable at best. See Bryon Moraski and William M. Reisinger, "Explaining Electoral Competition across Russia's Regions," *Slavic Review* 62 (2003): 278–301; and Andrei Morozov, "Izbiratel'nye tekhnologii i administrativnyi resurs: Pskovskii retsept sokhraneniia vlasti," in *Vybory i problemy grazhdanskogo obschestva na severo-zapade Rossii* (Moscow: Carnegie Moscow Center, 2001).

10. Vadim Shumilin, "Vtoroe dykhanie: Volgogradskii Gubernatori nameren ostat'sia u vlasti, perepisav zakon o vyborakh," *Nezavisimaia Gazeta,* February 8, 2000.

11. Aleksandr Kondratov, "Chestnye vybory: V Brianskuiu oblast' potianulis' dvoiniki kandidatov v gubernatory," *Kommersant Daily,* September 30, 2004; Aleksandr Kondratov, "Chestnye vybory: Genprokuratura zainteresovalas' brianskim "dvoinikom" kandidata v gubernatory ot "Edinoi Rossii," *Kommersant Daily,* November 18, 2004.

12. Aleksandr Kondratov, "Gubernatorskie vybory: Brianskii gubernator popal pod sud," *Kommersant Daily,* November 30, 2004.

13. Andrei Riskin, "I primknyvshie k nim gubernatory," *Nezavisimaia Gazeta,* January 12, 2003.

14. Jose Antonio Cheibub and Adam Przeworski, "Accountability for Economic Outcomes," in *Democracy, Accountability, and Representation,* ed. Adam Przeworski, Bernard Manin, and Susan Stokes (Cambridge: Cambridge University Press, 1999), 225.

15. Leonid Smirniagin, "Zakon dlia obrechennykh: Gosudarstvo gotovitsia udushit munitsipalitety v svoikh ob'iatiiakh,," *Novoe Vremia,* September 17, 2003.

16. Tomila Lankina "Federal, Regional Interests Shape Local Reforms," *Russian Regional Report,* September 29, 2003.

17. See Federation Council speaker Sergei Mironov's and first vice chair of the State Duma Committee for Questions of Local Government Gadzhiment Safaraliev's public statements in Irina Voitsekh, "Merov tozhe nasadiat na vertikal," *Utro.ru,* October 8, 2004.

18. For studies focusing on the impact of the media on popular support and elections, see Shanto Iyenger and Donald Kinder, *News That Matters: Television and American Opinion* (Chicago: University of Chicago Press, 1987); and Diana Mutz, Paul Sniderman, and Richard Brody, eds., *Political Persuasion and Attitude Change* (Ann Arbor: University of Michigan Press, 1996). For a normative argument about the media's appropriate role in a democracy, see Graham Ramsden, "Media Coverage of Issues and Candidates: What Balance Is Appropriate in a Democracy?" *Political Science Quarterly* 111, no. 1 (1996): 65–81. Studies looking at the role of the media in determining individuals' evaluations of the economy include Diana Mutz, "Mass Media and the Depoliticization of Personal Experience," *American Journal of Political Science* 36, no. 2 (1992): 483–508; Marc Heatherington, "The Media's Role in Forming Voters' National Economic Evaluations in 1992," *American Journal of Political Science* 40, no. 2 (1996): 372–95; For a challenge to the media's role in shaping economic evaluations, see H. Brandon Haller and Helmut Northrop, "Reality Bites: News Exposure and Economic Opinion," *Public Opinion Quarterly* 61, no. 4 (1997): 555–75.

19. Mutz, "Mass Media and the Depoliticization of Personal Experience."

20. Heatherington, "Media's Role in Forming Voters' National Economic Evaluations in 1992."

21. After a September 2000 presidential decree, directors of regional GTRK were appointed not by the regional executive but by the presidential envoy for that region's Federal District.

22. However, as the author's discussions (mostly conducted in 1999–2001) with a number of regional journalists, editors, and broadcast news personalities indicate, the degree of latitude can vary markedly. The editor of one municipality-sponsored paper suggested that only the most blatant attacks on city administration policy would result in some form of retaliation. Others spoke of self-censorship arising from the realization that the media outlet's facilities and funding were entirely dependent upon the goodwill of its sponsors. In a survey of owners of mass media organizations in nine cities conducted by the Center for Law and the Mass Media, 90 percent of the interviewees indicated that mass media reflected the point of view of the outlet's sponsors, the executive or legislative branch, or the governor and that one can "know precisely which publication works for whom"; Center for Law and the Mass Media, *Rossiiskie sredstva massovoi informatsii, vlast' i capital: K voprosu o kontsentratsii i prozrachnosti SMI v Rossii,* June 27, 2003, http://www.medialaw.ru/publications/books/conc1/2.html.

23. The increasingly ambiguous relationship between Samarskaia Oblast's Titov and the regional media from 1999 on provides an example of the latter. After Titov challenged Vladimir Putin in the 2000 presidential election, one of the region's most prominent business publications, *Samarskoe Obozrenia,* turned sharply against the governor and his supporters. Other private television and radio stations also changed allegiances as significant portions of the regional business elite aligned themselves with the federal government.

24. Drawing upon the Ul'ianovsk survey data, I present an initial investigation of these issues in Andrew Konitzer-Smirnov, "Jurisdictional Voting in Russia's Regions: Initial Results from Individual-level Analyses," *Europe-Asia Studies* 55, no. 1 (2003).

25. Timothy Colton, *Transitional Citizens: Voters and What Influences Them in the New Russia* (Cambridge, Mass.: Harvard University Press, 2000), 61.

26. These four outlets were ABC News, CNN, NBC News, and CBS News. See

Pew Research Center for the People and the Press, *July Omnibus–Media Update,* "Final Topline," July 8–16, 2002.

27. The data are from three separate surveys (1998, 1999, 2001) by the Public Opinion Foundation. The first two surveys asked specifically about the objectivity of political information, whereas the final survey asked about the veracity of the media "in general." Negative responses varied between 50 and 60 percent, and positive ones varied from 30 to 37 percent. The balance of respondents answered, "difficult to say." See "A voobshche o politicheskikh sobytiiakh v strane televidenie, radio, gazety rasskazyvaiut v tselom ob'ektivno ili neob'ektivno?" *Baza Dannykh FOM* [Public Opinion Foundation, Fond Obshchestvennoe Mnenie, or FOM], June 17, 1998, http://bd.fom.ru/report/cat/societas/mass_media/t8036910; "Kak vy schitaete, esli govorit' v tselom, to poluchaiut ili ne poluchaiut Rossiiane iz peredach televideniia, radio, i iz gazet ob'ektivnuiu, pravdivuiu informathiiu . . . o politicheskoi zhisni Rossii?" *Baza Dannykh FOM,* March 21, 1999, http://bd.fom.ru/report/cat/societas/mass_media/t904416; and "Informatsiia o politike v SMI," *Baza Dannykh FOM,* February 14, 2001, http://bd.fom.ru/report/cat/societas/mass_media/tb010509.

28. "A peredachi vashikh mestnykh telekanalov pokazyvaiut sobytiia, zhizn' vashei oblasti, regiona ob'ektivno, priukrashivaiut ili, naoborot, ocherniaiut deistvitel'nost'?" *Baza Dannykh FOM,* October 21, 1998, http://bd.fom.ru/report/cat/societas/mass_media/t8041617.

29. Colton, *Transitional Citizens,* 61–62.

30. As indicated in chapter 4, audience rates in *raion* centers, towns, and villages reached 64.1, 60.9, and 63, respectively.

31. Maksim Glinkin, "Vybory s zaviazannymi glazami," *Nezavisimaia Gazeta,* February 13, 2003.

32. Georgii Il'ichev, "Konstitutsionnyi sud razviazal zhurnalistam ruki," *Izvestiia,* October 10, 2003.

33. Besik Pipiia, Viktor Svinin, and Sergei Sergievskii, "Administrativnyi resurs rabotaet bez otpuska," *Nezavisimaia Gazeta,* September 23, 2003.

34. See Marina Volkova, "Zalozhniki politicheskikh tekhnnologi," *Izvestiia,* April 11, 2000.

35. Natal'ia Ratiani, "Stepashin ob'iavil Yakovlevu bol'shuiu federal'nuiu voinu," *Izvestiia,* March 31, 2003.

36. "Iskuplenie grekhov," *Izvestiia,* June 17, 2003.

37. Boris Vishnevskii, "Vizit k prezidentu mozhet izmenit' rasstanovku sil na vyborakh v Peterburge," *Novaya Gazeta,* September 8, 2003.

38. Georgii Kovalev, "Piterskie vybory: Markova protiv Matvienko," *Politkom.ru,* October 3, 2003.

39. Kovalev, "Piterskie vybory."

40. Dmitrii Volgin, "Popravki k zakonu 'o SMI' usiliat regional'nuiu vlast'," *Politkom.ru,* May 23, 2003, http://www.politcom.ru/2003/zloba2370.php.

41. Tim Carrington and Mark Nelson, "Media in Transition: The Hegemony of Economics" in *The Right to Tell: The Role of Mass Media in Economic Development,* ed. Roumeen Islam (Washington, D.C.: World Bank, 2002), 225–45.

42. Nonetheless, a study by David Barker and Kathleen Knight indicates that the problem of strong media bias is certainly not restricted to Russia. See these authors' examination of Rush Limbaugh's listening audience in, David Barker and Kathleen

Knight, "Political Talk Radio and Public Opinion," *Public Opinion Quarterly* 64 (2000): 149–70.

43. For a more detailed discussion on the erosion of Russian media autonomy, see Laura Belin, "Political Bias and Self-Censorship in the Russian Media," in *Contemporary Russian Politics: A Reader,* ed. Archie Brown (New York: Oxford University Press, 2000).

44. Of course, political scientists and other analysts have long emphasized the important linkage between political parties and democratization. For a recent example, see Seymour Lipset, "The Indispensability of Parties," *Journal of Democracy* 11 (2000): 48–55.

45. When speaking of the "unknown challenger" issue, interviewees often referred to a Russian saying about "buying a cat in a sack." Such a transaction puts the buyer at a disadvantage because the sack conceals the nature of the creature within.

46. Samuel Popkin, *The Reasoning Voter* (Chicago: University of Chicago Press, 1991), 51.

47. Of course, this is a simplification. As indicated at the end of chapter 3, a number of other factors may raise the costs for terminal incumbents and other candidates who practice dirty campaign tactics. Life goes on after the election and, unless the candidate leaves the region, he or she may face the consequences of a particularly *groznyi* campaign under an embittered and victorious opponent.

48. Terry Moe, "Political Institutions: The Neglected Side of the Story," *Journal of Law, Economics, and Organization* 6 (1990): 213–53.

49. Grigorii Golosov, *Political Parties in the Regions of Russia: Democracy Unclaimed* (Boulder, Colo.: Lynne Rienner, 2004), 3.

50. Golosov, *Political Parties,* 19–53.

51. Golosov, *Political Parties,* 3.

52. Golosov, *Political Parties,* 113–22.

53. Grigorii Golosov, "Gubernatory i partiinaia politika," *Pro et Contra* 5, no. 1 (Winter 2000): 69–108.

54. M. Lugovskaia, "Vvedenie proportsional'noi izbiratel'noi sistemy v regional'noe zakonodatel'stvo o vyborakh," *Dzhurnal o vyborakh* 4 (2003): 4.

55. Lugovskaia, "Vvedenie proportsional'noi izbiratel'noi sistemy," 8–10.

56. Dmitrii Solntsev and Ol'ga Popova, "Titov poshel na tretii srok," *Samarskoe Obozrenie,* December 29, 2003; "Titov udivil Sychevym," *Reporter,* December 26, 2003.

57. Aleksandr Kynev, "Krizis sistemy Titova," *Politcom.ru,* http://www.politcom.ru/2004/analit166.php.

58. Sergei Tatarenkov, "Kirienko khochet posporit'," *Delo,* November 9, 2001.

59. Thanks to Vladimir Zvonovskii, the director of the Samara Fund for Social Research, for his insights into the implications of Sychev's appointment for the presidential elections. Vladimir Zvonovskii, interview by the author, Samara, Samarskaia Oblast, December 26, 2003. See also Andrei Fedorov, "Regional'nye vybory: Samarskii gubernator reshil pereizbrati'sia dosrochno," *Kommersant Daily,* February 24, 2004.

60. See, e.g., Henry Hale, "Putin's Federal Reforms: Success or Failure?" comments presented during roundtable at the annual meeting of the American Association for the Advancement of Slavic Studies, Toronto, November 2003.

61. Andrei Riskin, "Gubernatory podmiali 'partiiu vlasti': Mikhail Prusak i Evgenii Mikhailov dobilis' sniatia neugodnykh regional'nykh partbossov," *Nezavisimaia Gazeta,* April 24, 2003.

62. Riskin, "Gubernatory podmiali 'partiiu vlasti.'"

63. As indicated above, though this process is certainly not new, it is interesting in the United Russia case because it goes against the popular conception of the party as a strong arm of the federal center. For earlier examples of party "privatization," see Nikolai Petrov and Aleksei Titkov, "Vybory-99 v regional'nom izmerenii," in *Regiony Rossii v 1999 g.,* ed. Nikolai Petrov (Moscow: Carnegie Moscow Center, 2001).

64. Steven Solnick, "Gubernatorial Elections in Russia, 1996–1997," *Post-Soviet Affairs* 14 (1998): 48–80; Andrew Konitzer-Smirnov, "Incumbent Election Fortunes and Regional Economic Performance during Russia's 2000–2001 Regional Executive Election Cycle," *Post-Soviet Affairs* 19 (2003): 46–79.

65. Georgii Il'ichev and Ol'ga Tropkina, "'Edinaia Rossiia' predpochitaet vybory bez konkurentov," *Izvestiia,* December 21, 2004.

66. Dmitrii Kamyshev, "Siuzhet nedeli: Altai-boltai i drugie," *Kommersant-Vlast,* April 12, 2004.

67. Dmitrii Kamyshev, "Velika Rossiia, a nastupat' nekomu," *Kommersantt-Vlast,* December 13, 2004.

68. Riskin, "I primknyvshie k nim gubernatory."

69. Vladimir Sokolov, "Politika: Regional'nye vybory: Edinorossy prodliat polnomochiia gubernatorov Rosselia," *Kommersant Daily,* March 6, 2003.

70. Iurii Dorokhov and Sergei Berg, "Regional'naia politika: Edinaia Rossiia dala Irkutskomu gubernatoru tretii srok," *Kommersant Daily,* November 27, 2003.

71. Sergei Obsiannikov and Nikolai Gul'ko, "Gubernatorskie vybory: Vybory Kirovskogo gubernatora proidut bez gubernatora," *Nezavisimaia Gazeta,* October 29, 2003.

72. These results are from the Central Election Commission Web site, http://www.cikrf.ru.

73. See Henry Hale, "Explaining Machine Politics in Russia's Regions: Economy, Ethnicity, and Legacy," *Post-Soviet Affairs* 3 (2003): 229–63.

74. The omnipresent nature of the mythical list in discussions of the 1999–2001 elections defies a complete listing of references. For one discussion of the list, see Andrei Cogrin and Artur Akopov, "Shestero prigovorennykh . . . Komy vygodny 'utechki' iz Kremlia?" *Vremia MN,* March 15, 2000.

75. Igor' Bunin, "Vsgliad: Zaklanie Gubernatorov," *Novye Izvestiia,* May 18, 2004.

76. Il'ia Sverdlov, "Peterburg proignoriroval vybory," *Novaya Gazeta,* September 23, 2003; Aleksandr Zadorozhnyi and Aleskei Bessudnov, "Politika: Gubernatorskie vybory: Kremlevskie resursy," *Expert,* September 29, 2003; Boris Vishevskii, "Osechka 'Avrory': Pochemu mnogie pitertsy ne prishli na vybory svoego gubernatora," *Novaya Gazeta,* September 25, 2003; Anatolii Golov, "Ravnodushnykh budet bol'she," *Novaya Gazeta,* September 25, 2003.

77. Worse was still to come. During the December 2004 regional executive election in Brianskaia Oblast, the region set a new record for votes cast "against all" candidates. After a heavy-handed removal of the incumbent governor Iurii Lodkin from the race for election infractions, a full 20.81 percent of the electorate voted against all candidates. "Pobit record golosovaniia 'protiv vsekh,'" *Izvestiia,* December 7, 2004.

78. See, e.g., Kathryn Stoner Weiss, "Central Governing Incapacity and the Weakness of Political Parties: Russian Democracy in Disarray," paper presented at the Annual Meeting of the American Political Science Association, Boston, August 2002.

Appendix: Methods and Measures

As indicated above in the main text, this study employs both qualitative and quantitative data to paint a picture of economic voting and accountability in Russia's regions. In combining these two approaches, I endeavor to present a fuller story of economic accountability that goes beyond anecdotes of specific high-profile election cases while still providing the detail necessary to place the quantitative results in context and provide the reader with a grasp of the shape and feel of regional executive election campaigns.

In presenting the quantitative data, I have made every effort to maximize the accessibility of these analyses to readers from a wide range of statistical backgrounds so that those with even the most basic understanding of these methods can negotiate the models. Aside from descriptive statistics like means, medians, and percentages, the book presents the results of a number of more sophisticated models; it is hoped that this brief primer will make these models more comprehensible for readers accustomed to other approaches.

The analyses in chapters 4 and 5 feature binomial and multinomial logit models that present the relationship between either a dichotomous dependent variable (in this case, whether or not the respondent will vote for the incumbent) or a multivalue categorical variable (in this case, party choice) and a set of independent explanatory variables. For a description of the binomial and multinomial logit models, see J. Scott Long, *Regression Models for Categorical and Limited Dependent Variables* (Thousand Oaks, Calif.: Sage Publications, 1997); and J. Scott Long and Jeremy Freese, *Regression Models for Categorical Dependent Variables Using Stata* (College Station, Tex.: Stata Press, 2001).

The values for each of the independent variables in a logit model can be presented in a number of different ways; however, one of the shortcomings of any categorical regression model (logit, probit, etc.) is that the raw values lack any logical substantive interpretation. To overcome this obstacle, I use Michael Tomz, Jason Wittenberg, and Gary King's CLARIFY software to derive quantities from the raw values that represent the "total effects" of the given indicator on the change in the predicted probability that the dependent variable takes on a given value for a particular respondent (chapter 4) or region (chapter 5) in question. (For more on CLARIFY software, see Gary King, Michael Tomz, and Jason Wittenberg, "Making the Most of Statistical Analyses: Improving Interpretation and Presentation," *American Journal of Political Science* 44, no. 2 [April 2000]: 347–61; and Michael Tomz, Jason Wittenberg, and Gary King, "CLARIFY: Software for Interpreting and Presenting Statistical Results, Version 2.1," Stanford University, University of Wisconsin, and Harvard University; available at http://gking.harvard.edu.)

For the first model in chapter 4, the total-effect estimate indicates the change in the probability of supporting a candidate as one moves from each independent variable's minimum value to its maximum value while holding all other indicators in the model at their means. For the model in chapter 5, the total-effect estimate indicates the change in the probability of an incumbent win as one shifts from the specific independent variable's minimum value to its maximum value. In both cases, the total-effect estimate allows one to concentrate on the individual effects of each independent variable across its entire range of values.

To take the example from table 4.3 above in the text, if "personal pocketbook" is a five-category indicator of a respondent's self-assessment of the change in his or her personal economic situation during the past year, then a value of 0.10 would indicate that, with all other variables in the model held at their means (again, to isolate the individual effect of the variable in question), the predicted probability of supporting the incumbent for a respondent who gave the highest ("5") assessment of her economic situation increases by a factor of 0.10 above that of a respondent who gave the lowest ("1") assessment. If the coefficient were –0.10, then the relationship would be reversed, with the most positive respondent being *less* likely to support the incumbent than her more negative counterpart. The model in chapter 5 also utilizes logit analyses; only in this instance, the results are displayed as the total change in the probability that an incumbent will maintain office after an election given a shift in the given independent variable from its minimum to maximum value.

Chapter 6 examines the relationship between economic conditions and the dismissal of Ukrainian regional executives. In this instance, the dependent variable differs from earlier models because, instead of measuring the outcome at a conveniently established point in time (an election), I am instead looking at the probability of removal at any point in time during a period of five years. This situation demands a different approach that more explicitly includes the element of time—something for which time-series analysis was designed.

Hence, instead of looking at preconditions and outcomes during elections, I instead set up a database that breaks the years from 1996 to 2000 into quarters. For each of Ukraine's twenty-seven regions, I include variables indicating whether incumbents retained office along with a set of other economic and political indicators measured over a period of twenty (five years times four) quarters. I then analyze the data using a fixed-effects logit model. This particular model works similarly to the standard logit models described above, in that it estimates the relative effects of a set of independent variables on the probability of a certain outcome on a dichotomous dependent variable (in this case, an incumbent win or loss). However, as a "fixed-effects" model, it also brackets out factors that are constant for a given region across time (e.g., location, relatively constant features of the local political culture) and estimates the effects only of those variables included in the model.

Aside from the use of a fixed-effects model, the results displayed in chapter 6 also differ from the models in chapter 4 and 5 in the way in which the values are presented. Because CLARIFY is not presently compatible with fixed-effects, cross-sectional, time series models, I present the results of the Ukrainian analyses using odds ratios. Odds ratios indicate the percentage change in the odds of a positive "1" outcome on the dependent variable given changes in the independent variable in question. These values are interpreted by subtracting 1 from given the value and treating the difference as the percentage change in odds.

Therefore, if the variable indicating whether Ukrainian president Leonid Kuchma carried the region in the most recent presidential election has a coefficient of 0.10, then, with all fixed effects held constant and all other variables held at their mean, a win for Kuchma in a given region lowers the probability of an executive's dismissal by 90 percent ($0.10 - 1 = -0.90$). For the "parties of power in 1998" indicator, a value of 7.18 indicates that the odds of removal for a regional executive ruling over a region where support for the parties of power fell below the national median are 618 percent

(7.18 – 1 = 6.18) greater than for his or her counterpart in a region where support was higher than the national median.

For each of the analyses presented in the book, I again give brief explanations of the methods involved. However, throughout the text, the reader may want to refer back to the above description of the methods employed. Following the presentation of the results, I make every effort to couch the discussion of the models in the most accessible terms possible, and I encourage the reader to take the time to understand the tables.

Aggregate-Level Indicators

The following indicators for Russia and for Ukraine are those from chapters 5 and 6. The indicators for chapter 4 are described in the chapter.

Russian Analyses

Turnover: A dichotomous variable indicating a "1" if the incumbent or his "heir" (*preemnik*) won the election, and a "0" otherwise. Instances in which the incumbent or a *preemnik* did not compete (as in Kursk Oblast, where the incumbent was disqualified just hours before the election), are coded as missing.

Effective number of candidates^{log}: A logged (to attenuate the skewed distribution) measure of the effective number of candidates adapted from the "effective number of parties measure" of Markku Laakso and Rein Taagepera, "Effective Number of Parties: A Measure with Application to West Europe," *Comparative Political Studies* 12 (1979): 3–27. The measure is:

$$N = \frac{1}{\Sigma p_i^2}$$

In simpler terms, the measure is derived by dividing 1 by the sum of the squares of each candidate's share of the popular vote during the first round of elections. The result is a number indicating how many viable candidates competed in an election.

Tours: A dichotomous variable coded as "1" if the election was concluded in two tours and "0" otherwise.

Δ *Adjusted wages:* A measure of change in adjusted wages standardized across all regions for the year before the election in question. In mathematical terms:

$$\Delta \text{ adjusted wages} = \frac{(Y_{rt} - Y_{rt-1}) - (\bar{Y}_t - \bar{Y}_{t-1})}{s_Y}$$

where Y indicates the economic indicator, r the region, and t the year of the election.

1997, 1998, 1999, 2000, 2001: Dummy year variables indicating "1" if the election occurred in a given year, "0" otherwise. The year 1996 acts as the baseline.

Ukrainian Analyses

Dismissal: A dichotomous variable indicating a "1" if the regional executive was dismissed from office during the quarter in question and a "0" otherwise. Instances in which an executive died in office or was promoted are coded as "0."

Kuchma win: A dichotomous variable indicating a "1" if Kuchma came in first place during the last round of the most recent presidential election and "0" otherwise.

Parties of power in 1998: A dichotomous variable indicating a "1" if, within the last two quarters, a Verkhovna Rada election occurred, in which the summed percentages of the "parties of power" (for a list of the parties, see note 22 in chapter 6) for a given region fell short of the national median. The variable takes a value of "0" otherwise.

% Δ GRP: The percentage annual change in per capita gross regional product.

% Δ employment: The percentage annual change in the number of individuals employed.

% Δ budget revenues: The percentage annual change in regional budget revenues.

% Δ avg. income: The percentage annual change in average regional incomes.

% Δ investment: The percentage annual change in fixed capital investments.

% Δ small enterprises: The percentage annual change in the number of small enterprises.

1997, 1998, 1999, 2000: Dummy year variables indicating "1" if the election occurred in a given year, "0" otherwise.

Index

absolute majority-based elections, 76
absolute sociotropic effects, 130, 132–34
accountability, 31–36; and appointed
 executives, 15, 22, 232; criteria for,
 35–36, 96–98, 103; and decentralization, 175–76; and economic outcomes, 11–12, 36–38, 54–61; and
 elections, 8, 10–15, 96–98, 174; and
 game theory, 33–34; hostile environment toward, 3; and incumbents, 83;
 and media, 214; and party consolidation, 225; and postcommunist
 elections, 50; subnational, 3, 4, 54,
 230–31. *See also* challenges to
 electoral accountability
accountability representation, 31, 33–35
administrative resources, abuse of, 7, 75,
 79–80, 82, 120, 226–27. *See also*
 chernaia tekhnologiia (dirty tricks)
 and *administrativnye resursi*
advanced industrialized societies:
 accountability and economic voting
 in, 20; concepts derived from, 30–31;
 voting studies from, 14, 39–42
aggregate economic performance and
 election outcomes, 158–73; data
 sources, 14, 159–60; elected vs.
 appointed executives, 171; model and
 final results, 167–71; preview and
 summary of results, 160–62; regional

growth and election outcomes, 9; test
 variables and controls, 162–67
aggregate-level analyses, 64
airline downings, 5
Alford, J.R., 40
All-Russian Coordinating Council
 (OKS), 86–87
anonymous pamphlets, 81
antireform protest, 6–7
appointed executives: and accountability,
 15, 22, 232; determining outcomes for,
 174–75; and economic growth, 22;
 elected vs., 171, 174–75; and market-
 preserving federalism, 177–78; in
 oblasti and *kraia*, 55; presidential
 appointments, 52–53; toward system
 of appointed regional executives, 5–7,
 8, 231–33; in Ukraine, 179, 183,
 184–89, 232. *See also* comparative
 perspective of Russia's regional
 elections
arbitrary federal intervention, 229–31
area specialists, 29–30
assigning responsibility, 28–70; accountability, 31–36; choosing issue for
 study, 36–38; economic accountability
 in evolving context, 54–61; economic
 voting, generally, 39–46; economic
 voting in Russia and Eastern Europe,
 46–54; looking ahead, 64–65;

assigning responsibility (*continued*)
methodological decisions, 61–64;
"portability of concepts," 29–31
Atkeson, L.R., 45
autonomous *okruga*, incumbent success
in, 94, 98

ballot confusion, 2
Basic Guarantees of Citizens Electoral
Rights and Right to Participate in
Referendum: article 63, 78; campaigning, restrictions on, 210–11; and
election challenges, 78; enactment and
provisions of, 72–73; and media, 75;
and regional election commissions,
80–81; and regional legislatures, 219;
and resignation of regional executives,
200
"Belgorod alternative," 82, 197–98, 200
Belgorodskaia Oblast regional election,
198
Belonuchkin, Grigoryi, 19, 160
Berezovskii, Boris, 229
Beslan hostage crisis, 5, 231
best assessment of regional voters, 166
best interests of citizens, defining,
10–11
bilateral treaties between republics and
Moscow, 17, 57–59
Blanchard, Olivier, 178, 179, 189
Bloc Zhirinovsky, 48, 135
Bloom, Howard, 40
Brianskaia Oblast, elections in, 2, 89–90,
199–200, 201, 225
"Briansk alternative," 198
Brody, Richard, 42
budgets: chaotic relations, 3; lack of
federal funds, 57–59; lack of
transparency, 177; and performance-
oriented policies, 177; regional
responsibility for, 57–59
Bunin, Igor', 229
Busygina, Irina, 11, 59

campaigning by candidates, 74–76, 79,
89, 210–11. *See also chernaia*

tekhnologiia (dirty tricks) and
administrativnye resursi
candidates: "clones" election strategy,
89, 171, 198, 200–201; "effective
number of candidates," 92, 94;
eligibility requirements, 72–73;
financial statements from, 74;
opposition, 98; phony, 171, 177;
from security organs, 62, 137, 140;
signature requirement for ballot, 74.
See also campaigning by candidates;
incumbents
Carrington, Tim, 214
"cassette scandal" in Ukraine, 179, 181
Central Election Commission, 4, 73, 124,
219
central government intervention in regional elections, 8, 10, 22, 61, 229–31
challenges to electoral accountability,
194–239; arbitrary federal intervention, 229–31; *chernaia tekhnologiia*
(dirty tricks) and *administrativnye
resursi*, 197–202; political parties,
215–29; poorly defined policy
jurisdictions, 202–5; post-Yeltsin
challenges and Putin's solutions, 197;
regional media, 205–14; toward a
system of appointed regional executives, 231–33
Cheibub, Jose Antonio, 202
Cheliabinskaia Oblast, elections in, 83
chernaia tekhnologiia (dirty tricks) and
administrativnye resursi, 89, 177,
197–202, 216, 217–18, 222. *See also*
administrative resources, abuse of;
political parties
China, 22, 171, 174, 177–78
Chubb, John, 43–44
Cities of Federal Significance, executives
in, 94
city council in Ul'ianovskaia Oblast,
113–14
CLARIFY software, 242, 243
Clem, Ralph S., 48–49, 54
"clones" election strategy, 89, 171, 198,
200–201

Cohen, Stephen, 30
Colton, Timothy, 46–48, 144–45, 207, 208–9
Communism, return to, 85
Communist Party, 48–49, 135, 138, 217
comparative perspective of Russia's regional elections, 174–93; appointee system in Ukraine, 184–89; preview and summary of results, 183–84; theoretical expectations and disappointments, 175–80; and Ukraine, 180–83
comparativists, 29–30
competition: elimination before election campaigns, 92; and elites, 13, 50–51, 162, 163, 177; poorly established norms of, 177; regional elections with, 92, 162–63; significance of, 171
consecutive terms of office. *See* term of office
Constitution: of Russia, 15, 17; of Ukraine, 180
Constitutional Court, 6, 211
consumer price index and regional executive electoral performance, 152
Cook's distance, 169
courts: and challenges to elections, 78–80; and media regulation, 211
Craumer, Peter R., 48–49, 54
criminal proceedings against regional executives, 229
Czech Republic, elections in, 49–50

decentralization, 8, 13, 59–60, 72, 175–76, 233
decision-making process of Ul'ianovskaia Oblast voters, 131–42
Demin, Oleg, 182
Denin, Aleksandr, 2
Denin, Mikhail, 201
Denin, Nikolai Vasil'evich, 2, 198, 201
Diamond, Larry, 176
"dictatorship of law," 195, 229, 233
dirty tricks. *See chernaia tekhnologiia* (dirty tricks) and *administrativnye resursi*

district-level electoral commissions, 73–74, 76
district-level presidential representatives, 4
Downs, Anthony, 39, 215
dublery (stand-ins), 199–200
Duma: and elected executives, elimination of, 6; election of 2003, 220; and elections, generally, 50; political party participation in, 218–19; single-mandate districts, elimination of, 5. *See also* laws

economic performance: and accountability in evolving context, 11–12, 54–61; and appointed executives, 22; as choice for accountability study, 36–38; and elected officials, 186; and incumbents, 40; and period of stability, 61; and subnational elections, 176. *See also* economic voting
economic voting, 8–13; and decision-making in Ul'ianovskaia Oblast election, 131–42; and ideal subnational jurisdictional voter, 128–31; and jurisdictional issues, 42–46, 53–54, 62; literature review, 39–46; and methodology, 61–64; in post-communist elections, 50; at regional level, 128–29; in Russia and Eastern Europe, 46–54; in subfederal-level elections, 9, 12, 42–45; in transition and Western countries, 13
"effective number of candidates," 92, 94
"effective number of parties," 92
"elected by recommendation of president," 6, 23
elected officials: appointed executives vs., 171, 174–75; economic performance of, 186. *See also* regional executive elections
election commissions, 73–74, 78. *See also specific commission or type*
"electioneering" by incumbent regimes, 200

elections of 1996–97 cycle, 54, 56, 84–87, 96, 127
elections of 1999-2001 cycle, 54–56, 60, 63, 71–102, 198. *See also* Ul'ianovskaia Oblast and regional jurisdictional voters
elections of 2001–4 cycle, 60–61
eligibility requirements for candidates, 72–73
elimination of regional executive elections: from central government intervention to, 10, 195–96; and defeats of 2004, 225; effect of, 22–23, 228, 234; as institutions worth saving, 232–33; justification for, 8; negative implications of, 183; process of, 5–7, 60–61
elites: and appointed executives, 87, 179; business, 206; and competition, 13, 50–51, 162, 163, 177; and control of election process, 9; and media, 210; and political parties, 217; predatory political, 171; and regional politics, 4, 50–51, 77, 88, 97–98, 180; replacement of, 88; ruling, 3–4; in Ukraine, 181; and Ul'ianovskaia Oblast elections, 120, 123, 125
employment status and voters' decision-making, 135
ethnic republics, 15, 17, 83, 94
Evenkiiskii Autonomous Okrug 1997 election, 169
executives. *See* regional executive elections; regional executives
exit polls, 62–63

Failed Crusade (Cohen), 30
Fair, Raymond, 40
federal context and incumbent support, 142–47
federal districts, 4–5
federalism, 3–5, 15–18; budgetary, 57–59; and Kozak Commission, 204; market-preserving, 15, 21–22, 177–78, 179; Yeltsin-era, 202–3
federal subjects, incumbent success across, 94–95, 98

Feldman, Stanley, 42
"fiefdoms," 7–8, 96
financial crisis of August 1998, 58
financial statements from candidates, 74
Fiorina, Morris, 39, 41, 127
FOM (Public Opinion Foundation, Fond Obshchestvennoe Mnenie) surveys, 7
fragmentation, political, 3–4

Gaidar, Yegor, 107, 108, 112
game theory and accountability, 33–34
Glinkin, Maksim, 210–11
Golosov, Grigorii: analysis of, 14; and election cycles, 18; and party rivalries, 86; and political parties, 216–17; study of regional executive election success, 51–52, 53, 54
Gorbachev, Mikhail, 220
Goriachev, Iurii Frolovich: administration of, 106–27; on candidacy, 103; and Communist Party, 138; defeat of, 125; and elections, 112–16, 120–23, 124, 125; and groups supporting, 138, 140; as head of regional administration, 82; on heating subsidies, 2; and presidential support, 144; "punishing" of, 148; term of governor of, 82; and Yeltsin's appointment procedure, 87
governors: and accountability, 13–14; appointment, 5–7; and elections in Russia, 6, 13–14, 51–53, 54; incumbent success and economic performance, 159; and jurisdictional issues in elections, 43–45, 128–29; as *khoziain,* 11, 165, 228, 232, 233; and "local authoritarianism," 56; and relationship to presidential support, 142–47; removal of rogue governors, 97–98; restrictions on power of, 4–5; role of, 11; term of, 87; U.S. gubernatorial elections, 43–44, 45, 56, 96–97. *See also* regional executives; Ul'ianovskaia Oblast and regional jurisdictional voters
Govorin, Boris, 227
gross regional product (GRP), 164, 166, 167, 174, 188, 189

GTRK Volga: effect on viewers, 133, 140, 209; and incumbent support, 139, 140, 141, 142, 143, 148–49; *selektornoe soveshchanie* and other shows on, 124; and Ul'ianovskaia Oblast 2000 election, 2, 122
"Gubernatorial Elections in Russia, 1996–1997" (Solnick), 51
Gusinskii, Vladimir, 229
Guzhva, Igor', 179

Hahn, Gordon, 195
Hale, Henry, 50
Hetherington, Marc, 205
Hibbing, J.R., 40
history and comparison of Russia and Ukraine, 178–79
Hungary, elections in, 49–50
Hyman, Lisa, 43

ideal subnational jurisdictional voter, 128–31; hypotheses, 129–30; measures, 133–37; preview and summary of results, 131–42; survey, 130–31
ideology and partisanship, 138
Kirovskaia Oblast elections, 226–27
illegal activities in election process, 89. *See also chernaia tekhnologiia* (dirty tricks) and *administrativnye resursi*
incumbents: and accountability, 83; and accountability representation, 33–34, 35; aggregate-level regional economic performance and success, 158–73; attrition rate for, 96; careers after office, 97–98; and economic factors, 14, 40, 52; "electioneering" by, 200; and enactment of incumbent-friendly laws, 88–90, 91–92, 97; entrenchment of, 83, 88, 89, 95, 96–97; evaluating success of, 51, 129–30; in federal context, 142–47; final-term, 97; and ideal subnational jurisdictional voter, 128–31; and information, 136–37; and litigation challenging elections, 78; and mandate responsibility, 31–32;

media and support for, 2, 140–41; and party success, 39–40; performance and electoral success, 9, 14, 54; and political parties, 39–40; presidential appointments, 52–53; regional status and success, 63, 94–95; and retrospective voters, 39; successful elections in Yeltsin and early-Putin eras, 82–88; successful elections of past decade, 88–94; voter response to, 4, 9, 35–36. *See also* economic voting; punishing or rewarding incumbents
industrialized societies. *See* advanced industrialized societies
information, effect on voters of, 12–13, 22, 135–37
Institutional Revolutionary Party in Mexico, 35
Internet reporting, 19, 20
Irkutskaia Oblast, elections in, 83, 226–27
Ivanchenko, A.V., 113
Ivanov, Sergei, 8

jurisdictional issues in voting, 42–46, 62; and ideal subnational jurisdictional voter, 128–31; and incumbent support, 158–59; pocketbook or absolute sociotropic considerations, 132–33; and regional elections, 53–54, 62; in Russia's regions, 125–28. *See also* Ul'ianovskaia Oblast and regional jurisdictional voters

Kabardino-Balkarskaia Republic 1997 election, 92
Kahn, Jeffrey, 17, 94
Kashkorova, Svetlana, 110
Kasianov, Mikhail, 122
Kazakov, Aleksandr, 5
Kazakov, Viktor, 220
Kazantsev, Vladimir, 112
"Kemerovo/Samara alternative," 199
Kemerovskaia Oblast, elections in, 199, 219
Key, V.O., 39
Khodorkovskii, Mikhail, 229

khoziain, governor as, 11, 228, 232, 233
Kiewiet, D. Roderick, 12, 41–42, 45, 46, 47, 62
Kinakh, Anatoly, 181
Kinder, Donald, 12, 41, 42, 45, 47, 62
King, Gary, 242
Kirienko, Sergei, 121–22, 125, 229
Kirovskaia Oblast, elections in, 198, 199
Kokov, Valerii, 92, 203
Korsunov, Aleksander, 203
Kozak, Dmitrii, 203
Kozak Commission reforms, 61, 203–5
Kramer, Gerald, 12, 39, 41
Kravchuk, Leonid, 180
Kruglikov, A., 114–16
Kuchma, Leonid, 179, 180–82, 184–85, 187–88
Kurskaia Oblast, elections in, 91, 123, 199
"Kursk variant," 123, 125, 198
Kyiv Rus, 178

Laakso, Markku, 92, 94
Landry, Pierre, 178
Lankina, Tomila, 203
Lavrov, Aleksei, 19, 57
Law of Power (Ukraine), 180
Law on Local Self-Government (Ukraine), 180
Law on the Formation of Local Government Bodies (Ukraine), 180
laws, 4; election law in Ul'ianovskaia Oblast, 113–14; incumbent-friendly legislation, 88–90, 91–92, 97; and Kozak Commission reforms, 204–5; legal basis for elections in Russia, 72–82; and media, 72, 209–11; term limits, 97; Ukraine, 180–81
Lebedev, Iurii, 110
legislatures: disbanding of, 4, 56; regional legislatures and regional executives, 81; in Ul'ianovskaia Oblast, 113–14; Yeltsin's showdown with federal legislature, 56, 81. *See also* laws
Liberal Democratic Party of Japan, 35

Lipetskaia Oblast 1998 election, 169
litigation challenging elections, 78–80
Lodkin, Iurii, 2, 89, 201
Logan, Mikal Ben Gera, 41
logit model, 241–42
lower-level electoral commissions, 73–74
low-turnout issues, 89
Lugovskaia, M., 219
Luzhkov, Iurii, 95
Lysenko, Vladimir, 71

Magadanskaia Oblast, election in, 224
Malafeev, Valentin, 87, 106
mandate representation, 31–33, 35
Manin, Bernard: and criteria for accountability, 35–36, 103; and electoral accountability, 10; and forms of representation, 29, 31–36; and pocketbook voters, 129; on survival in office, 162
maps: electoral geography of 1996 Ul'ianovskaia Oblast elections, 115; electoral geography of 2000 Ul'ianovskaia Oblast elections, 126; Russian Federation's administrative boundaries, 16
market-preserving federalism (MPF), 15, 21–22, 177–78, 179
Markova, Anna, 213
Marusin, Vitalii, 115, 116, 117
Maslow, Abraham, 37
mass media. *See* media
mass public meetings, restrictions on, 75–76
material welfare, accountability for citizens', 11
material well-being vs. support of regional executives, 8
Matsuzato, Kimitaka, 179, 184–85, 189
Matvienko, Valentina, 2, 212–13
McAllister, Ian, 207
McIntyre, Robert, 107, 111
media: and accountability, 36, 205–14; administration control of, 22; appointment of directors of regional broadcast

stations, 4–5; bias, 206–7, 208; biased and unprofessional, 9; and campaigns, 2, 74, 75, 79, 82–83; control over, 4, 22, 207; election analysis by, 20; and entrenched regional executives, 82–83; on governors, 11; and incumbent support, 140–42, 143; independence of, 36, 148; information, effect on voters, 135–37; Internet reporting, 19, 20; laws on, 72, 209–11; mobilizational effect, 208; newspapers and publications, 136, 140–41, 148, 206; and opinion polls, 74–75; orientation of media outlets, 123–24, 125, 135, 206; policy commentators, 19; printed material, regulation of, 75, 81; prohibitions, 4, 210–11; radio, 206; reelection reporting, 13; regional, 205–14; and Saint Petersburg gubernatorial elections, 211–14; and television, 141, 148–49, 205–6, 209–10, 212–13; treatment of campaign-period litigation, 79; trust in, 206, 207, 208–9; and Ul'ianovskaia Oblast elections, 123–24, 127, 131–32, 206, 208, 209. *See also* GTRK Volga

methods and measures, 241–46; aggregate-level indicators, 244–46; Russian analyses, 244–45; Ukrainian analyses, 245–46

Mickiewicz, Ellen, 207, 208–9

Mikhailov, Evgenii, 222

Molodezhnaia Gazeta, 140

monitoring election process, 77–78, 82

Montinola, G., 177

Moraski, Bryon, 29, 52, 53

Moses, Joel, 197–98

MPF. *See* market-preserving federalism

Murmanskaia Oblast 2000 election, 92

Mutz, Diana, 205

Nadezhdin, Boris, 1

Narodnaia Gazeta, 123, 142

national elections and regional results, 188–89

"national referendum" voting, 45

Nazdratenko, Yevgenii, 61

Nelson, Mark, 214

Nenetskii Autonomous Okrug, election in, 60–61, 232

newspapers. *See* media

Niemi, Richard, 45, 176

nomination requirements, 217

Novgorodskaia Oblasti, 92, 221–22

NPSR (Popular-Patriotic Union of Russia), 86–87

NTV, 148

Oates, Sarah, 207

Oates, Wallace, 44

oblasti, 15, 17, 55, 98; and taxes, 57. *See also specific oblast*

obstacles to accountability. *See* challenges to electoral accountability

October 1993 showdown with federal legislature, 56–57

oil revenue, 61

OKS (All-Russian Coordinating Council), 86–87

oligarchs, attacks on, 229–30

Omelchenko, Alexander, 181

opinion polls, 6–7, 62–63, 74–75

opposition in elections: candidates, 98; in Kurskaia Oblast elections, 123; parties, 36; in Ul'ianovskaia Oblast elections, 114–17, 123–24

"Orel alternative," 198–99

Oreshkin, Dmitrii, 84–85, 158

Orlovskaia Oblast 1997 election, 198–99

Orttung, Robert, 78

"partial-Belgorod alternatives," 82, 198

participation barriers, 90

parties. *See* political parties

Partin, R.W., 45

partisanship and ideology, 138

Periaslav Treaty of 1654, 178

Perspektiv Sociological Laboratory, 130–31

Peterson, Paul, 44

phony candidates, 171, 177

plurality-rule-based elections, 76, 90

pocketbook interests: and incumbent support, 14, 138; and jurisdictional issues in voting, 129, 132–33; measures of, 134; role of in voting, 41–42, 62, 147; and support for incumbent, 129; survey data, 47, 64. *See also* economic voting

Poland, elections in, 49–50

policy jurisdictions, poorly defined, 202–5

political fragmentation, 3–4

political parties: and challenges to electoral accountability, 215–29; and incumbents, 39–40; information from, 12–13, 22; loyalty to, 12–13; and partification process, 219, 221, 222–23; and presidential support, 146; regional and central government actors, relationship, 176; and regional elections, 12–13, 50; weak party system, effect of, 177. *See also* United Russia party

Popkin, Samuel, 215, 222

Popular-Patriotic Union of Russia (NPSR), 86–87

postcommunist elections: and accountability, 50; economic voting in, 50, 54–56

post-Soviet political, social, and economic environment, 3, 9

preelection surveys, 63

preemniki, 97

presidential envoys, 77–78

presidential referendum effect, 176, 177

presidential vs. gubernatorial support, 142–47

presidents of republics in Russian Federation, 17

Price, Douglas, 40

printed materials. *See* media

privatization, 55

proportional representation, 5

protest in provinces to reform, 6–7

proto-parties, 86

Prusak, Mikhail, 92, 221–22

Przeworski, Adam: accountability and elections, 10; criteria for account-

ability, 35–36, 103; and defining accountability, 202; and forms of representation, 29, 31–36; and pocketbook voters, 129; on survival in office, 162

Pskovskaia Oblast, elections in, 163, 199–200, 222

Public Opinion Foundation (Fond Obshchestvennoe Mnenie, FOM) surveys, 7

public opinion polls. *See* opinion polls

punishing or rewarding incumbents: and absolute standard of living, 160; and accountability representation, 31; and campaign platform, 32; and decentralization, 176; and economic voting, 55; and election outcomes, 14; and election reforms, 196; on factors beyond official responsibilities, 62, 176; and getting out vote, 183–84; and Goriachev, 148; and jurisdictional issues, 42–43, 103, 133; and levels of government, 142–43, 176; and national elections, 23; and performance, 4, 9, 62, 130, 160; and personal economic assessment, 129, 147; and regional factors, 127, 128, 131, 147, 165, 175; removal from office, 162; and second-order elections, 44; short-term increases vs. prudent long-term policies, 177; in U.S. gubernatorial elections, 45; use of ballot box for, 3, 228

Putin, Vladimir: and accountability, 4, 22; anti-decentralization efforts of, 72; and appointed regional executives, 5, 8; challenges to, 79; comparison between presidential and gubernatorial support, 144, 146; consolidation of power under, 5, 202; election of, 5, 144, 219; elimination of dirty tricks, 200; federalism under, 3; first term of, 195; and intervention in regional elections, 8, 10, 61; and Kurskaia Oblast elections, 123; and political parties, 218; reforms of, 4, 5–6, 23, 56,

71, 77, 195–96, 203, 218–19, 232–33, 234; relationship with incumbents, 60; September 2004 initiatives of, 7; and Saint Petersburg election, 212; support for candidates by, 27; television appearances of, 2; and Ul'ianovskaia Oblast 2000 election, 121, 122–23, 124
Putin, Vladimir Borisovich, 198

Qian, Yingyi, 177
quality-of-life indicators, effect on incumbent success. *See* aggregate economic performance and election outcomes
quasi-appointment of executives, 5–7, 13, 231–32. *See also* appointed executives

radio, 206
recentralization of Russia, 7
Reddaway, Peter, 78
reelection of executives, 13, 36, 97
referendum effect, 85, 176, 177
referendum voting, 45, 53, 60, 88
regional economic performance, responsibility for, 11
regional election commissions, 73–74, 76, 80–81, 218–19
regional electorate, 1–27; accountability and economic voting, 10–13; context, 15–18; data sources, 18–20; number of regional elections, 2–3; regional elections as failed institutions, 7–10; second look at elections and regional executive accountability, 13–15
regional executive elections, 71–102; and accountability, 3, 15, 23, 56, 96–98; assessing factors influencing, 9–10; central government intervention in, 8, 10, 22, 61, 229–31; competition in, 92; consumer price index, 152; and economic accountability, 54–61; election period studied, 17–18; election process, 73; eligibility requirements for candidates, 72–73; as failed institutions, 7–10; incumbent

success in past decade, 88–94; incumbent success in Yeltsin and early Putin eras, 82–88; Internet reporting of, 20; legal basis for elections in Russia, 72–82; manipulation of, 9; number of, 2–3; and political fragmentation, 3–4; and political parties, 12–13, 50; postcommunist elections, cycles of, 54–56; and problems with endlessly unfolding election contests, 13, 71; regional status and incumbent success, 94–95; success in, 51–52; voters in, 4, 50–51. *See also* comparative perspective of Russia's regional elections; elimination of regional executive elections; incumbents; *specific election cycle or location*
regional executives: criminal proceedings against, 229; and disbanding of legislatures, 56–57; power to remove, 4; and regional legislatures, 81, 219; role of, 4; term limits, 4. *See also* governors; regional executive elections
regional government responsibilities, 57–59
"regionalized autocracies," 3–4, 7, 229
regional jurisdictional voters. *See* Ul'ianovskaia Oblast and regional jurisdictional voters
regional legislatures. *See* legislatures
regional presidential representatives, 77
Reif, Karlheinz, 44
Reisinger, William, 29, 52, 53
removal from office, 97–98, 162
republics in Russian Federation, 17, 94, 98
rewarding incumbents. *See* punishing or rewarding incumbents
Riskin, Andrei, 222
Rivers, Douglas, 46
Rizhskaia metro station bombing, 5
Rodina faction, 7
Rogozin, Dmitry, 7–8
Romanenko, Pavel, 118
Rossel, Eduard, 226–27

Rostovskaia Oblast, elections in, 199
Rumer, Eugene, 8
rumors and disparaging activities in
   campaigns, 89. *See also chernaia
   tekhnologiia* (dirty tricks) and
   administrativnye resursi
Russian Constitution, 15, 17
Russian Election Commission
   Publications, 18–19
Rutskoi, Aleksandr, 1, 91, 123
Ryzhkov, Vladimir, 6

Samarskaia Oblast, 79–80, 117–18, 199,
   219–21
Saraevym, B.A., 107
scandals, 7, 8
second-order elections, 44, 85–86
security organs, candidates from, 62,
   137, 140
selektornoe soveshchanie, 124
Semashin, N., 116
Semenov, Victor, 222
September 2004 initiatives, 7
Sergeenkov, Vladimir, 198, 227
Shaimiev, Mintimer, 77, 92, 203
Shaklein, Nikolai, 227
Shamanov, Vladimir, 119–21, 124, 125,
   137, 140
Shevel', Olga, 199
Shishkin, Sergei, 227
Shleifer, Andrei, 178, 179, 189
*Short-Term Fluctuations in U.S. Voting
   Behavior* (Kramer), 39–40
short-term increases, voter focus on, 177
Shumpeter, Joseph, 176
Shuvalova, Valentina, 103, 130
Sidorenko, Viktor, 105–6, 109–10
signature requirement for ballot, 74, 217
Simbirskie Gubernskie Vedomosti, 123,
   124, 125
Simbirskii Kur'er, 123, 125
single-mandate districts, 5, 215
Slider, Darrell, 58, 59–60
Slovakia, elections in, 49–50
Smirniagin, Leonid, 203
Sniderman, Paul, 42

Social Democratic Party of Russia, 220
social organizations, law concerning, 72
sociological-psychological analysis of
   incumbent electoral success, 51–52
sociotropic interests: absolute sociotropic
   effects, 130, 132–34; incumbent's
   success as related to regional economy,
   130; and incumbent support, 14; and
   jurisdictional issues in voting, 129,
   132–33; role of in voting, 42, 54, 62,
   147; survey data, 47, 64
Solnick, Steven: analysis of, 14, 64; and
   election cycles, 18; evaluation of
   election cycle by, 21; and gubernatorial
   elections in Russia, 29, 51, 52–53, 54;
   and ideology and partisanship, 138;
   and proto-parties, 86–87; and
   referendum voting issues, 60
Solomonov, Vladimir, 28
Sorkin, Jill, 43
sploshnie vybor (endless elections), 71.
   See also regional executive elections
SPS (Union of Right Forces), 48, 135
Saint Petersburg gubernatorial elections,
   2, 211–14, 228, 229, 230
standard-of-living measures. *See*
   aggregate economic performance
   and election outcomes
stand-ins *(dublery),* 199–200
Stanley, Harold, 45, 176
Stein, Robert, 43, 45
Stepan, Alfred, 94
Stokes, Susan: and criteria for accountability, 35–36, 103; and forms of
   representation, 10, 29, 31–36; and
   pocketbook voters, 129; on survival
   in office, 162
Stoner-Weiss, Kathryn, 3, 58–59
Stroev, Yegor, 198–99
subnational elections: accountability of,
   3, 54, 175–76; in Russia, 50–54; and
   subnational economic performance,
   176
subnational jurisdictional voter. *See* ideal
   subnational jurisdictional voter
survey-based data, 62–64

Sverdlovskaia Oblast elections, 226–27
Sychev, Sergei, 220–21
Sychev, Valerii, 121–22
Sysuev, Oleg, 203

Taagepara, Rein, 92, 94
TACIS, 19
Tarkhov, Viktor, 79–80
Tatarstan, 163. *See also* Shaimiev,
   Mintimer
taxation, 57–58
Teibout, C., 44
television. *See* media
term of office, 4, 76, 87, 97
territorial electoral commissions, 73–74,
   76
terrorist attacks, 5, 81
third parties, role of, 126
Tidmarch, Charles, 43
Titov, Konstantin, 28, 79–80, 199,
   219–21
Tiumenskaia Oblast election, 164, 169
Tolz, Vera, 11, 59
Tomz, Jason, 242
transition countries: and appointed
   officials, 171; economic voting in, 13
transparency, lack of budgetary, 177
treaties between republics and Moscow,
   17, 57–59
Treisman, Daniel, 58
Tucker, Joshua, 49–50
Tufte, Edward, 40, 41
Tuleev, Aman, 199
Tulskaia Oblast, election in, 200
turnout thresholds, 89–91
Turret, Stephen, 43
TV-6, 148

UAZ (Ul'ianovskii avtomobil'nyi zavod)
   automobile factory, 105, 109, 118
Ukraine: and accountability of
   policymakers, 22; appointee system in,
   179, 184–89, 232; "cassette scandal"
   in, 179, 181; comparative perspective
   of Russia's regional elections, 15,
   180–83; executive turnover in, 15,

179, 182, 184–85; history and
   comparison with Russia, 178–79;
   presidential election of 2004, 182;
   preview and summary of results,
   183–84; United Russia party in, 228
Ul'ianovskaia Oblast and regional
   jurisdictional voters, 103–57; from
   behavior to outcomes, 149; decisionmaking process of voters, 131–42;
   federal context, application to,
   142–47; Goriachev administration,
   106–7; hypotheses, 129–30; ideal
   subnational jurisdictional voter,
   128–31; incumbent-friendly election
   laws in, 88–90; jurisdictional support
   in Russia's regions, 125–28; measures,
   133–37; model specification and
   results, 137–42; 1992–96 institutional vacuum and consolidation of
   administrations' control, 112–14; 1996
   and rise of viable opposition, 114–17;
   period between elections, 117–19;
   political control and adaptation, 112;
   preview and summary of results,
   131–42; socioeconomic and political
   history of Ul'ianovskaia Oblast,
   104–25; survey, 130–31; and threats
   of terrorist bombing, 81; 2000 election
   campaign, 119–25; "*Ul'ianovsk
   Phenomenon*", 107–12, 117, 125;
   United Russia party in, 225; and
   Yeltsin's appointment procedure,
   87–88
Ul'ianovskaia Pravda, 123
"*Ul'ianovsk Phenomenon*", 107–12, 117,
   125
Ul'ianovsk Segodnia, 123, 125
unfunded mandates, 203, 204
Union of Right Forces (SPS), 48, 135
United Russia party: antigubernatorial
   bloc in, 220; bloc in Duma, 6;
   candidates, 10; Duma elections of
   2003, 222; and election reforms, 219;
   endorsement by, 223–25; expansion
   and consolidation of, 202, 221–29,
   231; information from, 22; and

United Russia party (*continued*)
partification process, 222–23; "privatization" of, 222; publication support
by, 211; and Putin, 218–19, 221
United States, elections in, 43–45, 56,
96–97
Unity, 218

validity of elections, challenges to,
78–80
Verkhovna Rada (national parliament),
180, 185
Veshniakov, Aleksandr, 123
Vesti, 124
violations in election process, 61, 77, 78
Vogel, Ronald, 45, 176
Volgin, Dmitrii, 213–14
Volgogradskaia Oblast, election in, 200
Vologodskaia Oblast, election in, 92
Volzhskaia Kommuna, 79
voters: behaviors and outcomes, 8–9;
best assessment of regional voters,
166; decision rule of, 39; mobilization,
185, 188; in regional elections, 50–51;
turnout, 89–91. *See also* regional
electorate
votes, collection and tallying of, 76
VTsIOM (the All-Russian Center for
Public Opinion Research), 11

wage changes, effect on incumbent
success, 55
Weingast, Barry, 177
Western countries, economic voting in,
13
White, Stephen, 207
Wittenberg, Jason, 242

Yakovlev, Vladimir, 2, 61, 212
Yeltsin, Boris: and election victory of
1996, 13; federalism under, 3;
incapacitation of, 4; and incumbent
electoral success, 83–88, 91, 113;
presidential appointments of, 52–53,
72, 106; promoting regional-level
accountability, 4; and regional
administrations, 83; and regional
presidential representatives, 77;
resignation of, 60, 144; showdown
with federal legislature, 56, 81;
support for, 51, 52
Yermakov, Sergei, 113, 114, 115, 116
youth, issues concerning, 2
Yushchenko, Viktor, 181, 182–83

Zelenov, Evgenii, 221–22
Zhirinovskii, Vladimir, 1
Zimmerman, William, 144–45
Ziuganov, Gennadii, 85, 86